The Producers

Tim Adler is editor of film industry newsletter *Screen Finance*. He also writes for the *Financial Times*, the *Daily Telegraph* and the *Evening Standard*. He lives in London with his two sons.

The
Producers

Money, movies and who really calls the shots

Tim Adler

Methuen

Published in paperback by Methuen, 2006

10 9 8 7 6 5 4 3 2 1

Copyright © 2004 by Tim Adler

The right of Tim Adler to be identified as the author of this work has
been asserted by him in accordance with the Copyright, Designs and
Patents Act 1988

Methuen Publishing Ltd
11–12 Buckingham Gate
London SW1E 6LB

www.methuen.co.uk

ISBN 10: 0 413 77152 0
ISBN 13: 978 0 413 77152 0

A CIP catalogue for this title is available from the British Library

Typeset by SX Composing DTP, Rayleigh, Essex
Printed and bound in Great Britain
by Cox & Wyman Ltd, Reading, Berkshire

For Anne Phillips, with gratitude

The producer who is personally interested in every stage of a picture can afford to experiment with his interpreters.

Alfred Hitchcock[1]

Contents

Acknowledgements

First, I would like to thank the seven producers who have agreed to have their profiles written: Dino De Laurentiis, Michael Douglas, Marin Karmitz, Duncan Kenworthy, Andrew Macdonald, Jeremy Thomas and Christine Vachon. They are all busy people with better things to do than watch some journalist occasionally groping his way through shorthand outlines, trying to figure out what he has just scribbled down.

Second, I want to thank those people who have acted like a whetstone, sparking insights into producers and what they actually do: Chris Auty, managing director of Civilian Content; Steve Clarke-Hall of Skyline Films; Angus Finney, managing director of Renaissance Films; film director Mary Harron; Terry Ilott, chief executive of Hammer Films and former consultant editor of my own magazine, *Screen Finance*; Scott Meek of Deep Indigo; Bertrand Moullier, director general of the International Federation of Film Producers (Fiapf); Jonathan Olsberg, chief executive of consultancy Olsberg SPI and a producer in his own right; Simon Perry, former director of co-productions at Ingenious Media; Agnes Poirier, film critic of French newspaper *Liberation*; and Lord Puttnam of Queensgate, who remains the only European ever to have run a Hollywood film studio.

I would also like to thank Catharine Browne, who acted as my translator during my interview in Paris with the resolutely Francophone Marin Karmitz. Without Catharine, given the standard of my French, the interview would have ended after ordering a cup of coffee.

John Simmons of the Royal Bank of Scotland also deserves thanks for his patience during the three-year period it has taken to write this book.

Staff at the British Film Institute library, in particular chief librarian Sean Delaney, have gone out of their way to be helpful.

Also, I would like to thank my agent, Laura Morris, for taking a risk with somebody who just wrote to her out of the blue; Max Eilenberg, my publisher at Methuen, for pointing out that the theme of this book should run through each chapter like letters through a stick of rock; and Methuen editor Joanna Taylor for guiding me through the editorial process.

Finally, I would have liked to thank Alexander Walker, late film critic of the *Evening Standard*, for his encouragement when I first suggested writing about the producer as auteur. He was a man I was proud to think of as my mentor. We used to meet infrequently for lunch and I miss his impeccable manners, his occasionally malicious wit and, most of all, his dinning into me that writing about films and the movie industry involves moral conviction as well as ideas about what makes for good cinema. I only wish he was still alive to read this book.

The author and Methuen Publishing Limited gratefully acknowl-
edge the permissions granted to reproduce the quoted extracts
within this work.

Appleyard, Brian. 'The Road to Morocco'. *Sunday Times*,
2 September 1990.

Byrne, Bridget, 'Sam Spiegel: making cathedrals out of raw film',
Los Angeles Times, 2 January 1972.

Byron, Stuart, *Film Comment*, January – February 1977.

Champlin, Charles, 'A Ding-Dong King Kong Battle', *Los Angeles
Times*, 5 November 1975. Copyright © 1975, Los Angeles Times.
Reprinted with permission.

Cronenberg, David, *Naked Lunch: a screenplay based on the novel by
William S. Burroughs*, second draft. 5 March 1990.

Davenport, Hugo, *Daily Telegraph*, 19 November 1990.

Drew, Bernard, *American Film*, December 1976 – January 1977.

Elley, Derek, *Variety*, 12 February 1996.

Fitzgerald, F. Scott, *The Last Tycoon*. Copyright © 1941 by Charles
Scribner's Sons, renewed 1969 by Frances Scott Fitzgerald Smith
and Edmund Wilson. Used by permission of Scribner, an imprint
of Simon & Schuster Adult Publishing Group, and Harold Ober
Associates Inc.

Fixx, James F, 'The Spiegel Touch', *Saturday Review*, December 29,
1962. Reprinted by permission of the *Saturday Review*. Copyright
© 1962 by General Media, Inc.

French, Philip, *The Movie Moguls: an informal history of the Hollywood
tycoons*, Weidenfeld & Nicolson, 1969. Copyright © Philip French
1969, by permission of PFD.

Greene, Graham, *In Search of a Character*, The Viking Press, 1962.

Haigh, Peter, *Film Review*, volume 27, 2, February 1977.

Hitchcock, Alfred, 'Directors are Dead', *Film Weekly*, 20 November 1937. Courtesy of the Alfred Hitchcock Trust.

Hodge, John, *Trainspotting and Shallow Grave*, Faber and Faber, 1996.

Hoyle, Martin, *Financial Times*, 20 May 1999.

Humphries, Reynold and Suzzoni, Genevieve, *Framework*, vol. 11, 5, winter 1976–7.

Kaye, Annene and Sclavunos, Jim, *Michael Douglas and the Douglas Clan*, W. H. Allen, 1989.

Kesey, Ken, *Kesey's Garage Sale*, Viking, 1973.

Lawson, Alan, *Michael Douglas: a biography*, Robert Hale, 1993.

Levy, Emanuel, *Variety*, 6 September 1999.

Lightman, Herb A., *American Cinematographer*, January 1977.

Mailer, Norman, *Advertisements for Myself*, G. P. Putnam's Sons, 1959.

Mandell, Paul, *Cinefantastique*, vol. 5, 1, spring 1976.

McCarthy, Todd, *Variety*, 24 January 1994.

Negri, Livio, *The Sheltering Sky*, Scribners, 1990.

Parker, John, *Michael Douglas: acting on instinct*, Headline, 1994. Reproduced by permission of Headline Book Publishing Ltd.

Powers, James, *American Film*, July – August 1979.

Semple, Lorenzo Jr., *The Complete Script of the Dino De Laurentiis Production of King Kong*, Ace Books, 1977.

Tookey, Christopher, *Daily Mail*, 11 November 1994.

Tutt, Louise, *Screen International*, 22 August 1997.

Vachon, Christine, *Shooting to Kill: How an independent producer blasts through the barriers to make movies that matter*, Avon Books, 1998.

Vertrees, Alan David, *Selznick's Vision: Gone with the Wind and Hollywood Filmmaking*, University of Texas Press, 1997.

Walker, Beverly, *Sight and Sound*, autumn 1975.

Warren, Bill, *Cinefantastique*, vol. 5, 3, winter 1976.

Wood, Michael, *The New York Review of Books*, vol. 22, 1, 5 February 1976.

Every effort has been made to trace the current copyright holders of the extracts included in this work. The publishers apologise for any unintended omissions and would be pleased to receive any information that would enable them to amend any inaccuracies or omissions in future editions.

Thanks also to the following for permission to reproduce the photographs of the producers:

Michael Douglas – Twentieth Century-Fox
Dino De Laurentiis – Paramount Pictures
Duncan Kenworthy and Andrew Macdonald – Nick Wall
Jeremy Thomas – Recorded Picture Company
Marin Karmitz – MK2
Christine Vachon – Chris Buck

Introduction

The manager of the Cipriani poured us both a glass of Rosario, a rose-tinted liqueur which tasted like scented petrol. Beyond the window the lights of Venice shone across the blue-black lagoon. Natale Rusconi was a dapper, courtly man in his sixties with slicked-back hair and a wry expression behind his metal-framed glasses. Being married to a vivacious blonde from the East Coast, his English was very good.

'It was my first time as night manager of the Ritz Hotel in London,' Rusconi said. 'I was patrolling the corridors at about three in the morning, checking to see everything was all right – that room-service trays had been cleared, that kind of thing. You can imagine my surprise when a naked woman ran past me down the corridor. Especially when she was a big Hollywood star, Merle Oberon. And then I had an even bigger surprise. Running after her was a naked man with his hands cupped over his balls. And coming round the corner after them both was Sir Alexander Korda, the film producer, who was married to Oberon at the time. He was still in his dinner jacket and out of breath. It's not often that you see one of the world's biggest actresses caught *in flagrante delicto*.'

Thirteen years later and I was sitting having lunch on the terrace of the Eden Roc restaurant in Cap d'Antibes. The restaurant had its own swimming pool that overhung the bay, seemingly suspended in space. The terrace looked down on the water, where a shimmering white yacht rested offshore. Surely this was one of the most beautiful places in the world.

Each year during the Cannes Film Festival there is an annual invitation-only gathering of film producers and financiers – a kind of hoods' convention. As far as I was aware I was the first journalist to have penetrated this annual gathering ('Don't let them know you're a journalist; let them think that you're one of them' was the advice I had been given). I had the impression that I was inside a shark tank, surrounded by some of the most dangerous and exotic of the species.

I watched one producer walk past me with a Desperate Dan-sized helping from the buffet, his plate piled with lobster, salmon and oysters. Watching him, you'd think he was never going to eat again. Another man passed my table. I felt as if I had been buzzed by a dangerous fish, a manta brushing past me as it swam into the gloom. Frans Afman was a Jimmy Goldsmith type, dressed in the rich man's Mediterranean uniform of blazer, silk shirt and blue jeans. Next to him was a thin, chic, dried-up woman whom I took to be his wife. They were both talking to a short, bearded producer, who was building castles in the air with the tip of his cigar. Standing next to the producer was a pouty would-be actress, presumably the producer's girlfriend. The wife and the mistress could have been the same woman forty years apart.

Afman used to run the obscure film lending division of a French bank in a Dutch backwater. What his bosses didn't know was that he had embarked on a spending spree with the bank's money, lending about $2 billion to a gaggle of producers back in the 1980s. Some claimed that he unwittingly laundered Mafia money, enabling an Italian entrepreneur to buy Metro-Goldwyn-Mayer for $1.4 billion in 1991. In the end the bank was left owed billions of dollars as Afman's clients went bust one after the other. Eventually Afman resigned, before resurfacing elsewhere. Of course, nobody was ever blamed – nobody ever is. It is never anybody's fault, and you see the same faces ordering *coupes de champagne* on the terrace of the Carlton Hotel in Cannes year after year.

Film producers, rather than actors or directors, have always fascinated me. They have the power and know where the bodies are buried. Many mothers want their sons to become lawyers or doctors or accountants. Mine encouraged me to think about becoming a film tycoon, giving me a copy of *Charmed Lives*, Michael Korda's memoir of the Korda family, when I was a teenager. There was something about Korda, the Hungarian exile who made *The Third Man* and *The Private Life of Henry VIII*, which captured my imagination – the Knize ties, the Sulka shirts, the Lobb shoes, the way he called drinking champagne from special glasses 'chi-chi'. It all seemed a long way away from growing up in a small terraced house in the Midlands in the mid-1970s.

The stereotypical film producer is some kind of champagne-guzzling, cigar-chomping plutocrat. 'Contempt for these men comes easily,' wrote Philip French in *The Movie Moguls*, 'and the terms to describe them – mogul, cinemogul, tycoon, czar and the rest – have a certain sneer about them, conjuring up as they do an unfavourable image of a cigar-chewing, language fracturing, power-mad, philistine ignoramus.'[1] But the reality is more likely to be a seedy office and unpaid bills. The truth is that for many, being a film producer is a lifestyle, not a business. The popular image of the producer is that of the money man, his eyes fixed on the balance sheet. But there are many different types of producer, and some have trouble adding up on their fingers.

There is the so-called creative producer. Received opinion has it that the director is the 'author' of the movies – a distortion popularised by American film critic Andrew Sarris in the early 1960s. Sarris took the idea from influential French film magazine *Cahiers du cinéma*, founded in 1951 by journalist Jacques Doniol-Valcroze. By 1953 writers including Jean-Luc Godard, François Truffaut, Jacques Rivette and Claude Chabrol were banging the drum for a 'politique des auteurs' – a notion in turn inspired by an essay by director and critic Alexandre Astruc in the Communist-backed magazine *L'Ecran français* earlier in 1948. Astruc wrote that the cinema was becoming a means of expression, just like the painting and the novel. Cinema, according to Astruc, had evolved from a fairground attraction and working man's diversion into an art form. A film-maker could use film-making as a tool for self-exploration, using his camera just as in other art forms an author uses his pen or a painter his paintbrush.

By asserting that a film director writes with his camera just as a novelist writes with his pen, Astruc was tapping into the popular and enduring appeal of the mythical romantic artist. This nineteenth-century invention, popularised by Goethe's 1774 novel *The Sorrows of Young Werther*, believed that a work of art was a cardiogram of the artist's heart, rather than the disinterested work of many hands. According to auteur theory, the producer, the writer and actors (as well as everybody else involved in a production, such as the cameraman or composer – known in the industry as 'below the line' talent) simply execute the vision of the director. But people who work in the industry know that cinema is a collaborative business. Making a film is not so much the outpourings of a tortured soul as the patient, step-by-step building of a cathedral, employing many hands and minds. Art historian Erwin Panofsky, writing in 1947, compared a film to a medieval cathedral: the producer corresponding to an archbishop; the director assuming the role of the architect; the screenwriter analogous to a scholar advising the bishop on imagery for the stained-glass windows; and the actors, cameramen and sound technicians equivalent to the choristers, gargoyle sculptors and stone-masons of medieval times.

Sarris used the term 'auteur' to denote directors whom he judged to have a discernible message or attitude running throughout their work. The critic developed a simplistic theory, celebrating the director as the sole purveyor of film art surrounded by hacks and profit-mongers. Sarris valued the personality of the director because, for him, the studio system worked against individual creativity rather than supporting it. Therefore the only film-makers worthy of canonisation as author-artists were those whose personal style emerged in spite of the profit-hungry Moloch that was the studio system. Sarris spoke of a handful of directors escaping the gravitational pull of the industry.

But as Thomas Schatz has argued in his book *The Genius of the System*, surely there is a connection between the later drop-off in quality in the films of Alfred Hitchcock – the director most often singled out as being an auteur – and the fact that he no longer worked with his regular team? Cameraman Robert Burks, editor George Tomasini, assistant director (and later associate producer) Herbert Coleman, costume designer Edith Head and screenwriter John Michael Hayes all worked alongside Hitchcock on *Rear Window*, *To Catch a Thief* and *Vertigo*. Later, Hitchcock dispensed with his usual collaborators to work on *Family Plot*, *Topaz* and *Torn Curtain* mostly by himself.

Today the term 'auteur' could possibly be applied to some writer-directors such as Woody Allen, Quentin Tarantino and Rainer Werner Fassbinder, film-makers who have recognisably created worlds in their own image. But the truth is that most directors are just the hired help. Of course, back in Hollywood's classical era, certain directors including John Ford, Howard Hawks and Frank Capra enjoyed some degree of autonomy, having control over script development, casting and editing, for example. This is because they were trusted to be producers as well as directors. Mention 'auteur theory' to anybody in the industry today and you get polite throat-clearing and shuffling of feet. The word 'master' may be reserved for a handful of directors such as Stanley Kubrick and David Lynch, but I defy anybody to see much stylistic difference (or even a subject) in most of the films which fill our popcorn penitentiaries. It is important to remember that Hollywood's target audience is aged between eighteen and twenty-four.

Auteur theory even pulled the wool over the eyes of that most urbane and penetrating of critics, Kenneth Tynan. Writing in 1971, Tynan reflected on how bamboozled he had been by Orson Welles' claim to have conceived, written, directed and produced *Citizen Kane*, when the truth was that the script was mostly the work of Herman Mankiewicz. Tynan concluded that the final shape of most films was dictated by a combination of skills, and that directors were spared the basic pain of creation. In his diary, Tynan reflected that the principle of a work of art as solo performance had underpinned his thinking for years. It was undermining for him to discover that so much of his earlier ideas about creativity had been based on falsehood.

Film is a collaborative medium but the myth of the director as auteur is still being promulgated, mostly by directors themselves. Directors are keen to be in the limelight and get that important 'a film by' credit in the titles. There is a Hollywood joke about two producers driving past the home of a famous director. 'Look, there's Joe Smith's house,' says one producer, before correcting himself. 'Or should I say, a house by Joe Smith.'

Astruc and the rest of the *Cahiers du cinéma* gang blithely ignored the economics of film-making: the fact that films cost many millions of dollars to produce compared with a novel, which just needs pen and paper. According to the Motion Picture Association of America (MPAA), the average Hollywood film today costs more than $100 million to produce and publicise – and this is the cost of a typical romantic comedy, not a blockbuster (although I am sure this figure will seem quaint in a few years' time). Tim Bevan, producer of *Bridget Jones's Diary*, dismisses auteur theory because of the amounts of money involved. If somebody wants to make a film just to explore his personal demons, then they would be better off writing a novel or painting a picture because, says Bevan, they are cheaper. Film, because of its inherent expense, must appeal to a wide audience.

However, if some film-makers do clearly have a recognisable style or theme, then some producers can be auteurs as much as directors. David Selznick, producer of *Gone with the Wind*, believed that films which succeeded were made according to the vision of just one man. Selznick agreed with Sarris that a movie must have a single author, but for Selznick that author must be the producer. Back in the 1930s and '40s, when Hollywood was arguably at its creative peak, the producer's name was more prominent in the credits than that of the director. The director's job was just to handle actors on set. The producer's job, on the other hand, stretched from initial conception to screenplay, casting and production design through to editing and marketing. Directors were often changed midway through shooting if the studio was dissatisfied with their work. One may have been good with actors while another specialised in big production scenes. How many people know the names of the four directors of *Gone with the Wind*, once described as the Sistine Chapel of movies? (Victor Fleming replaced George Cukor after three weeks of shooting; Sam Wood replaced Fleming, and later split the job with Fleming again;

production designer William Cameron Menzies oversaw the burning of Atlanta sequence.) But as Gore Vidal wrote, Selznick alone created the motion picture of *Gone with the Wind* – only the pub-quiz bore would know the names of the frankly interchangeable directors.

Producers hiring directors to execute their vision continues to the present day. Arguably, David Puttnam, producer of *Chariots of Fire* and *The Killing Fields*, played a bigger role in those films than directors Hugh Hudson and Roland Joffe.

The idea for *Chariots of Fire* came from a book Puttnam picked up in a Los Angeles hotel bedroom. One February morning, feeling unwell, Puttnam came across a history of the Olympic Games. Reading the chapter about 1924, he followed the story of two competing British Olympic runners, and the conflict one of them had with running on a Sunday. Again, the idea for the film *Local Hero* came from Puttnam reading a newspaper story about a man in the Hebrides who negotiated a shrewder deal with an American company than anything the government had attempted.

Puttnam distributed a memo to cast and crew on the eve of shooting *The Killing Fields*, his film about genocide in Cambodia, telling them that the entire film had existed in his head and what he had needed was to find a writer with whom he could communicate his vision. Director Roland Joffe must have choked on his papaya when he read that memo over breakfast the next morning.

And Puttnam's 1974 breakthrough film *That'll Be the Day*, a coming-of-age story set in the 1950s, was basically the auto-biography of one David Puttnam, with pop star David Essex playing the producer as a young man. One scene in the film recreated the midnight return of Puttnam's father from the Second World War. Puttnam cast his own eight-year-old son as the child he had been. It was, his biographer noted, the first time Puttnam had etched his signature on the big screen.

Puttnam, who has now retired from film-making in order to concentrate on politics, always made a point of working with first-time directors, presumably because they were more biddable. On one early film, *The Pied Piper*, Puttnam made the mistake of being swayed from his first choice of director and instead plumped for Jacques Demy (*Les Parapluies de Cherbourg*, *The Umbrellas of Cherbourg*, 1964) – already well established and a director of whom Puttnam was somewhat in awe. As a result Puttnam gave in to Demy every step of the way, allowing the film to slip away from him. Puttnam vowed not to get stung by the same bee twice, and remained in control of his films from then on. 'People do not work with Puttnam more than once because he is a dominant, creative presence,' says Terry Ilott, a consultant and film executive. Michael Apted, director of *Stardust* – the sequel to *That'll Be the Day* – and more recently *Enigma*, thinks that unless Puttnam could run the show, unless he is captain of the ship, he would rather not be involved with a project. Director Hugh Hudson, who has worked with Puttnam twice, believes that Puttnam was a frustrated director, driven by the memory of his journalist father, whom he remembered as an artist and wished he could be one too. Puttnam once said that somebody in France decided that film was a director's medium, and, with the gleeful participation of directors, the press accepted it. He believes that auteur theory captured people's imaginations because there is a natural urge to hold an individual responsible for any work of art, as opposed to the many hands which shape, say, a circus performance. 'On balance, auteur theory possibly did more harm than good,' he says.

A theme that runs through Puttnam's films from *That'll Be the Day* to *Chariots of Fire* and *The Mission* is of two men in conflict over the right way to behave. 'It is not illegitimate today to look at the body of work I produced and say there is a consistency. There is a thematic that goes right the way through,' he says. Puttnam thinks that all of his best films are about men in moral crises – how people cope with apparently intolerable pressure; how much the human frame can stand; and how moral issues are argued and resolved or simply left to be resolved another day.

Jerry Bruckheimer, producer of *Pearl Harbor*, *Armageddon* and *Pirates of the Caribbean*, sees himself as the master builder, hiring the best writers, directors and actors to execute his vision. First, the writer draws up the architectural plans of the house. Secondly, you hire the best builders available to try and build it. Finally, you try and sell the house. But the producer oversees all three stages.

A retired naval admiral serving as a technical adviser on *Top Gun* would often see Bruckheimer wandering by himself on the beach near the film set. One day, Bruckheimer was standing on the boardwalk, looking at the teenage boys and girls sprawled on the sand. The admiral remarked that this must be where Bruckheimer got his ideas, trying to get inside the heads of teenagers and work out what they wanted to see. Bruckheimer seemed genuinely surprised by this comment. Oh no, he told the admiral. On the contrary, he dictated what teenagers wanted to see.

'Every picture I produce myself,' says Dino De Laurentiis, producer of *Blue Velvet* and *Hannibal*. 'I work very near the screenplay writer. I select the director. Then I select the cast. Then I leave the director alone.'

Then there is the nebulous executive producer. This is somebody who has helped raise money for a project or helped put the film together. When asked what Francis Ford Coppola had done to be given an executive producer credit on *Sleepy Hollow*, director Tim Burton quipped: 'I think he made a phone call sometime in the '70s.' An executive producer hires a line producer or associate producer to deal with the physical, day-to-day grind of movie production. How do you go about covering Trafalgar Square with fake snow at three o'clock in the morning? Who do you need to see to hire the Macedonian army as extras for your battle scene? Why is your female star insisting on wearing her own clothes when your Oscar-winning costume designer has spent months sweating over her wardrobe? Actor and producer David Hemmings once described this element of film producing as a thankless task more akin to hotel management.

Since the collapse of the Hollywood studio system in the 1950s, movie-making has become more expensive and complicated. The role of the producer has atomised and splintered, which is why one sees a baffling list of associate producers, co-producers and executive producers working their way down the credit crawl. Few individuals have all the skills necessary to control a film from conception to release. Often it seems as if there are more producers than electricians working on today's movies. But as Steve Clarke-Hall, line producer of the British comedy *Saving Grace*, points out, the real producer is the one who turns up on set each day at 7 a.m. before anybody else has arrived. (Contrary to the popular image, working on film sets is not glamorous. One producer best summed it up as 'standing around in mud'.) The ideal producer will have an understanding of the sometimes arcane world of film finance; a working grasp of the law; the charm to woo temperamental and self-obsessed actors, writers and directors; the ruthlessness to fire a director midway though shooting; and the knowledge how to market and publicise a film.

This is why producers often work in pairs, for example Bruckheimer and his late partner Don Simpson, or Tim Bevan and his partner Eric Fellner (*Dead Man Walking, Fargo*), or the Weinstein brothers (*Shakespeare in Love, The English Patient*). Working as a team allows them to play good cop/bad cop or, more confusingly, alternate roles, perhaps reflecting the left brain/right brain aspect of being a film producer, which needs to balance the creative elements with financial constraints. After all, having the charm to woo Julia Roberts is not the same thing as negotiating the star's fee with Julia Roberts' lawyer. (Actually, it is not dealing with stars which gives producers headaches, but dealing with secondary actors, often people 'on their way up' who feel they have something to prove. It is younger actors who are temperamental and obnoxious, and who fill the tabloid papers with their behaviour. Provided they are surrounded by their team – the unctuous personal manager, the trusted publicity man and the exhausted-looking 'best friend' – stars can afford to be gracious because they are secure about their status.)

What does a producer actually do? Selznick summed up his job as really being responsible for everything. Tim Bevan, co-chairman of Britain's most successful film company, Working Title, sees his role as creating the fabric within which the image you see on the screen is going to exist. A producer, according to Bevan, is responsible for his film from conception until years after release, when everybody else connected with the movie has forgotten about it. Another thing that makes the producer different from the director is that he has to think about the marketing of the film – how much to spend, the order in which the film is released, what campaign to use in each country. Bevan believes the movie business is all about selling – to the studio, to the writer, to a director – and frequently to somebody who is reluctant to buy.

Some producers spend years finessing a single project. Uberto Pasolini, producer of *The Full Monty*, works this way. Others, pressed for cash, work on five or six projects at the same time, hoping that at least one will go into production. The producer's fee is approximately 10 per cent of what the film costs to make, payable on the day shooting starts. Usually this is the only money he ever sees from the production. Some producers, desperate after years of banging heads against walls to get their films made, agree to defer their production fee until other investors have recouped. A bank, for example, will insist at being at the top of the revenue cascade, which, by the time it reaches the producer, may have slowed to a trickle. Indeed, accounting procedures at Hollywood studios are designed to stop producers from seeing any cash – an example of what the late Alexander Walker, former film critic of the *Evening Standard*, used to call the systematic dishonesty of the film industry. However, in the case of *The Full Monty*, Pasolini hit a 'gusher'. Certainly he will never have to worry about where his next meal is coming from – somebody will always want to have a lunch meeting with him.

In my job as a film journalist I often feel like an observer in a casino, looking over the shoulders of the players and providing a running commentary as I walk around the tables. Is this producer up or down? Is he holding a winning hand or is he bluffing? Is he betting everything – his home, his family's future – on one last roll of the dice?

Imagine a London casino where the carpet is so thick that it absorbs the sound of your footfalls. The salon privé of this Mayfair club looks like the sitting room in a country-house hotel, except this sitting room has blacked-out bulletproof windows. Cameras look down on the players from the dusty pink Wedgwood ceiling. There are also cameras secreted inside the candelabra fixed to the pear-wood walls. Good horse paintings hang above thick, comfortable sofas. Dinner-jacketed croupiers deal out cash chips in denominations of up to £100,000, watched by impassive gaming inspectors. Players in the salon privé are expected to feel comfortable losing up to five million pounds in a night. Perhaps not surprisingly, nobody touches any alcohol. In this imaginary casino three of the most creative movie producers ever, to my mind, are gathered around the roulette wheel. Sam Spiegel, producer of *On the Waterfront*, *The Bridge on the River Kwai* and *Lawrence of Arabia*, stands on the left of Joseph E. Levine, the maverick behind *The Graduate* and *Eight and a Half*. On Levine's right is David Selznick, producer of *Gone with the Wind* and *Rebecca*, spilling cigarette ash down the front of his suit.

The *Los Angeles Times* said of Spiegel: 'One expects him to be clothed in ermine and armor, not a business suit. The lines of hound dog sadness beneath the eyes balance out the hauteur of the eagle's nose.'[2] In 1962 another journalist described Spiegel as 'a baffling, complex person. His cultured Viennese accent, with its overtones of London and Park Avenue, can at once convey a meltingly persuasive charm, and at the next dismiss somebody's idea with one crisp word. He can be as guileless as a child, or, when it suits his purposes, he can plot with the patience and cunning of a grandmaster at chess. But above all, he knows how to get his way.'[3] Collaborators such as Harold Pinter, who adapted *Betrayal* for him, spoke of Spiegel's sense of responsibility and dedication, while John Huston, director of *The African Queen*, said that Spiegel's skill lay in being a good judge of people, weighing up talent and knowing what it was capable of. Spiegel instinctively knew who a good writer was but would not have been able to judge the quality of his writing, said Huston. His flair was in putting people together and knowing who would work as a team.

It was Spiegel who convinced Huston to give *The African Queen* a happy ending, persuading the usually pessimistic director that Humphrey Bogart and Katharine Hepburn should be allowed to escape the hangman's noose after their marriage. It was Spiegel who came across Pierre Boulle's novel *Le Pont de la Rivière Kwai* in a Paris airport and convinced director David Lean that this would make a worthy subject. It was Spiegel who not only first read a limited edition of T. E. Lawrence's autobiography *The Seven Pillars of Wisdom* back in 1926, but who years later hired playwright Robert Bolt to adapt the book, picking composer Maurice Jarre to write the sweeping *Lawrence of Arabia* theme.

And it was Spiegel who made writer Budd Schulberg spend another year rewriting what he thought was the already finished screenplay of *On the Waterfront*. The producer's favourite phrase with screenwriters was 'Let's open it up again', and Schulberg chafed at Spiegel's demands. He grew to resent the producer making him rewrite the script for a year before he would deign to produce it. (Schulberg's wife once found him standing in front of a mirror in the early hours of the morning knotting his tie. When she asked him what he was doing, he replied that he was on his way to kill Sam Spiegel.) On the other hand, Spiegel's bullying resulted in the most famous scene in the film, Marlon Brando's 'could have been a contender' speech when he confronts Rod Steiger in a taxi. And the structure of the film was completely different. Schulberg's original concept was the old tired cliché of having a journalist expose union corruption. It was Spiegel's idea to have the film concentrate on a docker who turns against his workmates after they kill his brother. The film went on to win eight Academy Awards, including Spiegel's first as a producer.

For director Otto Preminger, one of Spiegel's most important contributions to cinema was asking actors such as John Garfield to defer being paid a salary in exchange for a larger slice of hoped-for profits. In this way Spiegel could make important films outside the studio system on small budgets with major talent. Pinter acknowledged that while Spiegel may not have written his films or directed them, he took complete responsibility for them from conception to execution, from first idea to gala premiere. Historian

Arthur Schlesinger added that Spiegel's constant pressure often exasperated and enraged writers and directors, but when the ordeal was over his collaborators recognised that Spiegel's perfectionism had goaded them into bringing out the best in themselves.

Before we float away on a cloud of praise, it is worthwhile remembering that Spiegel also had a dark side. Katharine Hepburn once described him as a pig in a silk suit that sends flowers. In 1963 *Time* magazine reported that a new verb was doing the rounds in Hollywood: 'to spiegel' – meaning to con, to cajole, to manipulate by sleight of mouth. Spiegel needed to dominate, to divide and rule, and, according to director Fred Zinnemann, 'being a producer was the apt platform for that kind of psychology'.

In our imaginary casino, what the producers are betting on is their taste. Studios make large bets every summer, reasonably certain that audiences will pay to watch franchise sequels such as Batman or James Bond. On films the studios are less certain about they are prepared to share the risk or spread their bets. But what the independent producer wants is a big hit from a handful of chips. A small film like *The Blair Witch Project* or *My Big Fat Greek Wedding* can earn back the initial stake many thousands of times.

Watching the roulette wheel spin, Spiegel reflects that if he had lived in another era he would have built cathedrals. The producer's job, he thinks, is to conceive a picture, to dream it up, to have the first concept of what the film is going to be like when it is finished, before a word is written, a part is cast or a director thought of. Producers today, he believes, merely assemble the elements of a film and then let others take over. Spiegel himself prepares the script long before he knows who is going to release it, even before he knows who is going to direct it. A film is the result of a combination of minds applied to the subject in hand, thinks Spiegel. Furthermore, any film worthy of being good must begin with an element of friction between the producer, writer and director – and no good film has been made without screaming and abrasiveness. In short, he is a firm believer that artists work better under pressure. His friend Slim Keith used to say that Spiegel liked to have a bone to gnaw on to assist the creative mechanism. When people ask him when he is starting his next film, his stock answer is: 'When the script is ready.' He believes that all the trials and errors of a picture are fought out on paper, and the writing period is for the elimination of doubts. Once confronted by cameras and thousands of people who cost a fortune, one cannot have doubts. Pictures are rewritten, not written. However, it is important not to obscure the central idea by embellishing it so much that its spark is extinguished.

According to Spiegel, one of the greatest faults in the film business is looking down on the audience. You must never under-estimate the taste and intelligence of your viewers. They are just as quick to grasp an idea as you are to present it. Set your level and they will meet you there. Indeed, Spiegel thinks that the general level of film-goers has risen much higher than the general level of film-makers. Spiegel wants the audience to become co-author with the producer, writer and director. It is this emotional involvement that makes a picture successful. But there is no formula for creating good pictures. They are made with assiduous, concerted hard work. If there were any recipe for being a producer, people would go to cookery school to get it. There are no rules. Producing a film involves one's waking and sleeping hours, one's objective and subjective interest; it excludes nothing and it permits no sanctuary in which one can breathe on one's own. It is really a negative that makes you a success – you should never make a picture you are not excited about, and you must feel that unless you make this picture you will not be able to sleep. (Spiegel once asked rhetorically: 'How do you penetrate a wall?' The answer: 'Gradually.')

Selznick chain-smoking next to him irritates Levine, a lifelong non-smoker. Short, round and darkly attired, Levine was described by the photographer Yosuf Karsh as a benign Roman conqueror in a Savile Row suit come home victorious to Rome. Now in his seventies, Joseph Levine has been dogged with ill health just as he is taking the biggest gamble of his career. He would give all his wealth just for another five years – he knows he would recoup the money in that time.

A Bridge Too Far is the 493rd film he has produced, co-produced, financed or distributed, and the one which could break him. Levine has invested every single cent he has accumulated over his 32-year career into this picture, which is budgeted at $25 million in 1977 (a sum equivalent to $74 million today). He is personally at risk for $22 million, a mixture of bank loans and his own money (according to Levine, banks never want to lend money unless you don't need it. He is thinking about writing a book called *Banks I Have Known*). Levine is in the middle of assembling an all-star cast – Robert Redford, Sean Connery, Anthony Hopkins, Dirk Bogarde, Ryan O'Neal – which he hopes will be enough to sell this as yet unmade film to distributors overseas. Redford is getting $2 million for six weeks' work; James Caan, $1 million. He has come a long way since the days when he was known as One Print Levine, tramping cheap exploitation pictures around the hills of New England. One of his earliest hits was an educational film about sexually transmitted diseases titled *Body Beautiful*. Even though the subject matter disgusted him, he knew people would pay to see it. Another was an Australian film called *Walk Into Paradise*, which he cannily renamed *Walk Into Hell*. 'Advertise, publicise, exploit – and do it big' – that was Levine's motto. He once admitted that he did not so much publicise films as explode them.

His first big hit was dubbing an Italian gladiator movie, renaming it *Hercules* and spending a lot of money on publicity. He then threw a lot of money at Vittorio de Sica's breakthrough film *Ladri di Biciclette* (*The Bicycle Thief*, 1948). Before long Levine was not just marketing other people's films, but helping to make them. He alternated producing movies aimed at what he called the cocktail party crowd – *The Bicycle Thief, Darling, Carnal Knowledge* – with crowd-pleasers like *Zulu*. The writer Gay Talese once wrote that Levine never permitted culture to get the better of him.

According to Levine, one of the problems with the industry is that nobody is capable of making a big decision. He, on the other hand, is mostly guided by instinct. For example, the actor Stanley Baker sent him the script for *Zulu* one Friday and was surprised to get a phone call from the producer first thing Monday morning. Levine announced that he wanted to start filming as soon as possible. 'You liked the script that much?' asked Baker incredulously. Levine confessed that he had not actually had time to read it, he was just going on the title.

Now large corporations control the business, whereas Levine prefers to gamble with his own money. His biggest regret was selling his film company to the Avco Corporation in 1967 for $40 million. He quickly found himself reduced to rubber-stamping petty cash slips. The way he operates, he thinks of money as chips. If he thinks of it as money, he is lost.

Levine has pioneered a way of financing movies with *A Bridge Too Far* that he thinks will become the standard way of doing things for decades to come. If everything goes according to plan, a patchwork of cash advances will be sewn together, repaying Levine as the film goes along (actually, Spiegel would argue that it was he who pioneered this form of film finance). *If* everything goes according to plan, that is. But what if something goes wrong? What if Levine cannot get the stars he wants? Steve McQueen has already hustled for $1 million per week as well as a cut of the film's profits before being turned down. What if the overseas film companies don't come up with enough cash to fund the production? What if *A Bridge Too Far*, a war movie with thousands of extras, goes over budget without any Hollywood studio to step in and bail him out?

Selznick has by now knocked his ashtray onto the casino carpet, spilling ash and cigarette ends everywhere. Chronically clumsy, Selznick once reduced his wife to hysterics by slamming his genitals shut in a hotel bedroom drawer. He is also an inept gambler, either spreading his bets too thinly or, in poker, calling his opponent's hand at the wrong moment. Usually, but not this evening, he drinks when he plays, a cigarette stuck to his upper lip. In some years his gambling losses have outstripped his earnings as a producer. At the moment he is smoking between eighty and a hundred cigarettes a day.

Right now Selznick is struggling to stay upright and awake after working an eighteen-hour day on *Gone with the Wind* and surviving on three hours of sleep a night – with the help of the Benzedrine tablets he crunches. Like Levine and *A Bridge Too Far*, he faces financial ruin if *Gone with the Wind* is a flop. Because the film has gone so over budget he has personally borrowed $2 million from the Bank of America to fund production. One million will go to *Gone with the Wind* and another $600,000 will help fund *Rebecca*, an adaptation of the Daphne du Maurier novel. But Selznick has a fractious relationship with its director, Alfred Hitchcock, because the Englishman will not automatically bend to his will. In the past Selznick turned down a pet project of John Ford's called *Stagecoach* because the producer had not picked the subject himself. He is wary of letting directors get the upper hand.

Every morning Selznick comes into the office with a hundred notes from which he dictates memos, his secretaries' typewriters clattering away like an infernal machine. He sleeps with a notepad on his bedside table in case he is inspired in the night. These interminable memos – which have earned him the nickname the Great Dictater – spew out of his office. As one writer put it, Selznick seems to regard film-making as a sustained existential dilemma, an exercise in crisis management. At times he can be foolish and idealistic, at others an arrogant manipulator.

History has not been kind to David O. Selznick (the O, a self-invention, stands for nothing). As Thomas Schatz put it in his book, *The Genius of the System*, 'the governing perception of Selznick's role as producer, finally, is one of a necessary evil; at best, he is viewed as a well-meaning but troublesome meddler who managed to produce a masterpiece almost in spite of himself, and at worst he is reviled as a shameless self-promoter and vulgar philistine whom the top talent necessarily learned to ignore'.[4] But film historian Alan David Vertrees has argued that, on the contrary, Selznick was chief architect and prime mover in the creation of *Gone with the Wind*. Selznick supervised every major aspect of the film's making, from scriptwriting and production to editing and marketing. Leonard J. Leff, author of *Hitchcock and Selznick: The rich and strange collaboration of Alfred Hitchcock and David O. Selznick in Hollywood*, wrote that Selznick influenced everything he touched, from the acquisition of the literary property to screenplay development, cast selection, pre-production, production, post-production, distribution, exhibition, re-release, and, shortly before his death, recutting for television. As president, chief executive officer and sole producer of Selznick International Pictures, one is reminded of what Harold Pinter said about Sam Spiegel: total control, total authority.

Selznick was one of the first people to employ somebody to break down a script and draw it shot by shot – a process called story-boarding, which has since become ubiquitous. The producer borrowed the idea from Walt Disney, one of whose animators had devised a way of showing *Snow White and the Seven Dwarfs* in its entirety as a series of wall-mounted sketches. Selznick also, along with most of the producers profiled in this book, oversaw the marketing strategies of his films. He confounded market research and his own sales department by spending heavily on *Spellbound*, another Alfred Hitchcock project. Marketing experts predicted the film would be a spectacular failure after Selznick's tinkering delayed its release. But Selznick trusted his intuition, surely the hardest thing to learn to do in business, and spent heavily, making *Spellbound* a big hit.

One of Selznick's innovations was to release films simultaneously across America to capitalise on audience interest, a practice now standard with summer blockbusters. Another innovation was Selznick's becoming a prototype of the packaging agent who came to dominate Hollywood in the 1980s – agents who assemble stars, director and writer and then sell the package to a studio. Selznick packaged an adaptation of *Jane Eyre* starring Orson Welles after he decided that *Rebecca* was a veiled adaptation of the same novel. He had no desire to repeat himself. Twentieth Century-Fox bought the package for $250,000, and the practice has since become commonplace.

Now he has staked his whole career, the existence of his company, on *Gone with the Wind*. He has gambled millions of dollars on his own conviction. And he takes full responsibility for every inch of the film, for the writing and reading of every line, for every prop and every camera set-up. No matter how well the picture finally does, part of him will always question whether it was worth what he put himself, his family and his employees through. (In 1987 *Variety* estimated that *Gone with the Wind* earned theatrical rentals – money going to MGM after the exhibitor has taken his cut – of $841 million.) Just as Columbia is pressuring Spiegel to cut *Lawrence of Arabia*'s three-hour running time, so MGM is leaning on Selznick to do the same to *Gone with the Wind*. Selznick has already told Spiegel not to back down. Nevertheless, MGM is alarmed by what it sees as Selznick's constant rewriting of the script. Selznick has already fired George Cukor after the director complained about his so-called meddling. One reason why Cukor was fired was because he refused to allow Selznick approval of every camera set-up. Selznick told his production manager that he did not mean to put Cukor in a straightjacket, but he could only work with a director who did what he was told. Well, damn George Cukor, broods Selznick. George was only a director. Selznick alone is the judge of what is a good script. The producer today, thinks Selznick, in order to be able to produce properly, must be able not merely to criticise, but, if necessary, to sit down and write the scene. If he is criticising a director, he must be able not merely to say, 'I don't like it', but tell him how he would direct it himself.

Sometimes Selznick admits that his constant polishing of scripts rubs away the idea that excited him in the first place. Once he called in a scriptwriter to rewrite a big scene in one of his movies. Sure, said the writer, how did Selznick want it rewritten? Selznick replied that he didn't know, he hadn't had time to read it yet. But in the case of *Gone with the Wind* he estimates that he worked out about 80 per cent of the narrative himself, with a few other writers tossing in dialogue. After all, it was Selznick who altered the novel's final line of dialogue so that Clark Gable says, 'Frankly, my dear, I don't give a damn', echoing the producer's own speech patterns. And it was Selznick who devised the film's ending, with Scarlett O'Hara standing in silhouette as Max Steiner's music swells, and her final realisation of the power of home. In the end, five writers in addition to Selznick will work on the script, although the Academy Award for best screenplay will be given solely to Sidney Howard – just as best director will be given to Victor Fleming alone, perpetuating the legend of single-minded intent when it comes to authorship.

At times Selznick's attention to detail can be pitiless. Back at the Metro-Goldwyn-Mayer studio in Culver City, actors are coping with nineteenth-century costumes under the Technicolor lights. The temperature is like that of Death Valley. One actress, Ann Rutherford, has asked whether it is necessary for her to wear sweltering petticoats under lights when the camera cannot see them. Absolutely, Selznick told her, it helps you believe that you are in character. He will go grey trying to finish editing *Gone with the Wind* in time for its Atlanta premiere, strangled like Laocoon by 225,000 feet of celluloid printed out of the half a million shot. Like Irving Thalberg, production head of Metro-Goldwyn-Mayer, Selznick sees the first cut of any picture as raw material, with its eventual reshaping determined largely by reactions of preview audiences.

For Selznick, Hollywood is a business in which one has to fight every inch of the way. People who have not chosen to persist in violent tactics have fallen by the wayside. The studios continue to believe that if they hire a good director, buy a good property and put down a couple of casting names on paper, the picture is made. What they fail to realise is that picture after picture is a failure *despite* these elements, because they have not been produced. And by *produced*, he means with the skill and the experience and the showmanship to know what pays off, both dramatically and commercially.

Ironically, Selznick's later films, such as *Duel in the Sun*, show the producer wallowing in the kind of self-indulgence associated with auteur directors. On *Duel in the Sun* not a single scene was filmed without Selznick's approval, and the film chewed its way through eight directors. With Selznick's earlier films one gets the sense that, if anything, the project is the auteur, with its needs overriding the egos of its multiple creators. But Selznick overwhelmed his later productions, which became progressively less memorable. Ultimately, his domineering management would alienate nearly everybody who came into contact with him. He found himself in a downward spiral, working in self-indulgent isolation on occasional overblown vehicles starring his inamorata, Jennifer Jones.

So why have I chosen the seven producers in this book – Michael Douglas, Dino De Laurentiis, Duncan Kenworthy and Andrew Macdonald, Jeremy Thomas, Marin Karmitz and Christine Vachon? First, I definitely wanted to write about creative producers rather than people who, it could be argued, simply rubber-stamp other people's creativity. It seems to me that each of the seven represents a different facet of being a producer. Michael Douglas represents the Hollywood star as producer in the same way that George Clooney does. Dino De Laurentiis is perhaps the last of the old-fashioned movie moguls. Duncan Kenworthy, producer of *Notting Hill*, and his partner Andrew Macdonald (*Trainspotting*) show the way that producers often work in pairs, dividing the job between them. Jeremy Thomas is, to my mind, a truly creative producer, who assembled *The Last Emperor* – still the most ambitious and expensive film ever made outside the Hollywood studio system. Thomas also exemplifies Ralph Waldo Emerson's dictum 'Hitch your wagon to a star', working with auteur directors such as Bernardo Bertolucci or 'Beat' Takeshi and parachuting them into unfamiliar cultures. Marin Karmitz illustrates the way producers work differently in continental Europe, often acting as midwife to the director, in addition to being a fascinating character himself. And Christine Vachon seems to me to represent the future: a gay woman making explicitly homosexual-themed films is a long way from the stereotypical cigar-chomping tycoon.

Most of the producers profiled in this book are either compulsives or obsessives, anxious about power and where they fit in the food chain. Writing in *The New Yorker*, novelist Joan Didion observed that Hollywood is an industry predicated on the daily calibration and reassessment of status. Being a film producer is not a career for those who in banking parlance would be called 'risk averse'. It is a nerve-jangling job, where the project can fall apart with just a single phone call. Producing does not suit people who want a salary, as it is all about risk. In another life film producers would be racing-car drivers or Arctic explorers. After all, the human psyche can stand anything except uncertainty. But for a film producer every day is uncertain. The producer may have to put his security at risk just to get the film started – remortgage his house or, in the case of Richard Attenborough and *Gandhi*, sell his beloved painting collection. Often producers are gamblers in their private lives as well, although film production is more of a calculated risk than betting. Film producing also means joining the travelling circus, where the cast and crew become your family. This is why there are so many divorces in the business – it does not sit easily with the happy domesticity of family life.

Often people become film producers having first made a success of some other business. Bruckheimer left a successful career in photography and advertising to pursue bigger dreams in Hollywood. Saul Zaentz, producer of *The English Patient* and *Amadeus*, whose films in total have won twenty-two Academy Awards, started out as a rock concert promoter. Levine had a number of jobs, including selling religious statuettes for Daddy Grace, a Harlem evangelist, before owning a restaurant in Boston where he used to do magic tricks to entertain the customers.

Given the rejection that you must deal with, the financial risks involved, and the unscrupulousness of the people you come across, why would anybody want to become a producer? My own view is a simple one. Everybody interviewed for this book shares the same dream of raising the Academy Award for best picture on Oscar night. To paraphrase Milton, an Academy Award rather than fame is the spur. But what does the Academy Award represent? Obviously it represents profit, glory and power; and it is also a metaphor for the private Gulfstream jets, parties in the Hollywood hills and meeting fascinating, mythic beauties. More than that, however, the Oscar is a symbol that the producer has experienced that special high which comes from provoking an audience to laughter or tears.

What qualities does one need to become an independent producer? Persistence, for one. Dreams about Hollywood are as addictive and delusional as silky cocaine. Consider the odds stacked against a film getting made, and the mountain the producer must climb to get a movie into production (with a gradient that keeps getting steeper the nearer you get to shooting). For every ten ideas that a writer or producer has, only one will be written up as a treatment – two or three pages sketching the story. Out of every ten treatments, only one will be selected to become a first-draft screenplay. Of the ten first-draft screenplays, only one will be developed any further. Only one out of every ten finished screenplays sent to film companies will spark any interest. And out of ten projects being developed by a film company, only one will go into production. But the process does not stop there. Out of every ten films that go into production, five will lose money, and four will eventually recoup their costs once they have trickled through the ancillary markets of DVD and home videos, and pay and free television. But just one will be a hit – and these are the nerve-jangling odds the studios play every day.

A director once told writer Martin Amis that the only films Hollwoood makes are the ones it cannot get out of making. The decision to go ahead with a film, concluded Amis, is the result of fatalism, embarrassment or inertia. For example, *Shakespeare in Love* took eight years to come to the screen after co-writer Marc Norman first had the idea, and the project collapsed after stars Julia Roberts and Daniel Day-Lewis dropped out. It was recast years later with Gwyneth Paltrow and Joseph Fiennes, and went on to win seven Academy Awards, including best picture, in 1999.

Scepticism is another arrow in the film producer's quiver. Being the most glamorous business in the world (comedian John Belushi once described film as king and television as furniture), film-making attracts boasters, hustlers and those one step ahead of the law.

A new London-based film company called Alchymie was launched in October 1999 in one of the city's top restaurants. Jeroboams of champagne embossed with the company logo flowed all night. Alchymie claimed it would spend $250 million over five years producing movies. And there to give his blessing for the launch was the then culture minister Chris Smith, beaming his Cheshire cat smile for the cameras. Even as Smith was speaking, guests were exchanging glances which meant 'he is going to regret this'. Four months later, Alchymie had fired most of its staff because it had no money to pay them.

Another example is the producer who announced during one Cannes Film Festival that he had raised a multimillion-dollar investment fund. The result of this was that the phone in his hotel room never stopped ringing as companies fought to set up meetings and lunch dates. But when a friend congratulated him on the fund, the producer admitted that the whole thing was a complete lie. He had made the same announcement at last year's Cannes Film Festival because it was the only way he could get people who normally wouldn't give him the time of day to return his calls. (Both announcements were written up by the sometimes credulous and forgetful trade press, which occasionally has the memory of a goldfish.)

Ruthlessness is another quality that producers need. Most of the successful films of the last fifteen years or so involved a key member getting fired. Indeed, one producer's trick is to fire somebody on the first day of shooting just to instil the fear of God into cast and crew. And if you are not ruthless as a producer, the chances are that you will be the one who is fired. 'You can be loyal to only one thing, and that is yourself and your vision,' says British producer Jonathan Olsberg (*Head in the Clouds*).

But perhaps the most prized skill in an independent producer was best summed up by F. Scott Fitzgerald in his Hollywood novel *The Last Tycoon*. Narrator Celia Brady, herself the daughter of a producer, says that the complex business of movie-making can be understood, but only 'dimly and in flashes'. 'Not half a dozen men,' she asserts, 'have been able to keep the whole equation of pictures in their heads.'[5]

1 Michael Douglas

The star

Making contact with Michael Douglas must be rather like trying to set up an interview with the royal family, only harder. Hollywood stars employ a cordon of people to protect them from strangers – mainly because most people who come into the orbit of a star try to make money out of them. Michael Douglas, on the other hand, was gracious enough to agree to meet face to face when told about this book. Then September 11th happened and all travel plans were cancelled. I was told by his people that I would have to settle for a telephone interview or, in hacks' parlance, a phoner. But even with a phone conversation there are layers of security that one has to go through. First you are given the number of an answering service in New York. Then you are put through to a telephone operator at another number. But where is Douglas anyway? In New York or in the Bahamas? Or circling the world in a private Lear jet? By the time Douglas comes on the phone even he sounds apologetic.

Michael Douglas had had a unique career path in Hollywood, because he first tasted success as a producer, not as an actor. Other actors, such as George Clooney, have used fame as a platform from which to launch production careers. With Douglas it was the other way round. Indeed, when the very first film he produced, *One Flew Over the Cuckoo's Nest*, won the Academy Award for best picture in

1975, Douglas remembers sitting with director Milos Forman and co-producer Saul Zaentz and predicting that it would all be downhill from there on.

But of course it was not downhill from there. Douglas went on to produce, among others, *The China Syndrome*, *Romancing the Stone* and its sequel *Jewel of the Nile*, *Flatliners* and the John Woo action movie *Face/Off*. Fellow producer Jeremy Thomas describes Douglas as one of the nicest people in what can be a venal business. People can be laughing with you one moment, and then shove a knife between your ribs the next – and not feel any connection between the two. At the same time, his acting career took off. Douglas won his second Academy Award in 1987 for his portrayal of rapacious stockbroker Gordon Gekko in *Wall Street*. He said that he drew on his experience of constant rejection as a producer when he had to find the motivation for Gekko's anger. According to Douglas, Gekko thrived on the energy of anybody who ever crossed him, and cherished holding grudges – it gave him the energy to keep going. As a producer all the rejection Douglas experienced also gave him stamina. By the late 1980s he was one of the biggest stars in the world. He had carved out a niche for himself as a middle-class white male under pressure in films such as *Fatal Attraction*, *Basic Instinct* and *Falling Down*.

Douglas grew up in Hollywood surrounded by the film industry. Los Angeles is a one-industry city in much the same way that Detroit is the centre of the world's car business; and studio executives work in much the same way as managers in other corporations, despite the exoticism of their product. Each morning they scan the daily pages of *Variety* and the *Hollywood Reporter*, the film industry equivalent of the sports pages, for shifts in the market. Douglas' father, Kirk, was one of the first stars, along with James Stewart, to set up his own production company back in the 1950s, when anti-competition legislation weakened the studios' grip on the business. Now Kirk could develop his own projects rather than just be an actor for hire. Kirk launched his own production company in 1955, named after his mother, Bryna, fulfilling a promise to her that one day she would see her name in lights. Bryna's first film was *The Indian Fighter*, in which, for reasons best known to himself, Kirk offered a role to his ex-wife Diana, Michael Douglas' mother. Even more puzzling, she accepted. Michael said that growing up in Hollywood meant he had a sense of reality and perspective about show business. As a teenager, visiting Kirk on set at Universal Pictures, he would spend lunchtimes in the editing suites. One of the first pieces he saw being cut together was the shower murder in *Psycho*.

Douglas attended the University of California at Santa Barbara, a campus best known for its bikini-clad students and surfing. It was the peak of the 1960s counterculture, when it seemed as if even the government was about to be overthrown. Understandably, given the revolution around him, and perhaps still feeling rejected by Kirk after his parents' divorce, Douglas dropped out of university. First he got a job working in a petrol station, and was even voted Mobil employee of the month. But he gave that up and drifted into a commune outside San Francisco, where he spent most of his time taking LSD and swimming naked in the pool. However, he probably knew that he was running away from something, and realised that he could not spend the rest of his life studying his (metaphysical) big toe. Instead he decided to become an actor – against Kirk's wishes. Like most Jewish parents, Kirk wanted his son to join one of the steady professions, become a lawyer, for example. When Kirk went to see Michael in his first play he was not afraid to tell his son how rotten he was. But Michael persisted and soon found himself typecast as the sensitive young man against the Vietnam

War in a couple of films. By the early 1970s, however, the war was over and these parts dried up. Douglas was left with a dilemma. Should he admit defeat and go into television? More specifically, should he accept a job as the second lead in a low-budget cop show produced by Quinn Martin? (Remember the gravelly voice announcing 'A Quinn Martin production'?)

Douglas faced the reality that Hollywood was not hammering down his door and accepted Martin's job offer. Martin cast Douglas as a young cop opposite Karl Malden, a friend of Kirk's and another refugee from Hollywood, in *The Streets of San Francisco*. Douglas played an idealistic by-the-book rookie paired with Malden's grizzled flatfoot. *The Streets of San Francisco* was one of television's first buddy cop shows and became an enormous success, partly because the real star was San Francisco itself. The show had a gruelling schedule, requiring fifty-two minutes of footage every seven shooting days. This meant shooting twelve pages of script each day. Douglas and Malden would finish a scene, grab the film cans and camera, hop in the truck and take off to another location. According to Douglas, making *Streets* was like lifting weights in a gym for a young would-be producer. He stuck close to the show's production manager, watching how the script was broken down and budgeted scene by scene. Having spent four years making a one-hour film every six days, he could not help but notice how feature films got made. *Streets* also taught Douglas a valuable lesson – that if a feature film was going to work, then cast and crew had to pull together.

As if Douglas did not have enough to do working fourteen hours a day, six days a week on *Streets*, he spent his only day off zipping across the bridge to Berkeley. He was developing his first feature film with Saul Zaentz, owner of Fantasy Records, the record label of rock band Creedence Clearwater Revival. Eight years previously, Kirk had acquired the film rights to *One Flew Over the Cuckoo's Nest*, a first novel by Ken Kesey, an unknown writer at Stanford University. The publisher Viking had snapped up the manuscript, paying Kesey $1500 – its highest ever advance for a first novel. Kirk then paid Kesey another $20,000 for the film rights. Published in February 1962, *Cuckoo's Nest* stayed for 258 consecutive weeks on the US best-seller list. Jack Kerouac hailed Kesey as 'a great American novelist'. When he saw Kesey, critic Malcolm Cowley, who was lecturing at Stanford at the time, was reminded of the glow which surrounded the young Hemingway in Paris in the 1920s.

Put simply, the novel of *Cuckoo's Nest* is about the conflict between Randle P. McMurphy, a convict who has faked his way into a mental hospital thinking it will be easier than prison, and Big Nurse, head of the psychiatric ward or 'the Combine'. The book is written in a druggy paranoid style, which chimed with 1960s youth. The Combine's electric machinery controls the ward just outside the narrator's field of vision – patients are enveloped by 'fog machines'. Kesey's great inspiration was to tell the story through the eyes of Chief Broom, an apparently deaf and dumb Native American Indian. Using Chief Broom as the narrator allowed Kesey to present the schizophrenic state the way the schizophrenic himself felt it, while at the same time reporting on the escalating conflict between Big Nurse and McMurphy. Kesey was inspired to write *Cuckoo's Nest* when he was high on peyote and Chief Broom swam fully formed into his vision – even though the writer had never met or had any interest in Native American Indians. Kesey, along with William Burroughs, was one of the first writers to use hallucinogenic drug insights in his work. Kesey had volunteered to be a guinea pig for various drugs being developed by the CIA as truth-telling serums at Menlo Park war veterans hospital in Palo Alto, California. Up to that point he had been a first-class student and a top athlete. But he was so excited about his experiences under the influence of various drugs (for example, a squirrel dropping a nut outside the hospital window had sounded like an atomic bomb exploding) that he got a job as a night attendant on the psychiatric ward. The hospital authorities allowed Kesey to bring a typewriter into the ward, and he banged out sketches of hospital life which he said later came more easily to him than anything before or since. The job also allowed him to break into the medicine cabinet, and he wrote several passages of the book high on peyote and LSD. He even underwent electroconvulsive therapy (ECT) so that he could write the passage in which Chief Broom comes back from the 'shock shop'. One night Kesey swallowed a dose of mescaline and, as he wrote to a friend, 'managed the night by mopping fervently whenever the nurse arrived so she couldn't see my twelve-gauge pupils, and the rest of the time argued so heatedly with the big knotty pine door across the office from me that I finally chalked a broad yellow line across the floor between us and told the door, "You stay on your side, you goggle-eyed son of a bitch, and I'll stay on mine".'[1]

Kirk Douglas thought so highly of *Cuckoo's Nest* that he dropped out of Hollywood to go back to the theatre for the first time in eighteen years. He opened his stage adaptation at the Schubert Theatre in New Haven. He told one critic that he was hoping for a long run at the Cort Theater on Broadway before taking the project to Hollywood. But the play was not a hit and *Cuckoo's Nest* closed after about eight months. Kirk also had no interest from Hollywood, which bewildered him. 'Who wants to laugh at crazy people?' executives asked. But Kirk never saw *Cuckoo's Nest* as a difficult film, just a brilliant story with conflict running through it: conflict between individuals, and conflict between the individual and society – and conflict is what drama is about. After a while, Kirk got tired of throwing his weight against studio doors, trying to force them open. As Woody Allen once said, Hollywood is not so much a dog eat dog world, as dog does not return other dog's phone calls. Kirk then tried to sell the rights for $150,000 in 1970 but could not find any buyers. Eventually Michael stepped in and said he wanted to try. Kirk wished his son well but at the time did not rate his chances of getting the film made.

Looking for investors, Michael Douglas was told by an agent that Saul Zaentz of Berkeley-based Fantasy Records was interested in investing in *Cuckoo's Nest*. Born in Passaic, New Jersey, Zaentz had started out by taking a course in poultry husbandry at Rugers University before attending a small business school. His boyhood interest in jazz and big bands, however, led him into the music business. The agent informed Douglas that Zacntz was only interested in fully financing the $2 million project if he was allowed to choose both the star and the director. Douglas had his own ideas about director and star and was not prepared to give way. The agent was told to relay the message back to Zaentz. Once again *Cuckoo's Nest* was back in limbo. But a few months later Zaentz and Douglas made direct contact and realised they saw eye to eye about the project. After getting rid of the intermediary they then contacted Kesey, wanting him to write the screenplay. The three men met and Zaentz told Kesey that he would get a chunk of the profits even if he did not write the script. But Kesey would get an additional salary if he wrote the screenplay. In 1970 Kesey told *Rolling Stone* magazine that he wanted to write and direct a film of *Cuckoo's Nest*. He would make it so weird, he said, that people would have trouble finding the exit when it was over. Kesey submitted an unusable screenplay. In one scene a nurse wearing a Valkyrian helmet like a stock figure in a Wagner opera scratches the walls, producing streams of blood. Zaentz and Douglas remained optimistic and requested rewrites. But Kesey reappeared with an agent and a list of demands.

Everything stalled and, in the end, Kesey was dropped. He subsequently sued for damages over the unused script, complaining that he thought Douglas and Zaentz had diluted the book for the sake of commercialism. Douglas and Zaentz, railed the novelist, had taken out the conspiracy that is America. He wanted five cents of every dollar taken at the box office, together with $800,000 in damages. Douglas pointed out that he had already promised Kesey a slice of the profits. The author settled for a still generous 2.5 per cent of the box office gross. (Usually only stars get a share of the gross; directors and writers have to make do with an often meaningless share of net profits – what is left after the exhibitor and the film company have taken out their commissions. The film business has been compared to a bucket full of holes when it comes to making money, because of the number of commissions taken out along the way. Studio accountants are there to make sure that some films never become profitable.) The dispute left a bitter taste in Douglas' mouth because he had idolised Kesey, not only for his book but also for his lifestyle, which Douglas had tasted during his Santa Barbara commune period.

One example of the synchronicity running through the project was that, unbeknown to each other, both father and son wanted the same man to direct: a Czech director called Milos Forman. Early in 1963 Kirk and other Hollywood personalities had been encouraged by President Kennedy to become ambassadors, spreading a message of goodwill from America to satellite Soviet bloc countries. Kennedy was now dead but the idea of goodwill missions was still there. Kirk first toured Europe and Asia for two months at the beginning of February 1964. It was during another trip a couple of years later, either in Prague or at the Karlovy Vary Film Festival, that Kirk encountered the then 34-year-old Forman. The writer and director, born Tomas Jan in 1932 in Caslav, Czechoslovakia, was already making a name for himself as a comedy director. In films such as *The Firemen's Ball* Forman showed a flair for lampooning authority, so much so that the Czech fire brigade went on strike in protest. *The Firemen's Ball* and *Loves of a Blonde* were both nominated for an Academy Award for best foreign language picture. Kirk discussed *Cuckoo's Nest* with Forman, who showed interest, and the actor sent him a copy of the book when he got back to America. Not hearing anything, Kirk assumed that Forman was no longer interested, but in fact the package had never reached its destination. Presumably it had been opened and destroyed by the Communist authorities. Eventually Forman left his young family in Prague, having been issued with a visa for America, and moved into the Chelsea Hotel in New York. His first English language film was *Taking Off*, a hippy story about two runaway teenagers written by John Guare, a playwright friend of Michael Douglas. It was Guare who recommended Forman to Douglas. Forman set off to the first meeting with Douglas feeling sceptical. As far as he was concerned, Michael Douglas, because of his father, represented mainstream Hollywood; and the possible co-producer, Saul Zaentz, represented American business. In his opinion, *Cuckoo's Nest* was a subject neither for Hollywood nor for big business. Forman could not understand why Zaentz and Douglas were such fools as to want to film *Cuckoo's Nest*. Although Forman wanted to make it, why Douglas and Zaentz saw the project as commercial was a mystery to him. Of course, he did not tell them that.

One of the key things Douglas had learned about television was the importance of understanding from the director how he saw the episode. But all of the would-be directors he interviewed for *Cuckoo's Nest* held their cards so close to their chest that Douglas assumed this was the way things worked in films. (Presumably they just did not have any ideas.) So it was a relief to sit down with Forman and listen as the Czech director went through the script page by page telling Douglas what he liked and disliked about each scene. (It was only after this meeting that Douglas found out about his father's prior interest in the director.) According to Douglas, the philosopher's stone of any artistic collaboration is as follows:

> What you do is, you just talk it out. Talking it through helps you see whether the director has a vision, and whether there might be bumps in the road. Making people articulate you get a better idea of what the picture is going to be. I do a lot of my producing unofficially as an actor. I just make a point to the director as an insecure actor, whether I'm insecure or not. I say, 'I really need to talk this out.' We take the script and I force him, even if it might be a lazy director who has not thought about it; I make him talk before we start shooting the movie. I say, 'Let me hear the movie through your eyes', and it forces the director to have to talk it out.

To Forman's relief all three agreed on the basic concept of the film. First, *Cuckoo's Nest* would not pander to fashion by being self-consciously psychedelic and druggy, which would date it quickly. Second, the story must leave Chief Broom's head and be told objectively. Forman said that *Cuckoo's Nest* was the perfect book to stylise because it was all the vision of one mind put into words. But cinematography can only show surfaces, and you cannot step into somebody else's mind and describe thought without using voice-over. Forman felt the story was strong enough to be told objectively. He liked to reveal the inside through the surface. Forman was drawn to stories that dealt with individuals in conflict against the Establishment. He called *Cuckoo's Nest* a sort of a Czech book in that sense. The patients' difference from other people lies purely in their inability to adjust to rules. One character destroys all group games, while another needs to be an ally no matter what the situation. Forman defined mental illness as an inability to adjust to ever-changing, unspoken rules. It is people who are unable to follow these rules who are labelled crazy. Possibly for Forman the story resonated because it echoed the situation of those who disagreed with the Communist regime being locked up in mental hospitals. For Forman mental illness was a social disease, and therefore *Cuckoo's Nest* was a metaphor for society.

By now Douglas had spent two years trying to put *Cuckoo's Nest* together. Kirk Douglas was now too old for the part of McMurphy, and, in what could be interpreted as an Oedipal situation, Douglas approached Jack Nicholson. In another piece of synchronicity, Nicholson too had tried to buy the rights to *Cuckoo's Nest* in 1962, only to be told that Kirk had already acquired them. Although he was a fan of the book, one of the things which swayed Nicholson was the degree of openness Douglas and Zaentz brought to proceedings. Nicholson and Forman had never come across producers who were quite so collaborative before. However, this collaboration involved a lot of shouting, which often scared people around them. Forman would rant at Douglas and Zaentz for their stupidity. According to Zaentz, they were all novices, thrashing about in a business they knew little about. They may have fought, but, according to Zaentz, Douglas worked his fingers raw getting the film made. *Cuckoo's Nest* needed a star for the audience to identify with, because the rest of the cast would be unknowns. Once Nicholson was on board, financier Columbia allowed the budget to double to $4 million (a quarter of which was Nicholson's fee). Forman now had another $1 million to play with, which – although it did not change the way he wanted to make the film – gave him more time, more choices and a more experienced crew. In short, all of the agreeable things which a star brings to the director.

Douglas and Forman spent a year choosing the supporting cast. They interviewed more than nine hundred actors before whittling the list down to a final twenty. Forman believed that each of the patients had to be instantly identifiable and unique, but also had to work as part of a team. The producer and director spent between ten and fifteen minutes with each actor to get an idea of his personality. Every actor then took part in a make-believe therapy session with others auditioning. Those who walked in rolling their eyes and acting 'cwazy' because they knew this was a film about madness were immediately disqualified. Douglas and Forman then scoured Native American Indian communities for the right man to play Chief. They found him in Mount Rainier National Park in the state of Washington, where Will Sampson was working as an assistant warden. Sampson said that two men appeared on horses and offered him a career in the movies. At first he thought they were kidding, but he accepted over drinks that night. However, five actresses – Anne Bancroft, Ellen Burstyn, Colleen Dewhurst, Angela Lansbury and Geraldine Page – turned down the role of Nurse Ratched. In Kesey's book Big Nurse personifies America's crushing maternalism as she (symbolically) suffocates her charges between her breasts. Such misogyny was out of keeping with the women's liberation movement of the mid-1970s. Douglas and Forman had toned down the misogyny but such an unsympathetic part was a tough sell. In the end, Louise Fletcher, a fairly unknown television actress who had given up her career in 1962 to marry a producer, was finally cast. The film's Big Nurse – soft-skinned, petite and played in a saccharine monotone by Fletcher – kills more patients with kindness than electric shock treatment.

Douglas wanted to shoot inside a real mental hospital, but everybody he approached rejected his offer of a financial donation.

Because of the controversy surrounding the book, hospitals were afraid of receiving damaging publicity. The team ended up going to the hospital in Salem, Oregon, where Kesey had set the novel. Dean Rooks, director of Oregon State Hospital, loved *Cuckoo's Nest* and understood what had motivated Kesey to write it. The hospital used to have almost three thousand patients but at the time of filming had only six hundred in full-time care. An entire ward was given over to the team for both filming and production offices. Forman lived in the hospital for weeks, collaborating on a third-draft screenplay with Lawrence Hauben, a young writer who had already worked on two drafts by himself. Hauben was eventually replaced by a second writer, Bo Goldman. (Hauben and Goldman would win an Academy Award for *Cuckoo's Nest*, and Goldman would go on to win another Oscar for his screenplay *Melvin and Howard*.) Kesey's book had the feel of some kind of psychedelic cartoon, something Forman thought was totally unsuitable for film. 'There was a definite division in our points of view,' said Hauben. 'I created a warp and woof of time and space, like a trip in a nut house, using contrapuntal sound. Milos didn't want any of that. He was always asking, "But what happens next?" He goes from A to B to C – his main interest is how you get upstairs.'[2] (Hauben earned a million dollars from *Cuckoo's Nest* through his share of net profits. This was the only substantial money he ever made in his life. He invested the money in a dubious Panamanian tax shelter before dying of cancer in 1985. In December 1991 a Los Angeles jury found lawyers who had advised Hauben on the investment guilty of negligence. A judge awarded $1.8 million to Hauben's widow and daughter.)

Part of the deal Douglas made with Rooks was that inmates would be employed in technical departments during filming to give them extra money and a sense of responsibility. Therefore an arsonist who had tried to burn down the hospital the year before would work with the painters, a murderer was employed as an electrician and two paedophiles shifted scenery.

Filming began on 11 January 1975 for eleven weeks. One night Douglas and Nicholson were invited to something locals called a 'Hollywood party'. Curious to see what this was, they accepted the invitation and discovered it was a wife-swapping orgy. (Douglas and Nicholson refrained from joining in.)

One sour note during filming was when Douglas had to fire cameraman Haskell Wexler. The Oscar-winning cameraman wanted to give the hospital a harsh, depressing look, but Forman felt that through Nicholson's eyes the hospital should look faintly cosy – or at least better than prison. Wexler, whose concern for the misbegotten had been shown in political documentaries he had made and in his feature *Medium Cool*, disliked Forman's comic approach and did not hide his feelings. He complained that he was only being used to about 10 per cent of his ability. The flashpoint came when Wexler spent days filming the group therapy session. His camera had nothing to look at but faces. Forman said he had problems with Wexler because he was such a perfectionist. If you gave a cameraman his freedom, said Forman, he would exchange the actors for puppets because they would be less likely to disturb his lighting.

One Flew Over the Cuckoo's Nest opens and closes on an Oregon landscape, an image of liberty. Randle P. McMurphy, charged with assault and statutory rape – behaviour he cheerfully acknowledges – is transferred from a penal work farm to the state mental hospital, where, suspected of faking, he is held for observation. McMurphy is the only person who tries to make contact with individual patients on the ward. But the individual does not exist for this institution, only the group. Staff observe their charges with chill, impassive stares. Once a day half the ward gathers for a futile group therapy session with Nurse Ratched, who sets about embarrassing the men by washing their dirty linen in public. McMurphy – irrepressibly cheerful – soon clashes with Ratched, who sees her efforts to calm disturbed minds upset by his war on apathy. McMurphy substitutes a pornographic deck of cards for the one used in the ward, introduces cigarettes as gambling currency, and persuades hitherto submissive patients to demand changes in the ward schedule. He even organises a truant excursion for a deep-sea fishing trip one afternoon, accompanied by his hooker friend Candy. McMurphy is incredulous when he finds out that most of the patients are there voluntarily – and, unlike him, free to leave. He nearly causes a riot on the ward and is dragged off for shock treatment. Also waiting for shock treatment is Chief, a huge, morose and supposedly deaf and dumb Indian. Breaking his silence, Chief tells McMurphy that he is using the asylum as a refuge from the world that destroyed his father. If McMurphy symbolises the rebellious, aggressive side of the American psyche, then Chief is the vulnerable, terrified aspect. A delighted McMurphy invites the Indian to escape with him, but Chief says he is not ready. McMurphy decides to go it alone and one night holds a farewell party. He smuggles Candy and her friend Rose into the ward with supplies of booze, and the patients have a wild night – to the horror of the night attendant. But McMurphy makes the mistake of postponing his getaway so that a severely repressed boy, Billy Bibbit, can lose his virginity to Candy. Next morning McMurphy and the others are sleeping off their hangovers when Nurse Ratched and her staff arrive on the ward. Discovered in Candy's arms and harried back into his sexual trauma by Ratched, Billy commits suicide. An incensed McMurphy tries to strangle Ratched, but is hauled off for a lobotomy which leaves him catatonic. The party is the last straw for the authorities, and it is McMurphy's back they break. Contemplating the shell that was once his friend, Chief smothers McMurphy with a pillow. The Chief is the 'one' of the title who eventually escapes the asylum. But in a way McMurphy has been reincarnated through Chief. To break out of the hospital Chief lifts a stone drinking fountain in an action reminiscent of the rock being rolled away from Christ's tomb.

The film opened on 20 November 1975 to almost universal acclaim. Critics praised all of the performances, and immediately predicted Academy Awards for Nicholson and Fletcher. Forman's deft handling of the material was also appreciated. Even the editing and cinematography were singled out for being unobtrusive. However, the reviewer in *Films and Filming* said that watching the film he felt uncomfortably like one of those fashionable Parisians invited to laugh at the capers of inmates in Charenton mental asylum. And *Framework* magazine called *Cuckoo's Nest* dangerous and criminally irresponsible. It objected to the film's pretence that a game of basketball, an invigorating fishing trip and losing one's virginity can cure mental illness. In particular, *Framework* was alarmed by the film's anti-intellectualism. In *Cuckoo's Nest*, therapy – which in real life helps people and sparks insights into their problems – is seen as a form of castration. (Michael Douglas himself was later in therapy with Kirk, trying to work through their relationship, and also sought counselling for his drinking.) One patient, Harding, is derided for using long words. He has problems with his wife, and he is possibly impotent. The implication is that he is homosexual. 'And so the equation is built up,' noted *Framework*, 'the intellect equals impotence equals homosexuality.'[3] Michael Wood made a similar attack in *The New York Review of Books*: 'Can it be that the insane are merely scared, that it's all nurse's fault, and that a good fuck would cure many a pathology? Isn't there something unfeeling about such optimism? Kesey's novel doesn't prompt such questions . . . but Forman's movie does, and this reminds us how simplified it is both psychologically and poetically.'[4]

Audiences did not take any notice of this handful of squeamish reviews, and eventually *Cuckoo's Nest* grossed more than $112 million in the United States alone. It was nominated for nine Academy Awards in 1975 and won five. Kirk sat out the agony at home in Palm Springs. Forman would go on to win another Academy Award in 1984 for directing *Amadeus*, again produced by Zaentz, who also picked up a statuette. And Zaentz would win a third Academy Award for best picture in 1996 for *The English Patient*.

Now Douglas was left facing the classic 'second album syndrome'. How on earth could he top the success of his first movie? Once again he decided to look for a story that had a strong point of view or something thought-provoking to say. Douglas described this as the difference between reading a forgettable trashy novel and a haunting classic. After working his way through the slush pile, Douglas came across a script by Tom S. Cook and Michael Gray titled *Eyewitness to Power*. It was about the then fantastic notion of something going wrong at an atomic power plant, nearly triggering a nuclear explosion. An engineer tells a television reporter that a local power plant has had a number of safety problems. Filming inside the plant, the reporter and his crew are trapped when the plant nearly goes into meltdown. Douglas set up a meeting with Gray, the co-writer, and was surprised by his opening line: 'You know this is going to be a race,' said Gray. Douglas, taken aback, asked why. What race? 'A race to get the film released before there is a major nuclear accident,' said Gray. Douglas did not say anything, but he thought Gray was being a bit dramatic. Nevertheless, he optioned the script, which was renamed *The China Syndrome*. The title comes from the observation that if a nuclear power plant went into meltdown and sank through the earth's surface, there would be nothing to stop it from burrowing through to the other side of the world – in China. What interested Douglas about *The China Syndrome* was that it worked on a number of levels beyond the obvious political issue. It worked as a horror movie; and it had an interesting social message with all the aspects of a nail-biting thriller. Douglas also found a parallel with *Cuckoo's Nest* in that both projects were about individuals caught in a corporate or social structure that forces them to make a moral decision at the expense of their lives. In short, both films attempted to be Greek tragedy. Even so, there were times when he was working on the script that Douglas thought 99.9 per cent of the audience would not have a clue what he was talking about.

One might have thought that having just produced a film which went on to win five Academy Awards, Douglas would be fighting off people wanting to invest in his next project. Not so. He could not find anybody to put money into *The China Syndrome*. Even Zaentz turned him down. 'I kept smelling my armpits,' said Douglas. 'A lot of people I spoke to were real buddy-buddy, then they stuck it to me.'[5] A number of studios also passed. 'They really fucked around with me. Well, I keep tabs. I'll get even,' he said later.[6] 'What kept me going was the revenge factor. That's a key part of producers. It's like "some day, some day I'm going to get that son of a bitch. I'm going to have a hit picture." I think revenge is a very good emotion if you can direct it. It's healthy. Very healthy. It's like, maybe you happen to be in a restaurant somewhere and see somebody, and you just stop and say hello – "Hi, I'm celebrating passing a hundred million in grosses. Nice to see you again!" Revenge is great.'[7]

Gray originally wanted to direct – which Douglas supported – but his only experience had been directing low-budget documentaries. One of the hardest things is to persuade people to work with a first-time director. For an imaginative business, Hollywood does not have much imagination. One friend spent years trying to get a film with a first-time director off the ground, but the project was in production quickly once an established name was brought in (who subsequently ruined the film). Douglas' strategy would be to surround Gray with a strong cast attractive to an audience, provided these stars were prepared to work for slightly less than their usual fee. Early on he went to see Lenny Hirsham at the William Morris Agency, and asked the agent if he could think of anybody to play Cordell, who in the script was the 32-year-old plant manager. In classic Hollywood style, Hirsham asked Douglas whether Cordell had to be that particular age. (As the Hollywood joke goes, 'How many development executives does it take to change a light bulb? Answer: 'Does it have to be a light bulb?) Instead, Hirsham suggested 50-year-old Jack Lemmon for the part, knowing it would complement the actor's interest in environmental issues. Early in the 1970s Lemmon had narrated a series of documentaries for broadcaster NBC about ecological problems. The Pacific Gas and Electric Company One complained about one programme disclosing the dangers of nuclear energy, and NBC cancelled it. Douglas drove to Lemmon's house and pitched him the story. What impressed Lemmon most was Douglas' passion for the project. Lemmon deliberately stayed out of work for a year to be in the film.

Jack Nicholson dropped out of the role of the television reporter. Douglas cast himself as the television crew producer, with Richard Dreyfuss as the reporter. At the same time, Douglas was trying to woo Columbia Pictures. The package was now budgeted at $3.8 million. However, Dreyfuss priced himself out of the film by suddenly doubling his fee to $500,000. (Dreyfuss had reservations about Gray as director, but at the time he had need of a large amount of cash.) Eventually Jane Fonda – who had wanted to make a film about real-life nuclear whistle-blower Karen Silkwood but could not get the rights – replaced Dreyfuss as the lead. Fonda outlined her conditions over dinner in a restaurant on Melrose Avenue in Los Angeles. Gray had wanted an 'untraditional' look for the film but Fonda insisted on a straightforward Hollywood telling of the story. Gray was dropped as director. He commented later that Fonda may have been radical politically, but professionally she was quite conservative.

Once Fonda was on board, *The China Syndrome* became a co-production with her production company IPC. A new script was written taking Fonda into account. Columbia, where Fonda had planned to make her version of the Silkwood story, agreed to a pay or play deal. This meant that the studio agreed to pay Fonda's fee whether or not the film went into production. Effectively Columbia had more to lose by not putting *The China Syndrome* before the cameras.

James Bridges was chosen to replace Gray as director, despite the fact he had only made one film, *The Paper Chase* (1973), which had been successful. Even Bridges turned down Fonda and Douglas three times, although he later described Douglas as both meticulous and dogged. Douglas and Bridges thought that since *The China Syndrome* was a classic, formal thriller – a race against the clock – they wanted something different from a classic, formal editor. David Rawlins had just come off *Saturday Night Fever* and had what Douglas called 'a great, jamming style',[8] with a pace which never let up. Douglas also employed a team of technical advisers for expert information about atomic energy. The team included three former General Electric consultants who had resigned from the company because of their fears about safety. Their advice was useful when building the centrepiece of the film, an exact copy of a nuclear power plant control room. The project was allowed to film around a real nuclear power plant after promising its owner there would be no bad publicity. Of course, the script was kept well away from utility company executives and staff at the the plant. But a mischievous reporter leaked a copy to the workers. As a result they gave Fonda a fair deal of abuse, stemming from her days as 'Hanoi Jane' when she was photographed sitting smiling in a Vietcong anti-aircraft battery during the Vietnam War. One crew member remembered the last few days of shooting as being pretty frightening, with Fonda singled out for victimisation. The level of paranoia increased when Douglas discovered that his phone had been bugged after talking to the press about the film.

The China Syndrome opened on 650 screens in America on 16 March 1979, three years after Douglas had first optioned the script. Twelve days later a nuclear power plant at Three Mile Island in Pennsylvania caught fire and nearly went into meltdown. Bruce Gilbert, the executive producer, wondered if somebody had seen their film and – driven by some kind of delusion – had sabotaged the plant in imitation of Jack Lemmon. For Michael Douglas, the Three Mile Island incident was close to a religious experience. It was as if God were sending him a warning. There is even a moment in the film when experts discuss what would happen in the event of a meltdown, and one turns to another and says it would destroy an area the size of Pennsylvania. But contrary to what people thought, Douglas saw Three Mile Island as detrimental to the success of the film. What he had portrayed as an edge-of-your-seat thriller was now real. People stayed away from *The China Syndrome* because they thought they were watching it on the evening news. Nevertheless, *The China Syndrome* eventually grossed nearly $95 million.

Once again Douglas found himself in limbo. Although the stars and directors of his last two films had been offered other things, as producer he was left to start all over again. He soon realised that a producer is only as good as his next project. 'You've given your heart and soul to that one film, but it's on to the next one putting the elements together,' he told me. And just because he had enjoyed a couple of successes did not mean the studios were going to say yes to whatever he wanted to do. So it was a relief when Columbia offered his production company Bigstick a three-year first-look deal. A first-look deal means that the studio pays a producer's rent and salary bill in exchange for, literally, a first look at what he wants to make next. All the studios have first-look deals, often with stars' production companies. These 'vanity deals' rarely produce anything, and are kept on so that the star has a relationship with the studio. 'I have a special relationship with Tom/Nicole/Clint,' the executive will say, ignoring the truth that the only thing which motivates stars is getting their hands on the best script. However, in Douglas' case the studio was paying the overheads of a real producer. Leo Jaffe, chairman of Columbia Pictures, boasted that the deal was a coup for both Douglas and the studio. 'We're looking for pictures we can mutually agree upon,' said Jaffe. Douglas thought that he could produce a film a year. He hired Jack Brodsky, producer of Woody Allen's *Everything You Always Wanted to Know About Sex* and a marketing expert who had worked on *The China Syndrome*, as executive vice-president of Bigstick. As it transpired, Douglas made nothing for the next four years.

The first project that Douglas selected for Columbia eventually evolved into one of the most controversial films of the 1980s, one which would star Douglas himself. He bought the rights to *Virgin Kisses*, a novel about sexual obsession by Gloria Nagy, which would mutate into *Fatal Attraction*. Another project developed for two years was about American football coach Pop Warner. There was also a plan to produce a television miniseries about Cortez and the Spanish conquest of Mexico. Then in 1980 Douglas bought a script by Bruce A. Evans and Raynold Gideon entitled *Starman*. The story followed a cross-country trip made by a visitor from outer space and an attractive young widow. What attracted Douglas to *Starman* was the concept of everything on earth making sense to the alien except for human behaviour. Columbia was also developing a similar project with Steven Spielberg about a stranded alien who befriends a lonely human while on the run from pursuers. In the end Columbia decided to drop the Spielberg project, which was picked up by rival studio Universal. But by the time *Starman* was released in 1984 it was notorious for being the film Columbia made instead of *E.T. the Extra-Terrestrial* (1982). Douglas considered taking the lead role in *Starman* at one point, but in the end it went to Jeff Bridges. Shooting was due to begin in the autumn of 1982 but director John Badham dropped out and rewrites were ordered. By spring 1983 *Starman* was still without a director or cast. Writer Dean Reisner was called in after Evans and Gideon's second draft was rejected. Reisner struggled on for another two years with the script, emphasising the love story and diminishing aspects which resembled *E.T.* Meanwhile, directors including Adrian Lyne, Michael Mann and Tony Scott did a conga through the project until John Carpenter, a director synonymous with horror movies, took over. By the time *Starman* eventually went into production, Douglas was barely involved apart from choosing some of the cast and making notes on an early cut. (In 1986 Douglas was executive producer on the short-lived television series of *Starman* in which Robert Hays played the Jeff Bridges role.)

Meanwhile, a 33-year-old waitress called Diane Thomas – working at either the Cork Beach Cantina, a Mexican restaurant on the Pacific Coast Highway, or at Alice's Restaurant in Malibu Beach, depending on which version of the legend you prefer – was writing a screenplay between shifts. *Romancing the Stone* was a romantic comedy adventure about a female novelist, Joan Wilder, who has to survive in the jungle with a macho adventurer when searching for her missing sister. Brodsky came across the screenplay in autumn 1979, and within a week Douglas had bought it for $250,000. Douglas though the script had a 'virginal quality', totally fresh in its construction and theme. What appealed to him was that it failed to conform to normal screenplay structures. However, *Romancing the Stone* took a long time to get off the ground because it mixed up three genres: adventure, comedy and romance. People would ask Douglas what the project's genre was, and he would reply that it was an action adventure romantic comedy – at which point they would walk away.

At first Columbia insisted it would only do the film with Clint Eastwood or Burt Reynolds in the lead. Douglas then worked his way through the list of stars, and only suggested himself for the lead role of Jack Colton when Sylvester Stallone said no. But Columbia was lukewarm about Douglas starring in *Romancing the Stone* because he had never done comedy before. Columbia eventually passed when the project became bogged down in script and casting problems. Douglas took the project to Twentieth Century-Fox as soon as the Columbia deal expired. Robert Cort, a production executive at Fox, was a friend of Douglas who used to see the actor and producer goofing around in the office and could imagine him being both funny and romantic on screen. Fox badly wanted to make the film, said Brodsky. Douglas blamed Columbia's reliance on market research for souring his three-year overheads deal. Like fellow producer Dino De Laurentiis, Douglas believes that one of the problems with the studios now is that unlike the days when they were run by people like David Selznick, Irving Thalberg and Darryl F. Zanuck, there is nobody in charge with a single, visionary point of view. Instead, the producer gets a homogenised collection of script notes and the writer desperately tries to please all his masters, to the detriment of the original story. Douglas has been asked to run studios – both Universal Pictures and Warner Brothers – on three separate occasions but said no each time. Douglas knew he would lose all his friends as a result of trying to feed the maw of the studio distribution machine – at the end of which he would probably be fired and left with a face-saving producer deal, standard procedure for a superannuated executive. Douglas had thought that with two hit movies behind him, Columbia would want to make his next project, but he was left out in the cold. Kirk had taught him that a good business deal was one that was beneficial to both parties – which the Columbia deal was not.

Douglas picked a young, fairly unknown director called Robert Zemeckis for *Romancing the Stone*. He likes to work with new talents who want opinions, rather than established directors. It means that Douglas has a voice in the production. 'I'm just not happy with that style – the shouters, the hollerers, the tyrants.' He sees his job as supporting the director in any way he can, and being a sounding board for him. Directing is a lonely job. Because directors have to be in control all the time they become isolated with nobody to talk to. The key thing, according to Douglas, is to gain the director's confidence so that he trusts the producer. 'I enjoy more of a collaborative relationship than other producers who serve a maestro,' he told me. (Zemeckis went on to write and direct the *Back to the Future* films, and *Forrest Gump*, among others.)

Location shooting for *Romancing the Stone* started in Mexico in July 1983. Mexico had been chosen over Colombia, where the story is set, because it was cheaper and nearer to California. But the decision to shoot in Mexico turned out to be a nightmare. Because *Romancing the Stone* was, in Douglas' words, a linear chase film, this meant a different location every day – and consequently a new set of problems. Location shooting went on for months, roaming from a warehouse turned studio in Mexico City to weeks spent filming on narrow mountain roads. Unfortunately Douglas and his team arrived at the height of a fluke rainy season, at the end of which the region had more rainfall than it had seen in the past thirty-five years. One storm was so violent that a mud slide trapped the crew on top of a windy mountain road in Xalapa; another poured down on top of co-star Kathleen Turner and several crew members. Everywhere Douglas went the rain seemed to follow him. He joked about hiring himself out as a rain god. Douglas would arrive at previously scouted locations to find rivers and lakes had sprung up where before there had been dry land. Sometimes bridges had to be built just to reach locations. Kathleen Turner said that the crew was building Douglas-land throughout Mexico. If a road was washed away and the team could not get to its next location, Douglas would have arranged for thirty lorries full of gravel to be ready the next morning. Douglas' old friend and co-star Danny DeVito remembered the shoot like being stuck in a Hieronymus Bosch painting. Ironically, even though the script called for storms and fetid conditions, Zemeckis was unable to film in the rain. Natural rain seldom works on film because it has a softer register and can barely be seen. The director found himself in the ridiculous position of having to get wet and miserable waiting for the real rain to stop so that he could start his fake rain.

Douglas says that the difference between being an actor and a producer is that in acting you are paid to be selfish, but a producer has to have 360-degree vision. On one occasion he was in the middle of rehearsing a love scene with Turner, when a production assistant tapped the producer on the shoulder and asked him to come and solve a problem. Douglas had to ask his co-star to hold everything.

Completed at a below average cost of $9.5 million, *Romancing the Stone* was one of the biggest hits of 1984. It made $20 million in ticket sales in its first two and a half weeks, and earned another $15 million within thirty days. Within two years it had grossed more than $100 million. Fox told Douglas that it wanted a sequel by Christmas 1985; it would commit $40 million to produce and market it. Douglas had some loose ideas (mostly avoiding any plot involving rain or mud), and he started meeting writers. Diane Thomas was by this time under contract to Steven Spielberg, so Douglas tossed around ideas with various writers until he settled on Mark Rosenthal and Lawrence Kenner. Whereas the first film dealt with the emotional growing up of Joan Wilder, Douglas said that *Jewel of the Nile* would be about Jack Colton reaching maturity. The first draft was ready by early November 1984 and approved by Fox. Douglas worked on rewrites in New York while starring in *A Chorus Line* for director Richard Attenborough. He converted a dressing room in the theatre where the musical was being shot into an office. Douglas would sit upstairs and work on the script while the crew worked on dance numbers. The last day of shooting went on all night, and Douglas left for the airport to catch the 8.30 a.m. flight to Morocco.

But as soon as he arrived in Marrakesh he realised he was 'in deep shit', as he put it. He met director Lewis Teague at the airport along with the local production manager. These two comprised his entire Moroccan crew. The rest of the team was in Nice in the south of France. The production man explained that Nice was a good stopping-off point. Stopping-off point for what? Douglas wondered. Nice was a continent and three and a half hours away by plane. When Douglas realised he was six weeks from shooting without a single location having been found, he went to his hotel room and cried. The next day he spent deliberating what to tell the studio. 'I heard this screaming voice inside me shout, "Here you go. Life's been real good. You've been waiting for someone to do something really bad to you and this is it",' Douglas said.[9] In the end he decided to fly out his brother Joel to scout locations.

Kathleen Turner then changed her mind about doing the film because she did not like the script, which she thought was sexist and one-dimensional. Another factor was that Steven Spielberg had offered her the lead in *The Money Pit*. Douglas let it be known that he would replace her rather than postpone shooting, and both he and Fox followed this up with the threat of a $25 million lawsuit for breach of contract. However, to accommodate Turner, Douglas persuaded Diane Thomas to put some work into the lead characters and resolve some script problems.

Shooting *Jewel of the Nile* was another traumatic experience for Douglas. The production designer, location manager and their pilot died in a plane crash. Douglas then had to fire the production manager and other troublesome crew members after a row about accommodation. Two thousand posters and flags that had been printed for the sequence at a mass rally had to be destroyed and replaced just hours before shooting. Unwittingly, the design used on the flags was blasphemous in Arabic. Terence Smith, the new production designer, spent seven weeks in the desert building a set in an area which had been stricken by drought for six years. Just as he finished building one and a half miles of castle walls, bridges and roads, rain deluged the set for eight days – a local record. Finally an eight-foot-high torrent swept down through the dry riverbed, washing the set away in seconds. By the end of *Jewel of the Nile*'s five-month shoot, temperatures had soared to 130 degrees and the crew was suffering from sunstroke, dysentery, cholera and hepatitis. Douglas compared the shooting of *Jewel of the Nile* to a battle, with every day an advance into enemy territory. However, after a while, the battle-weary crew developed an esprit de corps, which Douglas said was the thing one hoped for as a producer.

By now Douglas' acting career had taken off and he was not able to devote as much time to producing. For example, tough police thriller *Black Rain* (1989) was produced 'in association with Michael Douglas', but this association mainly consisted of producers Sherry Lansing and Stanley Jaffe working through problems with Douglas over a drink at the end of each day.

In 1989 Stonebridge Entertainment, Douglas' new production company, struck another first-look deal with Columbia Pictures. Columbia agreed to contribute up to $1 million a year to Stonebridge's overheads, and would also fund development of projects approved by studio executives. But the million would cover only part of Stonebridge's operating costs; Douglas would have to find the rest himself. Stonebridge announced that it would produce two films a year in the mid-budget range of between $15 and $20 million. According to studio accounting procedures, this meant each project would have to make $60 million in order to make a profit. (This multiple has since risen so that pictures today sometimes have to earn seven times what they cost to produce in order to break even.) Rick Bieber, former head of production at Home Box Office Pictures, was taken on as Douglas' second in command. (Kirk Douglas was puzzled by the Columbia deal. He could not understand why his son persisted in wanting to produce now that he was a big star.) One project that Douglas developed was titled *Zoo Plane*, written by his cartoonist friend Garry Trudeau, about journalists on the presidential campaign trail. In the end Stonebridge produced five films, only one of which – *Flatliners* – was a hit. *Flatliners* cost $16 million to make and grossed more than $150 million. However, *Stone Cold*, *Double Impact*, *Hard Promises* and *Radio Flyer* all flopped. Looking back on the experience, Douglas remembered the adage 'Be careful what you wish for, because it may come true.' Stonebridge had forty projects in development, but

Douglas had negotiated such a shrewd deal in terms of his remuneration that it was almost in Columbia's interest not to put anything into production. In his own words, Douglas became producer as prisoner. He had also fallen into the Hollywood trap of having too many projects in development at any one time. He would come off an acting job and have to deal with a glut of mediocre screenplays, all of which required attention, and would then find it hard to concentrate on just one project. Bieber was released in November 1991 and the company was scaled back with many job losses.

Stonebridge's deal with Columbia ended on 30 April 1994. The next day, Douglas set up a new production company, Constellation Films, this time in partnership with Steven Reuther, former president of New Regency Films. Reuther's company had produced two of Douglas' films – *The War of the Roses* and *Falling Down*. Together they raised $500 million, most of it coming from Bodo Scriba, a German financier whom Reuther introduced to Douglas. Scriba would own 30 per cent of the company. The idea was that Constellation would produce twelve films in four years. The films would be distributed in North America by Paramount (Canada and the United States are treated as a single market by Hollywood), while Constellation would retain German and Eastern European rights. Paramount would sell other territories piece by piece.

There are three types of films in the world. Those that the studios fully finance because they know they are going to be global hits – franchises such as James Bond or Batman or Harry Potter. Then there are 'independent' films that are distributed territory by territory. These so-called 'art-house' films and non-English titles can be highly profitable. And then there are films on which studios want to share the risk. Although these projects – either made by the studio or 'picked up' from another company – deserve access to the studio's global marketing apparatus, they are not sure-fire winners. Often outside investors are brought in to share rights in what are known as split rights deals. These partners sometimes come from Germany, which has a history of getting into bed with Hollywood, lying back and thinking of the fatherland. Every couple of years or so there is a new film finance bubble somewhere in the world, which Hollywood will then burst, be it insured bank loans in Britain or tax funds in Germany. 'Anybody who does business with the US studios is effectively sticking their head in an oven, because Hollywood has been skinning outsiders since the 1930s,' one veteran told me.

Constellation announced its production plans in September 1995. The first film to go into production would be *Sabrina*, a remake of the Billy Wilder film, this time starring Harrison Ford and Julia Ormond, and directed by Sydney Pollack. Paramount and Constellation would split the risk on the $50 million budget of the film, which would be ready for release in December 1995. Constellation also paid $6 million for the rights to the John Grisham best-seller *The Rainmaker,* and Grisham would write the screenplay. The film would eventually star Matt Damon and Danny DeVito and be directed by Francis Ford Coppola. Then there was *Face/Off,* a futuristic thriller by Chinese action director John Woo which was to have starred Arnold Schwarzenegger but eventually co-starred Nicolas Cage and John Travolta.

Constellation arrived at Paramount with no projects in development or production. Because studios are notorious for developing huge amounts of material that is never made, Douglas' first instinct was to go through Paramount's inventory and see what the studio had on its shelves. One project that intrigued him was *The Ghost and the Darkness*, an unproduced screenplay by William Goldman, writer of *Butch Cassidy and the Sundance Kid* and adapter of Stephen King's *Misery*. Goldman's screenplay was based on a true story about a pair of man-eating lions that terrorised workers building a bridge in East Africa in the nineteenth century. Unusually, these lions hunted for pleasure and not for food. Even more sinister was the fact that they hunted as a pair; usually males have their own prides and keep very separate. During a nine-month period in 1898 the lions killed 135 railway workers. Eventually the railway engineer, John Patterson, was forced to become a big-game hunter. He taught himself how to hunt and track, and finally killed them. Douglas loved the screenplay and could not understand why it had not been made in the six years the studio had been sitting on it. Over the years he had gained confidence in his own taste. If he was interested in something, he suspected there might be other 'loonies' interested in it too.

But the most intriguing project was *A Song for David*, which was intended to bring together Kirk and Michael Douglas in a film for the first time. In 1994 Michael Douglas gave Kirk the script of *A Song for David* as a birthday present. Written by Dan Gordon, it was the story of a father and son and their construction business. Accompanying the script was a note from Douglas promising his father they would make it together in 1995. But Constellation got off to a rocky start when its questionable remake of *Sabrina*, which cost $58 million, took only $53 million at the box office. (One has to ask where the logic was in trying to improve on a Billy Wilder film starring Audrey Hepburn.)

The Ghost and the Darkness began shooting in Africa on 1 November 1995. Douglas had been keen to shoot in Tsaro National Park, where the killings took place, but there was no infrastructure to support a film of this size. Instead, most of the picture was shot in Songimelvo Game Reserve on the border between Swaziland and South Africa. (Douglas, a keen golfer, admitted he was partly swayed by Songimelvo's nine-hole golf course.) It still took a minimum of forty minutes to drive to the location, and even then only after the crew had built bridges and improved roads. Next – in a pattern which runs throughout Douglas' producing career – the rains came, washing away all the bridges and roads built by the crew two days before the start of filming. Eventually cast and crew had to travel to the location on rubber rafts accompanied by armed guards to drive off hippos which might capsize them. Shooting began without the supporting role of Remington, the big-game hunter, being cast. Eventually Douglas cast himself as Remington, and, according to screenwriter William Goldman, this was when the project went awry. Up to this point Douglas had been an exemplary producer, making perceptive comments on the script. Now he was the co-star, Douglas' insecurity as an actor surfaced, and the Remington character was built up and made more sympathetic. Goldman has described a good screenplay as being like a well-made piece of furniture. The story of *The Ghost and the Darkness* was now warped in order to accommodate Douglas the actor. The film cost $55 million to make, but only took $34 million in America and $75 million overseas, which meant that according to studio accounting procedures it was a flop.

Constellation was dissolved at the end of 1997 after Bodo Scriba decided to pull out of the company. Douglas and Reuther were unable to find anybody to replace the German financier and the pair decided to disband. But despite the split Douglas and Reuther were still developing projects together. One was *The Allegation*, a thriller about accusations of infidelity. Another was *Extreme Denial*, a kidnapping drama adapted from the novel by David Morell, creator of the Rambo character. Reuther set up Bel Air Entertainment at Warner Brothers, while Douglas decided to simplify his whole way of working. He realised that he worked best in a small office with just a reader and a secretary.

In January 2000 Douglas' new company, Further Films, signed a first-look deal with Universal Pictures. Based at Universal Studios in Los Angeles, Further takes its name from the destination sign on the front of the old school bus in which Ken Kesey and his merry pranksters drove across America in the acid-soaked 1960s. Calling the company Further Films was a nod to the spirit of San Francisco and *One Flew Over the Cuckoo's Nest*. Rather than get bogged down with screenplays, Further plans to put one project into production out of every two screenplays it is working on. And projects should have good parts for Michael Douglas the actor. Its first production was *One Night at McCool's* (2001), a comedy starring Liv Tyler. Further would develop projects with more material for Douglas himself to play. One of the disappointments of his producing career had been the lack of projects with roles for Douglas the actor. Now he was going full circle, going back to where he had started with *The China Syndrome*.

When it comes to a theme that runs through the movies he has produced, Douglas has said that most of his films have been contemporary, about people struggling to make the right decisions. He has compared the movie business to playing in an adult sandpit, where you might learn about mental hospitals and nuclear power plants, as well as get the opportunity to travel all over the world and meet charming, attractive and sexy people. It is a wonderful life, he says, and he could not imagine doing anything else. On the other hand he likes producing because of its grown-up nature. It involves taking adult risks and can be compared to a flying trapeze without a net.

Producing is very underrated, according to Douglas. There is an immense spectrum between the person who puts together or 'packages' a film, and the producer who sees a project all the way through. Unlike some other producers, Douglas does not put together a deal and walk away. He stays with a production and never takes a domineering role, preferring instead to be a sounding board. 'Some producers like making deals. I like making movies.'

As a producer you have to know what your strengths are and how they complement your weaknesses, Douglas told me. A producer must have a good sense of material, the ability to structure and understand a script and know how to bring the appropriate elements together – be they the cast, the director or the distributor – while always keeping in mind what is best for the project. One of his strengths is that he thinks logically, breaking down problems into their smallest parts and then working out which is the most pressing. Every step along the development process, which encompasses finessing the screenplay and setting up production, is important for him: doing his homework, selling the script, choosing the director, haggling with agents over actors, getting the locations right. It means he can never relax. 'That's a huge endeavour, so you have to be in love with the project.' His weakness is learning how to delegate and manage employees. The biggest problem with producing is that development is passed down to somebody else, often a junior studio development executive. 'You see this all the time in studios, where the person responsible for developing material is working on projects they have inherited from somebody else or it's a hand-me-down. Because my strength is hands on development it is difficult for me to relinquish projects to a studio.'

Douglas sees his greatest strengths as being his choice of material, and his ability to close his eyes and see the finished product, to picture it in his head and know if it is going to work or not. His approach is instinctive and most of the time his first feeling is the right one. Whenever he gets in a bind he tries to remember what his first instinct was and goes with that.

On average Douglas spends five years developing each piece of material. 'You get a vision, a kind of picture. For me, it's initially emotional. It makes you laugh or cry. Then I close my eyes and look at the script again and see whether it's got a good structure, a good foundation. I'm an old-fashioned structuralist – three acts and all of that. I have a theatre background, theatre training – so I go back and make sure I was not fooled or seduced. I close my eyes to see the act breaks, that it dramatically makes sense. And then it's the joy of completion, or trying to put all the elements together and hoping that the end result is at least as good if not better than what was on the page.'

Douglas sees his work as a labour of love, which is why each project takes so long to do. Like every producer profiled in this book, Douglas has to feel passionate about material before committing to it. He reads the script as if meeting a girl for the first time. What he is looking for is the moment when he becomes obsessed and cannot get the project out of his head. He has to become infatuated, sitting up in bed in the middle of the night and scribbling ideas – because he knows that this obsession is the only thing that will take him through the length of time it takes to make a film. If he finds this initial infatuation fading, then he realises the project was not right for him. After all, *Cuckoo's Nest* took six years to make; *Romancing the Stone*, five; *The China Syndrome*, four – and that, as he says himself, is a lot of time to spend knocking on doors.

2 Dino De Laurentiis

The mogul

It was a clear blue February morning when my car swung off Barham Boulevard in Los Angeles and pulled up outside Universal Studios. A security guard put his face close to my window and motioned for me to get out. Given the nervy atmosphere following September 11th my cheap hire car was given a stringent going over. A bomb mirror was even waved underneath the car, the guard looking for anything suspicious. One of the guards nodded and the barrier was raised. 'You want to go down James Stewart Avenue, turn right on Alfred Hitchcock Drive and go past King Kong Alley,' said a guard wearing mirrored sunglasses. I knew that Universal Studios had its own police force but once inside what nobody prepares you for is the scale of the place. Every street was lined with huge sound stages, each the size of an aircraft hangar. It was still early and I did not expect to see extras dressed as astronauts chatting with American Indians. But I could see why the expression 'dream factory' had been coined. This was exactly what Universal Studios was – a factory the size of a town producing the world's dreams. Everything had been provided to keep workers happy: restaurants, bars, a health club. Universal even had its own police station on City Walk. You could also see why sober accountants in foreign corporations such as Vivendi, the French water company, or

Japanese electronics manufacturer Sony lose all judgement when it comes to Hollywood. The atmosphere was heady. 'We must buy a Hollywood studio,' the chief financial officer will recommend to the board, using words like 'synergy' and 'convergence'. But within a month of arriving in Los Angeles the accountant has grown a goatee beard and is wearing an earring. He has even started vetting scripts. Meanwhile, shareholders angry at seeing their stock plummet demonstrate outside the company headquarters in Paris or Tokyo.

Dino De Laurentiis once described himself to a visiting camera crew as 'the last tycoon'. The producer of *Red Dragon* and *Blue Velvet* believes he is the last independent producer left in Hollywood. All the other producers, he says, are glorified executives employed by the studios to do what they want. He calls producers who rely completely on funding from the studios 'dependent' producers rather than independent ones. De Laurentiis claims he is the last independent left because he pays the cost of developing each project – buying a book, hiring the screenwriter – himself. Everybody else, including Jerry Bruckheimer (*Pearl Harbor*) and Joel Silver (*The Matrix*), relies on studios to fully fund their projects. De Laurentiis alone spends his own money. He puts together a package – writer, director and stars – which he presents to the studio. He never asks the studio to fund pre-production, because, again, that would make him beholden to an entertainment conglomerate. He prefers to remain independent, relying on the studio's distribution machinery.

The studio then haggles with De Laurentiis over the price for worldwide distribution rights. Or De Laurentiis will give Universal the film for North America and then strike deals with distributors overseas territory by territory. 'There are two ways of being a producer in the USA. Either you go to a studio and say, "I want to buy a book on Alexander the Great", and wait for the studio to agree or disagree. Or you can buy your own material and present the studio with a package – either for worldwide distribution or just North America.' He has always produced films with the international market in mind. For example, his Stephen King adaptation *The Dead Zone* did not perform as well in America as Paramount Pictures had hoped, but was a hit in France, Italy, Scandinavia and Spain.

De Laurentiis claims he invented the practice of financing films territory by territory in 1956 when he made *War and Peace*. Distributors pay an advance for a film that has yet to be made: known in film industry parlance as pre-selling. Then again, Sam Spiegel and Joseph E. Levine made the same claim (see Introduction). Trying to find out who invented this practice is like watching one of those television documentaries about the history of the blues. 'Uh-huh' croaks the wizened sharecropper rocking on his front porch. 'Selling films territory by territory began a hundred yards thataway,' he says, pointing a bony finger down the banks of the Mississippi. Perhaps the truth is that something was in the air. Nevertheless, most films begin life on the basis of a handshake in a hotel bedroom in Cannes, Milan or Los Angeles, the three big film markets held each year. Investors hand over money on the basis of little more than a script and a salesman's enthusiasm. Slowly, the patchwork of cash advances is sewn together.

De Laurentiis works out of a tidy white bungalow on Universal City Plaza. As you walk into his office you pass a vulgar trophy cabinet. There are sixty gold statuettes in the gaudy display case, and another twenty-six awards on the office wall. Pride of place has been given to the Irving Thalberg award he won at the Academy Awards in 2001 for his career in cinema. The two Academy Awards he won for *La Strada* (*The Road*) in 1956 and *Le Notti di Cabiria* (*Nights of Cabiria*) in 1957 stand on either side of it. In total De Laurentiis' films have been nominated for sixteen Oscars in various categories.

Today he is sporting a scrubby beard that gives him a salty sea-dog look. He sips an espresso and smokes a small cigar as he sits behind his enormous Italianate desk. Talking to De Laurentiis, one gets the feeling of soil that has been exhausted by the same old stories being trotted out, like a field which has been ploughed once too often. It takes an effort to jog the needle on to a tune one has not heard before.

According to official history, which has become as worn and smooth as old stone steps, Dino De Laurentiis was born in 1919 in Torre Annunziata near Naples in Italy. He enrolled in Rome's Film Institute when he was still a teenager and driving a truck at his father's spaghetti factory. When his scandalised father threw the eighteen-year-old out, De Laurentiis supported himself by working as an actor. He produced his first film when he was just twenty-two. De Laurentiis spent some of the Second World War in Capri waiting for the fighting to stop. There he read Homer's *Odyssey* and Tolstoy's *War and Peace* to pass the time, and decided to turn both into films. By 1950 he had formed a production company with Carlo Ponti, another Italian producer. Their first film, *Bitter Rice*, was a big domestic hit, and the film's star, Silvana Mangano, became the first Mrs De Laurentiis shortly afterwards.

In the first phase of his career, De Laurentiis' strategy was to finance art films with expensive historical epics. The man himself divides his work into two categories: auteur films and production films. Auteur films include *La Strada* (1954) and *Le Notti di Cabiria* (1957), both by Federico Fellini, and David Lynch's *Blue Velvet* (1986). The production films include *War and Peace* (1956), *King Kong* (1976); and, to an extent, the Hannibal Lecter franchise *Hannibal* (2001) and *Red Dragon* (2002). The breakthrough auteur film was *La Strada*, which won an Academy Award for best foreign language picture. *La Strada* is the story of a travelling strongman (played by

Anthony Quinn) who rejects the love of his moon-faced assistant (Giulietta Masina). She runs away after he kills another circus performer in a roadside brawl, and only then does the strongman realise what he has lost. *La Strada* is partly the story of the assistant's education as an artist. A puckish clown spells out the film's theme: everything has a purpose, even a humble stone, because if it does not then everything is useless – even the stars. However, *La Strada* is marred by its own sentimentality, which at times reminds one of a china Pierrot doll.

De Laurentiis already had a reputation for firing directors and taking films away from them. There was one sequence in the middle of *La Strada* that the producer felt slowed everything down, but Fellini did not want to cut it because he liked it so much. One night, De Laurentiis went to the laboratory, cut the whole sequence with a pair of scissors and threw it away.

La Strada received its premiere at the Venice Film Festival, and was destroyed by the Italian critics, the most generous of whom suggested that Fellini might offer something good in time. De Laurentiis was so annoyed by the critical drubbing that he took the film to Paris in a fit of 'I'll show them' pique, hoping to find an audience there. He could not find anybody willing to distribute it because of the disastrous reviews. Instead, he rented a cinema in the Champs-Elysées himself and the film became a hit with sophisticated Parisians. According to De Laurentiis, a critic's judgement never coincides, apart from some rare exceptions, with that of the public. Does a critic ever stand outside a cinema and watch people going in? Does a critic try to understand what kind of entertainment the public wants to see? Critics, he says, write to show their friends how intelligent they are. (One is reminded of the moment in *Waiting for Godot* when one of the tramps, thinking of the worst swear word he can imagine, shouts out 'Critic!' Beckett got the idea from listening to Brussels taxi drivers shout at each other after the Second World War. The worst insult in the heavily rebuilt city was 'architect'.) De Laurentiis remembers turning to Fellini at the end of a screening of *La Strada* and asking him what the film was about. 'I don't know,' replied Fellini. 'I'm waiting for the critics to tell me.'

When De Laurentiis and Ponti announced that they next wanted to film *War and Peace*, cynics on both sides of the Atlantic were bemused. Two other Hollywood producers, one of whom was Elizabeth Taylor's husband Mike Todd, were already racing to make Tolstoy's novel. De Laurentiis invited several screenwriters to work on the project but they only submitted synopses of the novel. It was De Laurentiis who decided that the story must concentrate on Natasha, a girl in love with a man who does not love her, who marries another man. Hearing that Todd wanted Audrey Hepburn to play Natasha, the Ponti and De Laurentiis press office announced that the Italians had just signed Jean Simmons for the role. At that moment, De Laurentiis was driving from Milan to the Swiss frontier to meet Hepburn and her husband, Mel Ferrer. De Laurentiis read the script to them, told them that King Vidor had agreed to direct, and returned home with both Hepburn and Ferrer under contract. *War and Peace* cost an eye-watering £3 million to produce in 1956 and met with indifferent reviews.

The next epic was *The Bible* (1966), which De Laurentiis got the idea for when he was separated from his luggage while visiting New York. Waking at 4 a.m. and desperate for something to read, he could only find a menu, a list of hotel rules on the back of the door and a copy of the Bible in a bedside drawer. He announced that John Huston would oversee the $90 million adaptation, which would be made up of two six-hour films. Orson Welles would direct the Abraham and Isaac sequence; French director Robert Bresson would direct the Creation; Luhino Visconti would direct the story of Joseph; and Fellini was chosen for the Flood. Maria Callas was to play Abraham's wife, Sarah, and Sir Laurence Olivier was to play God. And lastly, Stravinsky would write the music.

In the end the production cost $18 million and Huston was the only director. Peter O'Toole and Ava Gardner replaced Olivier and Callas, with George C. Scott as Abraham and Richard Harris as Cain. Huston himself played Noah after first offering the part to Charlie Chaplin and then Alec Guinness. The project's ambitions were also restricted to just the first twenty pages of the Old Testament, but De Laurentiis kept the original title. The producer then had the enjoyable job of interviewing three hundred prospective Eves before choosing Ulla Bergryd, the nineteen-year-old daughter of a Swedish language teacher. Unknown American Michael Parks, twenty-six years old, was chosen to play Adam, but in the end his mumbling was so bad that David Warner dubbed his voice on the soundtrack. When asked at the first press conference whether he was intimidated by the scope of the project, Huston replied that he had always wanted to create the heaven and the earth. Another reporter asked O'Toole how he had prepared himself to play God. O'Toole replied that he took cold baths, gave up drinking and submitted to daily birchings.

Production began on *The Bible* in May 1964 at the new Dino De Laurentiis Studios outside Rome. De Laurentiis milked publicity over the nude filming of the Adam and Eve story, perhaps even egging on ever-enterprising paparazzi by telling the press he had hired two dozen *carabinieri* to keep out unwanted visitors. Photographers bribed set workers, crawled over studio walls, crowded behind bushes and perched in treetops to snap the Garden of Eden. Renowned Italian sculptor Giacomo Manzú agreed to make the statue of Adam that God breathes life into. Manzu agreed to do the job as a favour to Huston but refused to be paid. De Laurentiis became so exasperated by this that the sculptor caved in and asked for just one hundred lire. Manzú counted on De Laurentiis being too grand to carry loose change. The producer dug around in his pockets and pulled out handfuls of large denomination bills. Finally, with his pockets inside out, De Laurentiis grimaced and shrugged.

Despite working with lions, zebras, giraffes, elephants and cheetahs – and even training them to walk two by two into Noah's Ark – Huston said the most difficult element of *The Bible* was dealing with George C. Scott's drinking. The actor had fallen obsessively in love with Ava Gardner and eventually followed her to London when filming was finished, forced his way into her suite at the Savoy and hit her in the face, nearly dislocating her jaw.

American Film magazine put its finger on why De Laurentiis' historical epics were often so turgid. 'The epics,' it noted, 'no matter how ultimately they turn out, are begun with the reasonable hope that the most expensive (and sometimes even the best available talents) will combine to make, if not an artistic triumph, at least a reasonable try – who is going to knock Tolstoy or God? – and the thunderous pageantry will take care of the commercial considerations. Since so many of them have turned out to be lifeless tableaux vivants, De Laurentiis has had more than his share of disappointment in this genre.'[1]

By the start of the 1960s De Laurentiis had become fed up with Italy. Too many bad producers, he said, were making too many rotten films. Quality and not quantity was what counted. In 1962 he announced that he was launching an American production and distribution subsidiary, the Dino De Laurentiis Group of America. This was the first time a European producer opened his own production and distribution business in America (known in the industry as vertical integration). The new company would be housed temporarily at 2 Park Avenue in Manhattan, pending negotiations to buy its own building in midtown New York. Meanwhile, the hits kept on coming throughout the decade, including *Barbarella* (1968). It was a time when American audiences were open to watching films from Europe – unlike today when the market share for foreign language European films in the USA is about 3 per cent.

In 1973 De Laurentiis announced he was moving to America permanently, partly because of what he perceived as jealousy over his success. He also said he was moving because of legislation that was forcing him to ensure two thirds of the actors in his films were Italian. Italy was, in some ways, an extremely provincial country, he sniffed. (The fact that he was also the second-highest taxpayer in Rome might also have been a deciding factor.) De Laurentiis announced that he was putting his studio complex, called Stabilimenti but nicknamed Hollywood-on-the-Tiber or, more cheekily, Dinocitta, on the market. The studio, fifteen miles south of Rome, reportedly cost over £40 million to build but was put up for sale for £15 million.

De Laurentiis' first American film was *Serpico* (1973), a thriller based on the true story of police officer Frank Serpico, who investigated corruption inside the New York Police Department. Al Pacino gave a gritty performance as Serpico, and the film hit a nerve with the public in the suspicious atmosphere of the Watergate era. The genesis of *Serpico* came when De Laurentiis rang up his friend Peter Maas, author of *The Valachi Papers*, and asked him what he was working on. Maas revealed that he had just written the first chapter of a new book describing the character of Frank Serpico. De Laurentiis read this opening chapter and liked it so much that he bought the as yet unwritten book for $500,000 (the equivalent of $5 million today). When De Laurentiis first arrived in New York he was unsure whether he had made the right decision. *Serpico* remains the film he is most proud of, he told me, partly because it proved to himself that he could make a go of things in America.

Death Wish (1974) again touched a nerve with the public. It seemed as if law and order was breaking down in American cities and New York itself resembled a war zone. Headlines about muggings and shootings screamed out from the *New York Post*. The city was also bankrupt. There were broken windows everywhere and holes in the steaming roads. (It could be argued, however, that some of the city's energy stemmed from its Wild West feel.) Charles Bronson accepted the role of a New York architect who takes the law into his own hands when muggers kill his wife. He becomes a vigilante, exterminating his wife's attackers one by one. Defending himself against criticism about the violence in *Death Wish*, De Laurentiis said that films held up a mirror to society. The reason why critics liked *Death Wish*, and audiences applauded at the end, was because it contained the idea that the conscience of society has to rest in the individual. Interviewed in 1974, De Laurentiis said it was impossible to make a realistic movie without crime and violence. Crime was inescapable whether you lived in New York, Rome or Paris, he said. However, he would change his tune when he saw how much his next project, a family film, earned at the box office. De Laurentiis' biggest film to date, both in terms of scale and folly, remains his 1976 remake of *King Kong*.

De Laurentiis moved to Los Angeles in 1976 and opened luxurious offices in Beverly Hills. His family was settled in a ten-acre estate called The Knoll, which reportedly cost him $3 million. He claimed he had the idea for a new *King Kong* after walking past the original movie poster tacked up on his daughter Francesca's bedroom wall. It showed the classic moment when Kong is on top of the Empire State Building swiping at biplanes. Suddenly De

Laurentiis thought, If this image has lasted almost half a century, why not show a new Kong on the towers of the World Trade Center?

However, one wonders what was going on in his mind when he decided to remake the 1933 classic. Although technically clumsy by 1970s standards, director Merian C. Cooper and special effects pioneer Willis O'Brien and his team made the 1930s *King Kong* with such attention to detail (for example, shadows of birds can be seen flying over trees way off in the distance), it is difficult to see how the telling could be improved. It was also a film of its time. Through a quite mad piece of identification, scenes of Kong destroying New York gratified Depression audiences. However, De Laurentiis was already in vague talks with Barry Diller, head of Paramount Studios, about making a monster film. Universal had had a big hit with *Jaws* the year before, the first mainstream film to be advertised on television – until then a medium used by cheap shockers and exploitation flicks. Before *Jaws*, most films opened on a small number of screens and grew in popularity by word of mouth. *Jaws* opened on 409 screens across America, leading to the situation today where you have films which are triumphs of marketing practically disappearing after their first three days when word gets out. The idea of releasing a film slowly and then building up an audience has all but disappeared. A film must do well immediately or it is yanked from the screens in order to make way for the studio's next release. Meanwhile, across the city at Paramount Studios in Melrose Avenue, Diller and De Laurentiis watched Universal's success and were determined to replicate it. De Laurentiis calculated that if *Jaws* made $240 million then his remake would earn at least $241 million, because unlike the Universal film his film would be aimed at a family audience. 'No one-a cry when *Jaws* die but when the monkey die, everybody gonna cry,' he predicted.[2]

Lorenzo Semple Jr., screenwriter of *The Parallax View* and *Three Days of the Condor*, was sitting in his office in Aspen, Colorado, when the phone rang. It was De Laurentiis. Semple Jr. had met De Laurentiis a few years previously to discuss a sequel to the erotic science-fiction film *Barbarella*. Most of the action would take place underwater and the working title was *Going Down*. 'Lorenzo, I give-a-you jus' a title, two words, you tell-a-me what you think,' said De Laurentiis. Dramatic pause. '*King-a-Kong!*'³ Semple went to see De Laurentiis the next day in an office so richly Italianate, said the writer, that one expected a Borgia pope to be working the Xerox machine. De Laurentiis asked Semple Jr. to update *Kong* with a modern environmental twist: the captors of the giant gorilla would not be explorer film-makers but unscrupulous oil prospectors. The script conference lasted a full fifteen minutes. Semple Jr. described De Laurentiis as a disciple of the written word. People who did not know him well were often misled by his flamboyant character, said Semple, only to be confounded when he caught them out on some tiny script detail.

Roman Polanksi, the auteur behind *Rosemary's Baby* and *Chinatown*, was the original, somewhat bizarre, choice for director. When he declined, De Laurentiis approached Milos Forman (*One Flew Over the Cuckoo's Nest*) and Sydney Pollack, director of *Three Days of the Condor*, but had to settle for John Guillermin, an English director who had just finished another special effects picture, *The Towering Inferno*. De Laurentiis was criticised for confining himself to known quantities to direct his films and asking them to repeat themselves. He never took a risk as fellow producers Richard Zanuck and David Brown had done with hiring 28-year-old Steven Spielberg for *Jaws* or William Castle had done with Roman Polanski on *Rosemary's Baby*. Instead, wrote *Film Comment* magazine, De Laurentiis had an inordinate fondness for faceless hacks who could be counted on to bring in a film on time and under budget. (Despite this, Guillermin described *Kong* as 'a very personal little film'.) Most recently, eyebrows were raised when De Laurentiis picked the relatively unknown Brett Ratner, director of *Rush Hour 2*, to make *Red Dragon*. Respected directors Michael Mann, Jonathan Demme and Ridley Scott had all directed Hannibal Lecter films in the past.

The truth is that De Laurentiis is somewhat dismissive of most directors. Like other auteur producers such as Jerry Bruckheimer, De Laurentiis is in charge of the ship. He only allows directors whom he considers to be of the first rank to choose their collaborators. Others he tells whom to work with, because as far as he is concerned, he is investing his own money. A Fellini is allowed to do what he wants but everybody else follows orders. And if De Laurentiis does not like the rushes, the director will be told to reshoot until the producer is satisfied.

As we have already seen, De Laurentiis is not intimidated by the cult of the director either. He took *Ragtime* away from Robert Altman because he felt the director had reneged on promised changes to the script of *Buffalo Bill and the Indians*. Worse, Altman had made a self-indulgent movie which might have held significance for him but which was lost on the audience. Not thinking about the audience is the worst crime, according to De Laurentiis. Auteur mentality, he believes, just exists in Europe. Nobody in America ever asks what a film is about; they understand that studio executives are showmen working for cinema-goers.

John Guillermin described his relationship with De Laurentiis on *Kong* as follows:

Dino runs the show but he doesn't interfere. He lets everybody function but he's able, in his utter crazy wisdom, to get people to give their 100-

per-cent best and yet be the Godfather – in the same way that Darryl Zanuck was or like Thalberg, I'm sure, was. No one in his right mind could have started this bloody picture in January and finished it in November. So, in that sense, he's crazy – just as Zanuck was crazy and Thalberg and Mayer and all the others. How many people do you find that would spend the amounts of time that Dino puts in? His whole life is film. After putting in a long day he has a movie delivered to his house at eight o'clock in the evening. Then at five in the morning he's sitting there making transatlantic phone calls. I've never met anybody like that before. Making films is a very passionate business, and Dino has so much bloody passion.[4]

However, horror and science-fiction fans were also passionate in their distaste for the remake. Jessica Lange, chosen to play the Fay Wray character, was dismissed as a model with no previous acting experience. Indeed, Lange was not the first choice; the part was originally supposed to go to Barbra Streisand, who would fit in with the script's somewhat campy feel – Semple Jr. wrote the *Batman* television series in the 1960s – but she was not available until spring 1976. Valerie Perrine was also approached but she was under contract for Universal, which was planning its own *King Kong* remake (see below). Bette Midler was proposed and then Cher. At the press conference announcing the film, one reporter said that in the opinion of one famous science-fiction writer, any remake of *King Kong* would be pointless. The original involved painstaking stop-motion work, multiple hand-drawn matte paintings and relentless technical ingenuity; De Laurentiis was talking about using a man in a monkey suit. What was De Laurentiis' view? 'Intellectuals gonna love *Kong* – even film buffs who love the first *Kong* are going to love ours. Why? Because I give them no crap. I no spend two, three million to do quick business. I spend $16 million on my *Kong*,' said

De Laurentiis, illustrating the chasm between him and the fans.[5] His attitude was that the remake could not fail if he threw enough money at it. In a widely circulated story, no doubt apocryphal, when asked why he was not using model animation like the original, De Laurentiis was said to have answered: 'Model animation? What's-a-dat?'[6]

Kong was rushed into production against a ticking clock. Everybody was trapped by a line of copy in Paramount's poster announcing the remake: 'One year from today, Paramount Pictures and Dino De Laurentiis will bring you the most exciting and original motion picture event of all time.' The film had to be ready by Christmas 1976. De Laurentiis had made a rod for his own back by deciding on the December deadline. In his experience audiences stay away from a good movie if it is released at the wrong moment. *King Kong* would be the most expensive film in history made in the shortest amount of time, he warned.

A further complication was that just as De Laurentiis had competed with Mike Todd to make *War and Peace*, so he was now in a contest with another charismatic rival, Lew Wasserman, the inscrutable chairman of MCA – owner of Universal. When Paramount and De Laurentiis advertised in the trade papers that they had won the rights to remake *Kong* from RKO, Universal sued in early June 1975 for $25 million. Universal claimed that RKO, the studio which made the original *Kong*, had reneged on a deal to give it licensing rights. Then in November Universal changed its legal strategy. It now claimed in another lawsuit that the story of *King Kong* was in the public domain and that RKO had no legal right to sell the story, which was not protected by copyright. De Laurentiis told the *Los Angeles Times* on 5 November 1975: 'I've made hundreds and hundreds of pictures. And my experience is, if there's any doubt, pay the money. If we bought rights we didn't need to buy that's a waste of money. But I'm a private company. I prefer the benefit of doubt. I don't want to risk making a picture for $12 million and then find suits from RKO.'[7] Universal argued that in 1932 Grosset & Dunlop published a novelised version of the *King Kong* screenplay co-written by Edgar Wallace and Merian C. Cooper. Universal claimed that the novel and screenplay were both based on the Wallace/Cooper treatment. De Laurentiis might own the remake rights to the 1933 movie but the actual story had been public property since copyright expired in 1960. RKO then jumped into the legal mire and sued Universal, claiming that Wasserman's planned remake would infringe RKO's copyright, and asked for $5 million in damages. De Laurentiis also sued Universal in December, seeking $90 million in damages for 'copyright infringement' and 'unfair competition'. The producer also sought an injunction against Universal to prevent it from interfering with his remake. Universal was not eager to abandon its version of *King Kong*. The case dragged on, filling the pockets of the lawyers, until a mediator was found in the form of lawyer Sidney Korshak, former adviser to Al Capone's gang, who still, according to the California Attorney-General, counselled organised crime groups in Chicago, California, Las Vegas and New York. Both sides came to an agreement over lunch in the office of Charles Bluhdorn, chairman of Paramount. Wasserman and fellow MCA director Sidney Sheinberg agreed not to produce their version, *The Legend of King Kong*, in exchange for a percentage of net profits from the Paramount film. Nevertheless Universal's case against RKO rumbled on.

Deciding what Kong should look like was the next problem. De Laurentiis thought of Kong not as a mean gorilla but as an animal with the powers of a jungle creature and the mind of a man. His version of the story would not be frightening like the original but would arouse sympathy. Lange should fall in love with the ape like

Belle fell in love with the monster in Jean Cocteau's *La Belle et la Bête* (*Beauty and the Beast*, 1946). Italian puppeteer Carlo Rambaldi was put in charge of reinventing Kong, whom Dino imagined as 'the most human ape possible'. Rambaldi and his team remade Kong countless times because they wanted him to look intelligent and charming. It was decided to build three different Kongs: a mechanical arm that could pick up the heroine, a full-sized mechanical monster, and a man in an ape suit. This meant building a full-sized and a miniature set for every scene in which the mechanical and ape-suit Kongs appeared. Eventually, 109 full-sized and miniature sets had to be built. According to *Black Film Review*, when De Laurentiis advertised for somebody to play Kong the advertisement said the production was looking for a 'well-built' black man to fill the ape suit. The National Association for the Advancement of Colored People (NAACP) gave De Laurentiis a rap across the knuckles and the advertisement was withdrawn. The original budget for *Kong* had been $16 million, but this crept up because of De Laurentiis' unhappiness with the gorilla design, which he felt had to be more human if the film was to work as a *Beauty and the Beast* love story. According to De Laurentiis, all films go over budget, not because of mistakes made but because of everyday decisions during filming. Happily, De Laurentiis had underpinned his risk on the budget. Paramount had agreed to pay $25 million for worldwide distribution rights, regardless of whether anybody bought a ticket. This is known in the industry as a minimum guarantee.

De Laurentiis decided to be the line producer on *King Kong* – the man who makes sure the film is running smoothly down to its smallest detail – the first time he had done so since his old European productions. He made all the major decisions from budget costs to the colour of Lange's dress in the New York finale. After one exasperating discussion about finding an ocean-going supertanker to film scenes of Kong being ferried to New York, De Laurentiis was reported to have sat back in his chair, slapped his forehead and exclaimed that if only Aristotle Onassis were still alive, he would have helped.

King Kong started shooting on 15 January 1976. As if *Kong* was not enough for one man to deal with, De Laurentiis also started work on two other productions that same week. *Drum* was a sequel to the vaguely racist slave movie *Mandingo* – surely one of the worst films ever made – and John Wayne's last film *The Shootist.* According to the publicity handout, *Kong* occupied seven sound stages at Paramount, together with one set on the backlot. This was the wall where the islanders who worship Kong make human sacrifices to the ape god. The wall was 47 feet high and 170 yards long and had been built using 5,500 pounds of nails, 8,157 eucalyptus poles, 126,000 yards of grapevine, 1,350 gallons of paint and 50,000 staples. The team building it worked in two shifts and finished the wall in eight weeks at a cost of nearly $1 million. However, by February the budget had crept up to $20 million and the production had run out of sets to film. One executive told Semple Jr. that the movie was in terrible trouble because De Laurentiis had already fired two costume designers. Semple Jr. felt relieved at this bit of news because he knew that De Laurentiis would keep going until he found the *right* costume designer. De Laurentiis' character was to keep driving forward to make the best possible production. Actress Mia Farrow would later describe the producer as an immovable force. If you come into conflict with him, said Farrow, all you can do is go separate ways because you will never win. However, even De Laurentiis grumbled about *Kong* being too difficult and too expensive. The pressure rattled Guillermin, who knew of De Laurentiis' propensity for firing directors. Production shut down in March because none of the Kongs were ready. De Laurentiis had accepted from the outset that production might have to shut down if the special effects team could not keep up with the shooting schedule. Work had begun on the full-sized Kong and the moving hand at the end of February. The rudimentary hand was the first to be ready, its fingers closed in an arthritic-looking fist. A demonstration was laid on to show how the hand worked. But once everybody was assembled the hand failed to respond to the hydraulic system, and the crew had to prise its fingers apart. Slowly the middle finger rose up and gave designer Carlo Rambaldi and his team the classic sign.

Rather than waste time with a 40-foot Kong that might or might not work, De Laurentiis decided to shoot most of Kong's scenes with a man in an ape suit, just like Japanese monster movies such as *Godzilla*. Production started up again with Hawaii standing in for Skull Island, the mysterious tropical paradise where the oil engineers discover Kong. Once shooting in Hawaii was completed, the production moved to New York to shoot the climax of the film. Again, De Laurentiis found himself trapped by the now classic advance poster for the film. The poster showed Kong bestriding the twin towers of the World Trade Center in daylight, screaming with fury as he crushes a jet fighter in one hand. De Laurentiis, perhaps wanting to cover up the limitations of a man in an ape suit, decided to shoot the climax at night. He allowed a completely fictitious press release to be issued that the Port Authority in New York had refused permission to put the 40-foot robotic Kong on top of the World Trade Center for safety reasons. Then De Laurentiis advertised for two thousand New Yorkers to come and see Kong die at the foot of the building. After all, it would save Paramount $47 per person per day for the cost of hiring extras.

Eventually *Kong* cost $24 million, of which $3 million had been spent on various mechanical apes and ape suits. Rambaldi would go on to win an Academy Award for best visual effects. But the truth was that despite all the publicity hype – the 6.5 tons of aluminium, the 3,100 feet of hydraulic hose and 4,500 feet of electrical wiring – the 40-foot model only appeared in the finished film for about three seconds. The whole thing had been a publicity stunt. 'Monsters of our imagination do not merely dwarf us in the manner of a huge billboard cut-out,' wrote animator Paul Mandell. 'Narrow-minded, money-hungry film producers who could not care less about the chemistry which made the original *King Kong* work, who are out merely to exploit it for a fast buck, are doing the film world and the public a grave injustice.'[8] The 40-foot Kong, noted *Cinefantastique* magazine, looked about as lively as a cigar-store Indian on roller skates.

De Laurentiis' mastery of English can sometimes be likened to a magician twisting balloons into party animals. During one interview he said that *Kong* stood a chance of winning the Academy Award for best picture: 'Is more difficult to convince you that *Kong* is good movie than it would be for any other movie. Here we have practically unknown director – and big ape. And all unknown people around him. It's not easy. Because is *big head*; they have to act with *big head*.'[9] De Laurentiis went on to praise special effects man Rick Baker's performance in the monkey suit, calling *King Kong* the greatest love story ever made. The man in the gorilla costume was so good, De Laurentiis deadpanned, that he deserved an Academy Award nomination for best actor.

Just before the film's release De Laurentiis flew to Russia to discuss a sequel, *King Kong in Moscow*, ignoring the fact that Kong dies at the end of the film. The initial print run was to be for 2,200 prints worldwide: 1,000 in the USA and 1,200 in the rest of the world. It would be simultaneously released in dubbed versions in French, Italian, Spanish, German and Japanese. There would also be subtitled versions in Portuguese, Swedish and Japanese.

Shortly before De Laurentiis announced his remake, the radical *Free Paper* said that young audiences saw the 1933 Kong as black, beautiful and bound in chains by the white oppressor. Kong was any simple peasant bombed by the United States airforce, said *The Free Paper*, with Denham, the film-maker and explorer of the original, playing the part of the imperialist aggressor, the bomber of Hanoi. This is the basis of Semple Jr.'s version, with the Petrox Oil corporation representing the collective evils of big business, advertising, Watergate and imperialism. The corruption theme is introduced early on, when Charles Grodin, playing a Petrox Oil executive, reveals he has bribed somebody at the White House to get hold of photos of Skull Island. Kong's capture is made to resemble a defoliation manoeuvre in Vietnam. And soldiers on top of the World Trade Center keep Kong at bay with napalm-like flame-throwers. This is the striking thing about *Kong* and also its weakness. The whole thing feels as dated as disco, tank tops and astrology. 'You goddam chauvinist pig ape!' Lange tells Kong at one point before enquiring about his birth sign. 'The kids would burn down every Petrox gas station from Maine to California,' says another character, harking back to a time when young people actually felt angry about something.

That said, De Laurentiis' *King Kong* starts enjoyably enough as a piece of slick hokum. You settle down in your cinema seat knowing that you are in a safe pair of hands. In Semple Jr.'s version, Jessica Lange's character, Dwan, is a would-be actress floating to Hong Kong on a shady producer's yacht. He is below deck watching a porn film and she is on deck asleep when the yacht explodes. The crew of an oil exploration ship pulls Dwan, the only survivor, from the sea. As she is hauled up from the water, she breathlessly asks her rescuers: 'Ever met anyone before whose life was saved by *Deep Throat*?' The impossibly lovely Lange plays Dwan as a Marilyn

Monroe *manquée* in fetching hot pants. De Laurentiis never misses an opportunity to show Lange stepping in and out of showers or waterfalls. Most of the time she spends cupped in Kong's hand she has an orgasmic expression on her face. Jeff Bridges, however, playing the palaeontologist hero, looks like a hippy with the munchies who has made too many trips to the refrigerator. The overweight actor spends most of the film huffing and puffing after Kong – goodness knows what went through his head when confronted by the stairs in the World Trade Center. But the film becomes laughably bad the moment we see Kong. Even the script cannot take De Laurentiis' monster seriously. 'Well, that sure as hell wasn't a man in a monkey suit,' says Bridges after Kong has lurched off in slow motion clutching a Barbie doll. Whether wrestling a fake-looking snake or destroying Hornby train sets, De Laurentiis' Kong looks about as convincing as a four-year-old who has raided the dressing-up box.

The *Listener*, for one, was enthusiastic about De Laurentiis' remake. In pushing the old story to its disillusioned limits, said its reviewer, De Laurentiis had not cheapened the myth but deepened and darkened it. But film historian William K. Everson in *Films in Review* pinpointed what was wrong with the 1976 version when he said that De Laurentiis' Kong gave the minimum it could get away with, whereas the original gave you the maximum it could conjure up. There was nothing in the new Kong to inspire a second visit, Everson noted presciently, unless it was an opportunity to study Miss Lange in her first film. *Kong* grossed over $80 million around the world and turned a profit of $46 million but De Laurentiis later dismissed the film as a business decision.

Nevertheless, out went sex and violence as De Laurentiis' credo. Fantasy and spectacle for family audiences was now the thing. For *Hurricane* (1979), a remake of John Ford's torrid 1937 film about forbidden love in the South Pacific, De Laurentiis bought the Hotel Maraa in Bora Bora, Polynesia, and installed his own electricity generator, radio transmitter and water desalination plant at the cost of $4.5 million. He also bought a 265-foot long freighter to move equipment and supplies from Los Angeles.

He spent two years in pre-production on his risible version of 1930s comic strip *Flash Gordon* (1980), which was meant to cash in on the *Star Wars* phenomenon. Instead, Bergman regular Max von Sydow, rock band Queen and hearty Welsh actor Brian Blessed collided somewhere above the planet Mongo. *Flash Gordon* took over seven stages at Shepperton as well as four stages at Elstree, including the *Star Wars* stage together with a converted aircraft hangar at the Brooklands Industrial Park near Weybridge. The production also had the largest special effects backdrop ever built, a blue screen, 99 by 55 feet, built for an aerial battle. Again, De Laurentiis had a bizarre first choice for director: Nicolas Roeg, whom he then dismissed as being 'too intellectual'. Mike Hodges, whose best film remains glum thriller *Get Carter*, replaced Roeg. De Laurentiis then brought in Danilo Donati, Fellini's production designer on *Satyricon*, *Amarcord* and *Casanova*, to design the garish sets and costumes.

At about this time, stories began to appear in the American press that De Laurentiis was supported by the Mafia and laundered Cosa Nostra money. De Laurentiis knew that at one time or another every Italian living in America was considered Mafioso, but he wanted to stop the gossip before it became too annoying. When one journalist approached him for an interview on the subject he invited her on a trip to Europe, promising to reveal Mafia secrets. The journalist, understandably excited, flew to Amsterdam with him to meet his underworld financiers. Meanwhile, De Laurentiis got on the phone to his banker Peter Slavenburg, chairman of blue-chip Dutch bank Slavenburg Bank of Amsterdam (subsequently acquired by Crédit Lyonnais). De Laurentiis explained that a journalist was shadowing him intent on discovering Mafia connections. Would Slavenburg organise a small cocktail party in De Laurentiis' honour attended by the Slavenburg board of directors? They could all pretend to be Mafiosi and have a good laugh before revealing the truth. But in her *New West* article, Mary Murphy did not mention the cocktail party but rather a meeting with Frans Afman, the bank's director of external affairs (who would later become a film financier himself). 'We're not the Mafia,' Afman assured her. And no backing from mysterious Arab oil sheikhs either, another rumour doing the rounds at the time.

By 1982 De Laurentiis was growing bored with just being a film producer. He indulged his love of Italian cooking by opening the DDL Foodstore in New York. It sold fancy olive oils and other ingredients that are now standard in chi-chi supermarkets. In 1984 he opened the second DDL Foodstore in Beverly Hills, 11,000 square feet of upmarket delicatessen with a 2,500 square foot kitchen. One might argue with the quality of his movies, De Laurentiis told reporters, but you could never argue with the quality of his food. (He could always be counted on to provide good copy.)

However, in 1984 he took the first steps in what remains the greatest debacle of his career – an attempt to rival the Hollywood studios head on which would cost investors $69 million. Like his hero Alexander the Great, De Laurentiis has always had an empire-building streak in him, as evinced by the studio he built in Rome. Now he began building a $1.2 million studio in North Carolina equipped with wardrobe and property stores, production offices and two sound stages. The plan was to extend the facility to include eleven sound stages at a cost of $10 million. Although the North Carolina authorities did not offer De Laurentiis any tax incentives, they did introduce him to local bankers and urged them to offer the producer the best possible terms.

In 1985 De Laurentiis was advised to buy the Embassy Pictures library from Coca-Cola for between $35 million and $50 million. His first instinct was to reject the deal as he felt it would compromise his freedom as a producer. But Coca-Cola was ready to let the library go 'cheaply' and the offer was too good to turn down. The acquisition transformed De Laurentiis into, in his own words, 'a real and proper Hollywood studio'. Embassy's library consisted of about 275 titles ranging from *The Graduate* and *Carnal Knowledge* – when Joseph E. Levine ran the company – to John Carpenter's horror movie *The Fog*. De Laurentiis knew that the way to make money in the film business was to be in distribution. Distributors are first in line to be paid after cinema owners take their fifty cents out of every dollar spent at the box office. Warner Brothers or Columbia TriStar, for example, will then deduct their marketing costs – known as prints and advertising, or P&A as well as a distribution fee, and whatever money they put into the production in the first place, before the producer sees a cent. Arcane studio accounting methods ensure that so many overheads are loaded onto a film that it is rare for a producer to see a penny of what is called net profit. In November 1985 Embassy changed its name to De Laurentiis Entertainment Group (DEG) Inc. By now DEG Studios in North Carolina had grown to six sound stages and a 32-acre backlot.

While all this was going on De Laurentiis embarked on another costly epic that would eventually accelerate the collapse of DEG. Once again, it was one of his daughters who put the idea into his head. Back in 1979 he had bought the rights to science-fiction novel *Dune* for $2 million at the urging of his daughter Raffaella, who was a fan of the book. Frank Herbert's novel had by this time sold two million copies and been translated into fourteen languages, despite being 'blokes in cloaks' nonsense about messianic sand worms and hallucinogenic space travel. Two previous attempts to make a film of the book had failed. Herbert wrote the first draft of the script, which came in at an unworkable 176 pages (the rule of thumb is that one page of screenplay equals one minute of screen time). Novelist Rudolph Wurlitzer (*Pat Garrett and Billy the Kid*, 1973) was then hired to write another version. That year Ridley Scott had an enormous success with *Alien*, and De Laurentiis offered the project to the British director. Scott got to work with H. R. Giger, Swiss designer of the *Alien* monster, and came back with a proposed $50 million budget. De Laurentiis baulked and Scott dropped out, partly, said De Laurentiis, because he was looking for a director with more heart and a less technological approach. Rafaella, who by now was co-producing the massive project, suggested David Lynch, director of the nightmarish *Eraserhead* and *The Elephant Man*. Lynch agreed and started adapting *Dune* with his *Elephant Man* co-writers Eric Bergren and Christopher de Voie. Their first draft was even longer than Herbert's, weighing in at 200 pages. De Laurentiis eventually accepted Lynch's sixth solo draft of the script a year later, after suggesting Lynch drop his co-authors. Lynch said that De Laurentiis wanted to make a science-fiction film about people rather than ray guns and spaceships.

Dune began shooting at Churubusco Studios in Mexico City. Production designer Anthony Masters, who had worked on *2001: A Space Odyssey*, built seventy-five sets on eight sound stages. The look of the film was inspired by a trip De Laurentiis and Lynch had made to Venice. But within a fortnight at least half of the 1400-strong cast and crew had come down with dysentery. De Laurentiis decided it would be more economical to build a new restaurant at the studio, and flew over his personal chef Gigi to supervise catering. Although budgeted somewhere between $30 million and $40 million, the costs began to escalate, owing to unforeseen circumstances. De Laurentiis had to buy six emergency generators because of Mexico City's random power cuts; and air-conditioning had to be installed at Churubusco to stop actors wilting in the 100-degree heat. In the end the film cost $45 million to produce.

Lynch's first assembly of footage ran to four hours but De Laurentiis insisted that the picture must last no longer than two hours and seventeen minutes. Drastic editing made the plot even more incomprehensible. Nevertheless, De Laurentiis had a touching faith that *Dune* would be a hit and bought the rights to all five novels in the series. Actors were signed up for sequels. But when *Dune* was released in 1985 the consensus was that it was boring and incomprehensible. *Variety* called the film hollow, unimaginative and cold. *Empire* magazine said that *Dune* looked like a million dollars – unfortunately it had cost fifty. Film critic Rex Reed told *New York Post* readers that this 'pretentious exercise in pointless insanity' was so bad that it was in a class by itself. The film grossed only $27.4 million in the USA. Looking back, Lynch said he had ignored his own instincts and made a film for De Laurentiis. The producer had indicated his expectations for the film and Lynch had made every decision trying to live up to them.

One postscript to *Dune* was that Lynch's contract said that De Laurentiis would have to fund a low-budget film of the director's own choosing after the science-fiction epic. De Laurentiis did his best to make the terms as unattractive as possible. In exchange for complete artistic freedom, Lynch would have to defer his salary and only receive a minimal share of whatever profits there might be. The budget would have to be no higher than $6 million. Filming began at the North Carolina studio in spring 1985 and De Laurentiis took no interest in the project except for the first day, when he stopped by to watch some rushes. De Laurentiis asked why everything on screen was so dark. Lynch fibbed that the camera lens was broken. De Laurentiis shrugged and left the projection room. Lynch's low-budget film was *Blue Velvet*.

In spring 1986 the selfsame financial advisers convinced De Laurentiis to become a public company and float on the stock exchange. According to the financial plan, DEG needed to raise $500 million, an enormous amount of money at the time. The idea was to raise $300 million on Wall Street and the remaining $200 million through US government tax shelters that were available for film. De Laurentiis later said that the decision to go public transformed DEG into a nightmare. He took part in elaborate presentations across the United States in April 1986, talking up DEG to small and large investors. The $300 million was quickly raised. By now there was also a 47 per cent holding in an Australian offshoot, De Laurentiis Entertainment Limited, and talk of investing $10 million in a studio near Surfers Paradise in Queensland, Australia. While all this was going on, however, tax legislation changed and the film tax break was shut down, leaving DEG $200 million short of its target. De Laurentiis convinced everybody, possibly himself included, that the shortfall could be made up through income from DEG's films. In addition to the difficult financial framework was the pressure of having to produce a number of films very quickly.

De Laurentiis had wanted to run his own studio since MGM and UA made such a mess of releasing Michael Cimino's police thriller *The Year of the Dragon* (1985). Another reason was the extortionate distribution fees other studios were demanding to release his films. De Laurentiis knew he could not just rely on his own productions to feed the distribution pipeline. However, bureaucrats who, De Laurentiis claimed, had never produced a foot of film in their lives ignored his suggestions that DEG acquire and release *Good Morning, Vietnam* or *Crocodile Dundee*, both of which became big hits for Disney and Paramount respectively. De Laurentiis found himself blocked whichever way he turned.

DEG planned to make fifteen films with a combined budget of $150 million. De Laurentiis was only going to invest $23 million of his own money; the balance was to be borrowed. Bank of America arranged a $65 million credit line with another $65 million to $75 million coming from a group of individual investors. The pressure to release movies in order to generate fees meant DEG put things into production before they were ready. The tail was now wagging the dog. In particular De Laurentiis regretted distributing four titles: *Maximum Overdrive*, *Raw Deal*, *Crimes of the Heart* and *Tai-Pan*. Being as yet unproven, DEG also had a credibility problem when it came to getting hold of material. One former DEG executive admitted that he was frustrated to be told by an agent that DEG was sixth on the list to be sent a hot script doing the rounds.

During this period De Laurentiis was convinced that horror writer Stephen King, author of *Carrie* and *The Shining*, would provide DEG with a hit if only he could find the right project. De Laurentiis produced screen adaptations of *The Dead Zone*, *Firestarter*, *Cat's Eye*, *Silver Bullet* and *Maximum Overdrive*. With the exception of *The Dead Zone*, directed by Canadian auteur David Cronenberg, all of them flopped. De Laurentiis was, according to King, persuasive, hypnotic and magnetic – one of the most fabulous creatures the novelist had ever met in his life. King concluded that no matter whoever was nominally director of De Laurentiis' films, really De Laurentiis was in charge of the set. But the experience of working for the Italian producer and then coming back for more left King feeling somewhat bruised. He compared his time at DEG to a girl who is raped and then turns over and offers herself again.

By now De Laurentiis realised that studios release films close to quarterly earnings reports in the hope that a success will prevent share prices from dropping. In order to meet these quarterly deadlines all the studios rush through post-production work, which went against the grain of De Laurentiis' way of doing things. For De Laurentiis the post-production stage was especially sensitive and it pained him to see corners being cut.

As things went wrong DEG sought not only to reschedule bank loans worth $65 million but also to stretch out payments on the $58 million it already owed to producers of finished films. DEG eventually lost $36 million over a nine-month period. De Laurentiis was told that the company could only be saved if he resigned from his $850,000-a-year job as chairman and chief executive. He agreed on two conditions: first, his name should be removed from the company and replaced by the original name, Embassy; second, the company must never declare itself bankrupt. In the end both of these promises were ignored. In August 1988, despite selling its 350-film library to British financier Michael Stevens for $54 million, DEG was forced to protect itself from creditors and file for Chapter 11 bankruptcy with losses of $69 million. De Laurentiis claimed he only learned about this disaster when he read about it in a newspaper. Others thought the former chairman and chief executive protested too much. Looking back on the mess, Stephen King compared De Laurentiis to a James Bond figure with a life jacket under his tuxedo, floating serenely away while everybody else is drowning.

Two years later De Laurentiis unveiled Dino De Laurentiis Communications (DDLC), his new production and sales company. During the 1990s he restored his credibility with a string of well-received productions, including *Breakdown* (1997). In 2000 he made his six hundredth project, *U-571*, an $80 million Second World War submarine adventure. The film, which reprised everybody's favourite moments from other submarine films such as *Das Boot* (*The*

Boat, 1981), was shot over a period of three months in a giant water tank in Malta, followed by another three months at Cinecitta Studios in Rome. But the *Sunday Times* sneered that the lack of stars in the film – the leads were Matthew McConaughey and Bill Paxton – showed how little interest the script drummed up when it was doing the rounds in Hollywood. It is true that the story has enough holes in it to sink the *Bismark*. Throughout the film the heroes have been struggling to get to England, but when they reach land, for some unexplained reason, a US Navy coastguard plane flies across the screen. When the submarine surfaces one almost expects a farmer to be standing on the beach saying, 'Welcome to Cornwallshire.' The lack of plausibility did not alienate audiences, however, and *U-571* went on to gross $77.12 million in the USA and Canada alone.

Like Duncan Kenworthy, who has hit a rich seam collaborating with writer Richard Curtis (*Four Weddings and a Funeral*, *Love Actually*), De Laurentiis is not afraid to offer the public an improved version of a film he has just made. For example, he rushed out *Drum* (1976) a year after his vaguely racist *Mandingo* was a hit.

In 2000 *Variety* reported that De Laurentiis had paid $10 million of his own money for the rights to *Hannibal*, the sequel to Thomas Harris' thriller *The Silence of the Lambs*. Back in 1986, De Laurentiis gave director Michael Mann (*The Insider*) his first big break with an adaptation of Thomas Harris' first Hannibal Lecter novel, *Red Dragon*, retitled *Manhunter*. Though praised by critics, *Manhunter* earned less than $9 million, and De Laurentiis was warned off making *Silence of the Lambs* by his staff. Instead, De Laurentiis gave Orion the sequel rights for free. *Silence of the Lambs* went on to win five Academy Awards: best picture, best director, best actress, best actor and best adapted screenplay. De Laurentiis was not going to be stung by the same bee twice. He still had first option on producing the screen version of any *Silence of the Lambs* sequel Harris might write. MGM, which had bought Orion's library, agreed to split the costs of making the $80 million *Hannibal* in exchange for marketing the film in North America. But when Jonathan Demme, director of *Silence of the Lambs*, declined to work on the sequel, De Laurentiis offered the job to Ridley Scott. The British director, whose credits included *Alien* and *Blade Runner*, was in Malta at the same time as *U-571*, shooting *Gladiator*. At first Scott refused, thinking De Laurentiis wanted him to make a film about the Roman emperor crossing the Alps on elephants. The next problem was Jodie Foster, who had won an Oscar for her performance as FBI agent Clarice Starling. Foster turned down the sequel because she disliked David Mamet's screenplay. Julianne Moore was chosen to replace Foster. Somewhat churlishly, De Laurentiis said Foster needed *Hannibal* more than the project needed her. Foster's last film *Anna and the King* had flopped, he claimed, because of the actress's lack of sex appeal.

De Laurentiis then decided to remake *Manhunter* as *Red Dragon*, going back to Thomas Harris' original novel. His thinking was that most people would not have seen *Manhunter*, Michael Mann's first major outing as a director. Mann, creator of cop show *Miami Vice*, had bathed *Manhunter* in the hot pinks and cool blues of the television series. Furthermore, his Hannibal Lecter was almost a cameo, whereas De Laurentiis wanted the franchise's most interesting character brought much more into the foreground in the remake. He persuaded MGM to allow him to reproduce the look and feel of *Silence of the Lambs*. Kristi Zea, production designer of *Silence*, was hired to plagiarise herself inch by inch.

Anthony Hopkins agreed to reprise his role as Lecter; Ed Norton signed on to play his nemesis, FBI agent Will Graham; and Ralph Fiennes was chosen to play serial killer Francis Dolarhyde, otherwise known as the Tooth Fairy. De Laurentiis then approached both Barry Levinson and Michael Bay (*Pearl Harbor*) to direct the film, but they turned him down. In the end De Laurentiis chose Brett Ratner, director of *Rush Hour*, *Rush Hour 2* and . . . *Rush Hour 3*. According to De Laurentiis, these films – fairly amusing buddy movies starring Jackie Chan and Chris Tucker – showed that Ratner was a director with his own style, even though Ratner himself admitted that the series was based on upbeat 1980s cop movies such as *48 Hours* and *Beverly Hills Cop*. Perhaps more importantly, the four films which Ratner had made to date had generated more than $700 million worldwide. Despite Ratner's batting average, De Laurentiis was on set first thing every morning keeping a close eye on his investment. Ratner compared the experience to being watched over by a parent. Now De Laurentiis is talking about a fifth film in the series, *The Lecter Variations*, starring Macaulay Culkin as the young Hannibal Lecter.

Like all of the producers profiled in this book, De Laurentiis is a hard worker. Unlike Sam Spiegel, who would laze around in the Mediterranean in his yacht for months on end, De Laurentiis goes to the studio five days a week. Whatever time he has gone to bed the night before, he wakes up at 5 a.m. including Sundays, Christmas and New Year's Day. After a cup of espresso and half an hour of exercise he is driven in his Mercedes to Universal. On the way to work he reads the *New York Times*, the *Los Angeles Times* and two Italian papers including a daily sports paper. At 7.30 a.m. he arrives at his office – 'I practically open the place up,' he says – and starts phoning Europe, which has a nine-hour time difference. At noon he stops and has a sandwich sent up from the Universal restaurant. Then he leaves for home at 1.30 p.m. and spends the rest of the afternoon reading scripts or negotiating deals. He eats dinner early with his wife Martha and daughters Carolyna and Dina once they have got back from school. He rarely goes to Hollywood parties, but if he does he will eat at home first because he thinks most party food is inedible. When the girls have done their homework and gone to bed, their father may watch the news or sport on the television. He believes that sport is the entertainment of the future. Now in his eighties, he claims that his stamina comes from having 'three Cs – cuore, cervello and coglioni', referring to heart, brains and balls. Cinema is something you have to love with 100 per cent of your attention, he says, otherwise, forget it.

Danilo Donati, production designer on *Hurricane* and *Flash Gordon*, has said that De Laurentiis is so driven because he burns all his bridges. He can only go forward because he cannot go back. *King Kong* screenwriter Lorenzo Semple Jr. saw De Laurentiis' decisiveness as impulsiveness: at one three-minute meeting at the start of *Hurricane*, De Laurentiis changed the setting to Bora Bora rather than the original Western Samoa, and requested that they have a white girl at the centre of the love story rather than a Polynesian.

Like French producer Marin Karmitz, De Laurentiis regards each film as a prototype with its own problems. Not surprisingly for a man in his eighties, he is gloomy about the future of Hollywood. The cost of distributing and advertising films keeps spiralling upwards (the average amount of money spent marketing a studio film in 2001 was $33 million – an increase of 14 per cent year-on-year). The market for pre-selling films to television stations has all but collapsed, and the studios are putting themselves out of business by each releasing between twenty and twenty-five films a year. Half of any studio's schedule are flops simply because there are not enough good projects to go around. In De Laurentiis' view, each studio should cut back to eight or nine good releases.

De Laurentiis blames himself completely if a film is not a success. After all, he has chosen the storyline, the script, the writers, the director, the actors and crew, and put them all together. If it flops, he considers that he has made a bad choice in one or all of the key positions. However, if a film is a hit he does not take sole credit. Instead he believes that credit should go to everybody involved, because the producer has evidently made the right choices. De Laurentiis believes, like Selznick, that a movie must be a one-man operation, just as the studios used to be in golden age of MGM boss Louis B. Mayer or Darryl Zanuck at Warner Brothers.

According to De Laurentiis, a producer should never be surprised when a problem arises. A producer should only be surprised when a problem does *not* arise. Problems are always different because they are all about creation. Or as director Roland Joffe (*The Killing Fields*) once put it, the director's eye is always fixed on what is going right and the producer's on what might go wrong. Every time De Laurentiis has made a film with no problems there is nothing to show for it on screen. Only when you have a film with problems is there something that audiences want to watch, he says.

De Laurentiis told me that he could teach the mechanics of what a producer does very simply. First, you buy a book or a screenplay. At the time of writing, his latest project was a life of Alexander the Great, the king who conquered Greece, Egypt and the Persian Empire and who founded Alexandria. He bought the rights to a trilogy of historical novels by Valerio Massimo Manfredi. De Laurentiis sequestered himself away for two weeks in a bungalow on the Universal lot and drew up an outline of the three books. He then gave this to writer Ted Tally, screenwriter of *Silence of the Lambs*. De Laurentiis will work with the writer kneading the material. When the script is ready, then you choose a director. And then you decide on what sort of marketing campaign is best for the project.

The star of the film is the script. Any director can make a good movie with a good script, and a great director can make a great one.

All a star is looking for, says De Laurentiis, is good material. When a big star appears in a flop it is because the script did not appeal to the audience. 'Nobody understand the secret,' he says. What he first looks for in a script is emotion, which is the first thing the audience wants to see. The type of emotion does not matter. 'It can be a war movie or a love story, but you need an intuition this would be a great movie.' A star is no guarantee. 'When people realise that the secret is the script they will make better movies.'

But what De Laurentiis cannot teach is what makes a great producer: 'To become a great producer you must have something inside of you that I cannot teach you. If you have nothing inside your personality I cannot help you. You need an artistic feeling inside you, something which divides artists and non-artists.'

And with that insight the last tycoon toddles off to the bathroom.

3   Duncan Kenworthy and Andrew Macdonald

The team

A run-down comprehensive school in south-west London is not somewhere you would expect to find Britain's biggest movie star. Hugh Grant is in Putney filming his latest romantic comedy in a secondary school on the edge of Roehampton. Various film crew members, all wearing fleece jackets, mill around outside the school, speaking into walkie-talkies. It is unclear what any of them might be doing, except possibly ordering more fleeces.

I am here to see Duncan Kenworthy, producer of two of the most successful British films ever, *Four Weddings and a Funeral* and *Notting Hill*, who, in tandem with writer Richard Curtis, has created the nearest Britain has to a franchise – Hollywood-speak for a successful film series such as James Bond or Star Wars. True, this franchise is based on a writer's work, but Kenworthy's romantic comedies to date have been about a tongue-tied Englishman, played by Hugh Grant, supported by a group of friends as he woos an enigmatic American girl. Francis Ford Coppola once pointed out that the reason why people like sequels goes back to childhood, and being tucked up in bed at night by your parents and told a familiar story.

My theme in this chapter is partnership: why some producers work best in teams. Working as a team allows producers to split the creative and financial aspects of the job. One producer may be good at reassuring actors, while the other partner is happier scrutinising a balance sheet. Working as a team also allows producers to play good cop/bad cop and then, to keep everybody on their toes, swap roles. Or perhaps producing a film has become such a complicated job that you need more than one person to do it.

Duncan Kenworthy and his partner, fellow producer Andrew Macdonald have produced some of the biggest hits in British cinema, including *Notting Hill*, *Trainspotting* and *28 Days Later*. Their joint company DNA Films (Anthony Minghella came up with the DNA moniker, which stands for Duncan 'n' Andrew) has forged a partnership with Twentieth Century-Fox, making it the second most powerful film company in Britain after Working Title, the London arm of Universal. Both producers became successful in the late 1990s at a time when young British producers were rejecting dour kitchen-sink dramas. Instead this generation wanted to make the kind of bright, energetic American films which they saw at multiplexes.

The main crew is filming inside the school hall, which – disconcertingly given that outside it is a warm summer day – has been dressed up for Christmas. You can smell school dinners somewhere in the middle distance. Kenworthy is filming his third collaboration with Curtis, *Love Actually*, which the studio backing the film, Universal Pictures, hopes will earn even more than the $363 million *Notting Hill* took at the box office. It is the start of the fourth week of shooting during a thirteen-week shoot. Kenworthy looks brisk but tense, dressed in his uniform of black jeans and a fleece (those fleeces again). Despite the twelve-hour days and six-day weeks, Kenworthy looks like a healthy man in his late thirties – despite the fact he is actually fifty-four – a prime advert for the benefits of not smoking or drinking. On a deeper level, Kenworthy has been compared to George Cukor, the American director of *The*

Philadelphia Story and *The Women*, who coaxed great performances out of his actresses. Kenworthy even managed to get a good performance out of Andie MacDowell in *Four Weddings*, even if she couldn't quite hide the furrows of perplexity around her eyes when she spoke Curtis's witticisms, as if unable to grasp what she was saying.

Orson Welles once described film directing as playing with the biggest toy train set a boy ever had. If so, Curtis looks like one of those swotty boys who read *Look and Learn* rather than *Whizzer and Chips*. He comes across as an inspirational science teacher, and is, everybody says, frightfully nice. Kenworthy sits next to him behind a stack of video monitors. A school band with actors playing teachers playing backing singers flanks a spotlit stage. A camera crane is out in front with a spotlight trained on a ten-year-old girl. A warm Tamla Motown track starts up and the little girl begins singing; her voice is like that of a young Michael Jackson. The stage is rocking, with musicians swaying and backing singers snapping their fingers. Then, inexplicably, the whole thing stops. The stage is swept and everybody gets ready for another take. Once again, just as the band gets going, Curtis waves at everybody to stop. The schoolchildren's frustration is palpable. It is all quite maddening. The ten-year-old's hair is twitched and primped and teased for the umpteenth time. Kenworthy's erstwhile business partner, Andrew Macdonald, describes film-making as a lot of standing around in muddy fields. Certainly the process does seem to involve a lot of 'hurry up and wait'. While all this is (not) going on, Hugh Grant slips into the back of the hall almost unnoticed. He appears to have 'do not approach' written all over his face. His co-star, Martine McCutcheon, is busy signing autographs for children like the stage school trouper she is. Interestingly, the children seem too intimidated to approach Grant – perhaps an assistant director has already forewarned them. Or perhaps kids just recognise McCutcheon from her days in the television soap *EastEnders*.

Kenworthy leans across and explains that Curtis has spent two years writing this episodic script. As is usual with their collaborations, Kenworthy made sure there was some tart taste in *Love Actually* to counter Curtis's overwhelming saccharine style. Curtis first pondered ideas for what would eventually become *Love Actually* while walking along a beach in Bali. He had taken his family there for an extended five-month holiday during 2000, but had to keep flying back to London to rewrite *Bridget Jones's Diary*, another Hugh Grant movie for Universal. To date, films written by Curtis for Grant have grossed $1.2 billion. Sitting next to me is a man from Universal, keeping an eye on proceedings. He is tapping figures into his calculator with a pen.

Duncan Kenworthy was born on 9 September 1949 in Yorkshire, England. He grew up in the village of Uppermill on the edge of Saddleworth Moor, where his father owned a woollen mill. Kenworthy gained a first at Cambridge University in English Literature, and then won a scholarship to the University of Pennsylvania. He stayed on in the United States and got a job in New York at the Children's Television Workshop, home of pre-school programme *Sesame Street*. Kenworthy was in charge of foreign 'cultural adaptations' of the show, the biggest being a two-year project in Kuwait. Jim Henson, the Muppets' creator, became Kenworthy's mentor. One of the things that impressed Kenworthy about Henson was his ability to screw money out of broadcasters to spend on audiences with the least amount of spending power – something which went against market forces. Henson also passed on to Kenworthy that what you see on screen often reflects the atmosphere behind camera. 'Another thing was Jim's own spirit. He was the only genius I've ever met,' Kenworthy told me one gloomy afternoon in his office. But the key lesson Henson taught the young producer was to do everything at 100 per cent of its potential and never accept second best.

Kenworthy returned to England in 1979 and co-created the children's series *Fraggle Rock*. By the late 1980s he was producing *The Storyteller*, another series for the Jim Henson Organization, written by future Academy Award-winner Anthony Minghella. Kenworthy also produced another television movie written by Minghella, *Living with Dinosaurs*, about a boy whose pet stuffed dinosaur comes to life. Slowly Kenworthy was working his way into the British film industry, building contacts and alliances with people he would work with in the future. Most importantly, agents – gatekeepers of talent – knew that if Kenworthy wanted one of their clients, he was serious, unlike some of the time-wasters who spent their nights in trendy Soho drinking clubs. To paraphrase the Peter Cook joke, first producer says: 'I'm producing a film', to which second producer replies: 'Neither am I.'

For a British producer, the success of a homegrown movie can be something of a mixed blessing. What it usually means is that the British talent involved is now on Hollywood's radar screen and already halfway across the Atlantic. The usual British reward for success, in other words, is getting a shot at an American pay day. Contrary to popular belief, Hollywood is not really American – an Australian, after all, owns Twentieth Century-Fox; the Japanese own Columbia TriStar; and, until recently, the French owned Universal. Although more British actors and directors want to stay and work in the UK, Kenworthy believes British producers must figure out how to reward them financially for their loyalty, and not simply ask them to stay on the breadline just for the pleasure of sleeping in their own beds.

Kenworthy's next project was *Greek Myths*, eight half-hour adaptations of ancient stories with Michael Gambon as the storyteller.

Again, the chief writer on the series was Minghella. For some time Kenworthy had tried to get the rights to Mary Renault's historical novel *The King Must Die*, having loved the book when he was a child, but this proved too complicated. Kenworthy believes that Greek myths appeal to our basic human instincts and can understand why Freud chose them as his paradigms. Unlike fairy tales, they have sad or gruesome endings which are often arrived at through violence.

In 1990 Kenworthy suffered a double tragedy. Both Henson and his father died within four months of each other. In my interview with Kenworthy I venture to suggest that losing both his father and father figure within a short space of time liberated him in some way. Kenworthy leans forward and agrees: 'I know I wouldn't have done *Four Weddings* if Jim hadn't died, because the seductive part of Henson was that it was a family. Jim was definitely a mentor and father figure to me. If Jim hadn't died I wouldn't have dared to do something that was very much my own.'

Kenworthy was forty-four when he took a sabbatical from his job as senior vice-president of production to produce his first film. At this time Richard Curtis was best known as a television scriptwriter, producing sketches for *Not the Nine O'Clock News* and creating the Rowan Atkinson comedy series *Blackadder*. The idea for a film based around weddings came to him when he calculated he had been to sixty-seven weddings over an eleven-year period. Curtis then approached Kenworthy with his first-draft screenplay because he believed that the Muppets producer was somehow good at making things deeper on an emotional level. He also admired the writing in *The Muppet Show* and appreciated Kenworthy's professionalism. But Kenworthy had previously turned down other scripts Curtis had written because none of them had been quite good enough to make him think about quitting his job. Curtis first showed Kenworthy an early draft of *Four Weddings* at the beginning of 1992. When

Kenworthy read it he knew this was the best thing Curtis had done so far. However, it still needed to be made more three-dimensional. As a television writer Curtis had to keep his characters the same week after week, whereas Kenworthy felt that a feature film needed more emotion. Kenworthy influenced the story by making it more realistic and giving the characters psychological depth. Curtis went on to rewrite the script twenty times under Kenworthy's supervision. Kenworthy drove Curtis so hard because in the producer's opinion, a drama can probably survive at less than 100 per cent but a comedy is funny or it is not, and the gap between funny and unfunny is the thickness of a cigarette paper. At this point the script was called *Four Weddings and a Honeymoon*. It was Curtis's friend Helen Fielding, who would go on to write best-seller *Bridget Jones's Diary*, who suggested the title *Four Weddings and a Funeral*. Slowly Curtis's screenplay moved away from people just being funny and became more about individuals who use comedy either to suppress feelings or to deflect intimacy. Simon Callow, one of the stars of *Four Weddings*, compared the finished screenplay to flicking a stone across a pond. The script had extraordinary bounce to it but was quite deep beneath the surface.

The producer's next job was to find a suitable director. Both Curtis and Kenworthy admired *Ready When You Are, Mr McGill*, a television drama made in the 1970s about an annoying film extra. Like *Four Weddings*, *Mr McGill* was repetitive but had a real-life feel. The danger with *Four Weddings* was that it could end up just being one shot after another of people clinking champagne flutes and being witty. When *McGill*'s director, Mike Newell, read the script he thought it was fairly funny, but he too wanted to give it more depth. Kenworthy and Newell both thought this was a serious film whose technique, whose medium, was comedy. After all, the best comedy is played straight.

Anglo-Dutch film company Polygram Filmed Entertainment agreed to put up 70 per cent of the $4.3 million budget, with UK broadcaster Channel 4 providing the remaining 30 per cent in exchange for showing the film on television. Then Channel 4 got cold feet and demanded another rewrite, which with hindsight Curtis thought was crucial in getting his script soufflé-perfect. As Kenworthy points out, talk is the cheapest part of a film and the six-month delay enabled producer, writer and director to chew through every possible permutation of the story. Not everybody was as ambivalent about the project as Channel 4 though. When an Australian distributor, Richard Sheffield-Maclure, read the finished script he was so excited he could hardly wait for the ten-hour time difference to telephone London and make an offer.

Kenworthy cut the shooting schedule from eight weeks to thirty-nine days. Andie MacDowell agreed to play the female lead for only $250,000, a quarter of her usual asking price (her share of profits, however, would eventually earn her $3 million). Shooting began on 28 May 1993. Typically freak English weather meant that thermal underwear was worn under flimsy summer frocks when shooting what was supposed to be a glorious outdoor wedding reception. Wanting to keep everything as realistic as possible, Kenworthy made sure that the posh metropolitan wedding had some real aristocracy in the congregation, including a viscount and two earls. Kenworthy later said it was easy to spot the aristocrats among the extras because of their confidence – they looked as if they really did belong at a grand wedding. Simon Lycett, the florist who had recreated Hampstead Heath for Jim Henson's memorial service at St Paul's Cathedral, was hired to decorate churches and receptions. (Lycett was subsequently hired to decorate the White House because of his work on the film.) But a last-minute change of heart by Southwark Cathedral meant that the fourth wedding was filmed at St Bartholomew's Church in Smithfield, east London, rather than south London as planned.

Interviewed on set, Kenworthy described weddings as one of the universal themes in life. Hugh Grant's character Charles, said Kenworthy, preferred self-deprecation to self-promotion, dissembling rather than telling the truth, all those things one recognises as being typically English. But an American agent damned the script as being 'Noël Coward-like'. And Russell Schwartz, head of the film's US distributor Gramercy Pictures (a Polygram subsidiary), told Kenworthy during editing that no American would sympathise with an English guy who couldn't make up his mind. Schwartz advised Kenworthy to dump the title, since no American alpha male would pay to see a film with 'wedding' on the poster. Over the next few weeks Kenworthy considered 112 alternative titles, including *Holy Misery* and *Lots of Weddings, Some Sex and a Cup of Tea*. Gramercy's suggestions included *The Pleasures of Merely Circulating, Loitering in Sacred Places, Skulking Around, Strays* and *Tales of True Love and Near Misses*. Finally the team plumped for *The Best Man* until they discovered a 1964 Henry Fonda film of the same name.

Executive producer Tim Bevan said that when his production company, Working Title (another Polygram subsidiary which was subsequently bought by Universal), was first approached with the script, he never had any doubts that the film would work in Britain. However, he was not sure how the film would be received in America. *Four Weddings* was given test screenings in Secaucus, New Jersey – an upmarket but suburban area – and in Santa Monica, Los Angeles, home of expatriate British. In Santa Monica the film got a 75 per cent approval rating compared with an average of 55 per cent. Studios rely on test screenings to tweak finished films. Most famously, Adrian Lyne reshot the ending of *Fatal Attraction* because audiences did not like its existing finale. Instead of Glenn Close's stalker character killing herself to *Madame Butterfly*, audiences voted for an air-punching ending with the wife of Michael Douglas' character shooting Close dead. Despite their squeamishness, most film-makers point out that test screenings are not editing by committee. They are especially useful for a comedy in that they show you where the laughs are – and how to pace the film accordingly. Market research companies are brought in once a project has been given the green light to ask the public its reaction to the proposed cast. Market researchers then gather public reactions to a film right until the test screening. Reshooting after test screenings is so common that money for reshoots is often built into budgets of films. David Puttnam, an advocate of this kind of research, said that test screenings date back to silent director D. W. Griffith: 'What we think of as the golden age of Hollywood, the 1930s and 1940s, was in fact the golden age of reshoots.' MGM, the most regimented of studios, was nicknamed Retake City during Hollywood's classical era. Irving Thalberg once said that films aren't made, they're remade. Interestingly, market research consultancy National Review Group (NRG), which is used by all of the studios to shape marketing campaigns, says that women almost invariably choose the films when twenty-something couples go to the cinema.

Four Weddings is unusual in that it saves its biggest laugh – Kristin Scott Thomas marrying Prince Charles – for the final few seconds of the film. Test audiences said they wanted to know what happened to the characters after the story ended, and Curtis thought of the idea for the credit-crawl photo montage on his way to have dinner with executive producer Eric Fellner. (Kenworthy puts in a cameo as John Hannah's new lover in the photo sequence.)

Despite encouraging test screenings, Polygram's down-to-earth president Stewart Till thought his company's other release, *Backbeat*, looked much more promising. After all, *Four Weddings* starred an actor who was known, if at all, for being just a pretty face and was directed by somebody who had just come off a flop. *Backbeat*, on the other hand, which followed the early years of the Beatles, had a built-in fan base, a great soundtrack and a sexy young cast. Till thought the little English comedy might gross between £5 million and £8 million in Britain; but its lack of foreign potential meant it was only scheduled to open on five screens in America – two theatres in New York and three in Los Angeles. If the film was successful Polygram would open the film on more screens – approximately twenty to twenty-five screens in twelve US cities in its second weekend, broadening to more than two hundred screens, and so on. According to Kenworthy, Newell was so depressed by the time he started dubbing the soundtrack that he had lost all confidence in the film being remotely funny.

Four Weddings had its world premiere on the opening night of the Sundance Film Festival in January 1994. Word of mouth was good but *Backbeat* received a much better, even ecstatic, reception. Nevertheless, Polygram's owlish president Michael Kuhn decided to give *Four Weddings* a push, eventually spending three times what it cost to make. The bottom line, said Kuhn, was that films had to be sold hard in America, like soap flakes. But when he scrutinised the opening weekend's figures from New York they were lower than expected. What had happened was that *Four Weddings* had been booked into the smallest screen of a multiplex. The film had sold out with people unable to get in. By contrast, other screens were mostly empty, showing Hollywood films which had been around for some time. Why not put our film on a bigger screen? Polygram suggested. The theatre manager said he was frightened of what the studio in question might do if it discovered its film had been demoted. The manager eventually agreed to show *Four Weddings* on a big screen at night and just hoped the studio would not notice. Polygram's sleight of hand bumped up the gross and meant it could justify rolling the film out across America. *Four Weddings* went to number one in the United States on just 721 out of the 26,586 screens in the country with a combined gross of just over $4 million. (This is why press releases claiming that, for example, the latest Bond film is the highest grossing so far are meaningless. Films are released on more and more prints to cope with the growing number of screens in America. The crucial thing to look for when measuring a film's success is how full each screen is, known in the business as the screen average.) Eventually, *Four Weddings* earned $52 million from 1500 screens across the USA. *Times* columnist Kate Muir commented that perhaps what Americans (and particularly women) liked about *Four Weddings* was that one of their own brings Hugh Grant in from the cold, unbuttoning him both metaphorically and physically. According to Muir, many American women assume that it is hard to pull a handsome, suave British man because he is both terribly clever and terribly cold.

In contrast to his current diffidence, Grant threw himself into promoting the film, appearing in more than a hundred features and items in the British national press and 450 times in the regional press. He also gave numerous television and radio interviews to the extent that he felt he was beginning to make a fool of himself.

Critics were pretty much unanimous in liking the film. Beguiling romantic comedy was one of the hardest things for a modern film to pull off but a winning British team had done it with *Four Weddings*, said *Variety*. 'Original in every sense of the word . . . Mike Newell's pic is knowingly funny about sex and structurally unusual enough to set it apart from countless other films in the genre, old and recent. Newell sets a sly tone at once and keeps characters' humour and libidos bubbling throughout.'[1] *The Times* said that everything about

Grant suggested that years of breeding and education had produced not a single advantage apart from the ability to look delightful in a morning suit. Grant's character, said the reviewer, was an absolute virtuoso of embarrassment. The *Daily Mail* raved that the film had been impeccably produced by Kenworthy and was the funniest British comedy since *The Lavender Hill Mob*. In New York, the *Village Voice* reviewer admitted she got engaged immediately after seeing the film. David Puttnam was quick to jump on the bandwagon, claiming that *Four Weddings* was the perfect model of what his new lobby group for commercial film-makers was trying to achieve. However, Polygram Filmed Entertainment president Michael Kuhn later described Puttnam's assertion as ridiculous.

Polygram originally estimated that *Four Weddings* would make a 23 per cent return on its investment. It went on to gross $246 million worldwide having cost just $4 million to make. Channel 4 earned £7 million from its £800,000 investment. In Britain it grossed more than £27,763,000 at the box office; it earned another £20 million in Australia, £20 million in France and £13 million in Germany. The song of the film, a cover of the 1960s Troggs' hit 'Love Is All Around' by pop group Wet Wet Wet, sold 1.4 million copies in the UK. Everybody connected with the film was brushed by its success. Kenworthy was voted producer of the year at the 1995 London Film Critics' Circle Awards. There was even talk of Hugh Grant becoming the next James Bond.

One year after the release of *Four Weddings*, another low-budget film became the first British movie in years which audiences were actually eager to see. You could feel the anticipation in multiplex foyers as people queued for tickets, wondering if the film was as good as everybody said. *Trainspotting* literally hits the screen running with the dustbin-lid drumming of the Iggy Pop song 'Lust for Life'. A skinhead and his pals are running away from the police down a side street in Edinburgh. A car swerves to avoid hitting the skinhead, Renton, played by Ewan McGregor. He bounces off the bonnet, gives a manic, incredulous laugh and hares off again. At the same time McGregor speaks the film's theme in voice-over:

> Choose life. Choose a job. Choose a career. Choose a family. Choose a fucking big television, choose washing machines, cars, compact disc players and electrical tin openers. Choose good health, low cholesterol and dental insurance. Choose fixed-interest mortgage repayments. Choose a starter home. Choose your friends. Choose leisurewear and matching luggage. Chose a three-piece suite on hire purchase in a range of fucking fabrics. Choose DIY and wondering who the fuck you are on a Sunday morning. Choose sitting on that couch watching mind-numbing, spirit-crushing game shows, stuffing fucking junk food into your mouth. Choose rotting away at the end of it all, pishing your last in a miserable home, nothing more than an embarrassment to the selfish, fucked-up brats you have spawned to replace yourself. Choose your future. Choose life.[2]

Intercut with this are shots of McGregor and his junkie gang playing football. It is a seductive, energetic opening that the rest of the film somehow fails to live up to.

Based on Irvine Welsh's best-selling novel, *Trainspotting* gets its title from heroin users injecting themselves up and down the main vein in their arm. Station to station, they call it, as they hunt for a new place to inject. The film takes its biggest risk in its first few minutes, showing the pleasures of drug use, which, asserts Macdonald, it would have been unrealistic not to show. Everybody knows that drugs are pleasurable, says Macdonald, which is why people take them – at least in the beginning. Renton and his gang spend their days getting high in a tenement slum. The first half of the film is often funny, especially the scene where the boys meet their girlfriends in a nightclub and Scottish accents become so impenetrable that subtitles flash up on the screen. *Trainspotting* also has a strong sense of place and time, with a thumping soundtrack (which went on to sell two million copies) and perfect period details. But things sour quickly when one of Renton's clean-living friends becomes addicted and dies of toxoplasmosis. The film then turns into a caper movie when Renton moves to London, becomes an estate agent and betrays his friends over a bag of drug money. (Macdonald puts in a cameo as a yuppie being shown round a revolting flat.) The film ends with Renton accepting the middle-class values he once despised – a Pauline conversion which makes no sense, except as an inducement for the censor not to cause any trouble.

Macdonald first read the book on a plane going back home to Scotland. He decided *Trainspotting* would be his next film even if it meant cutting fees to work on a Channel 4 budget. He passed the book over to his regular screenwriter, John Hodge, who started work on adapting it even before Macdonald had secured the rights. There was a problem here in that another production company, Noel Gay, owned the book, although it had no plans to make a film. Hodge, who wrote Macdonald's first feature, *Shallow Grave*, finished his first draft in December 1994. Hodge said that what attracted him to the book was that despite the horrors of drug addiction, Renton still had a good heart, albeit a slightly damaged, bitter one. Irvine Welsh liked Hodge's script so much he wanted a cameo role as a drug dealer. A fan of rave culture at the time, Welsh compared Hodge's adaptation to a record being remixed by a top DJ.

By March 1995 Noel Gay agreed to relinquish the rights in exchange for a share of net profits and its name in the credits. Macdonald admitted that a film about drugs, especially heroin, made the project difficult to finance. The film's budget was set at

£1.7 million, which Channel 4 covered by selling the unmade film all over the world on the basis of the film-makers' reputation.

Macdonald and his directing partner Danny Boyle were influenced by 1960s British movies – the zaniness and energy of Richard Lester's Beatles films, for example. For Macdonald the 1960s were the last period when the British made films about contemporary subjects that were exciting and popular with local audiences. Macdonald says that the challenge of adapting the book was an important impetus for making the film. It was important that *Trainspotting* remain Scottish but nonetheless it had to be understood by the rest of Britain. Therefore, the working-class setting of the film – pubs, housing estates and unemployment offices – could be anywhere in the UK. However, having decided to set *Trainspotting* in central-belt Scotland, the film-makers did not want to make a realistic film. With 230 scenes and a tiny budget, Macdonald made a decision to shoot as much of it in the studio as possible. Rejecting the grey feel of other drugs films such as *Christiane F* and *The Man With the Golden Arm*, production designer Kave Quinn saturated sets in vibrant acid colours to subliminally counteract feelings of repulsion that audiences have when watching scenes of heroin use.

Shooting was scheduled to last for thirty-five days. Boyle put the camera on the floor for some shots because, he reasoned, addicts spend a lot of time sprawled on the ground. And for Macdonald:

> For me the shooting process is the bit I least enjoy because it's just about negative problems. It's just standing around in mud. There isn't enough money and there isn't enough time. Everybody has his or her own agendas. The art director wants all the money to make the sets better, the cameraman wants all the lights to make them look better, the production department wants to keep all the money and get more drivers. I enjoy the editing and distribution process much more.

Indeed, Macdonald says he would have become a distributor if he had not become a producer. He worked with distributor Polygram Filmed Entertainment on the film's marketing campaign right from the start. He knew that he did not want to sell *Trainspotting* as a drugs movie but as a buddy film. According to Macdonald, *Trainspotting* is about friendship and betrayal, not about heroin. Polygram spent £850,000 marketing *Trainspotting*, hoping to tap into a young audience. Its fluorescent orange poster campaign, dreamt up by a record designer, was so successful it was widely imitated. Apart from *Trainspotting* mugs and T-shirts bearing the legend 'It's shite being Scottish', there were book and music tie-ins. As writer Geoffrey Macnab has pointed out, back in 1997 half the bus shelters in Britain seemed to be decorated with posters of Spud, Begbie and the rest of the *Trainspotting* crew leering at the camera.

Thankfully, the core cinema-going demographic of 18- to 24-year-olds responded to the campaign. *Time Out* called *Trainspotting* the first British film to speak to the way the 90s generation live here and now. *Variety* called *Trainspotting* 'a *Clockwork Orange* for the 90s . . . [its] most striking accomplishment – which will appall moralists as much as it will delight others – is the way it takes a bunch of goal-less losers and a subject [guilt-free drug-taking] that's ripe for downbeat grunge and turns this material into a sustained piece of cinema that's often wildly funny'.[3] *Sight and Sound* said *Trainspotting* established Macdonald and his collaborators as one of the most dynamic and exciting forces in British cinema, while *Evening Standard* film critic Alexander Walker praised the imagination of Macdonald's production values. However, the *Sunday Times* sniggered that the film was governed by an indiscriminate regard for the spunky spirit of renegade youth that you only find in advertisements for building societies worried about their image. And the *Daily Mail* fulminated that *Trainspotting* would receive a warm welcome in the liberal ghettos of north London, where residents have never had to worry about their children stumbling across a discarded HIV-infected needle.

Andrew Macdonald was born in Glasgow in 1966 and was brought up in countryside north of the city. He went to boarding school in Perthshire. His grandfather was Emeric Pressburger, writing and producing partner of director Michael Powell. Together Powell and Pressburger made fifteen features together, including *A Matter of Life and Death* (1945) and *The Red Shoes* (1948). Macdonald said his grandfather was an inspiration in that Pressburger made high-quality European films aimed squarely at the international market, something which Macdonald aspired to. He made his first film on Super 8 at school at a time when *Chariots of Fire* was being filmed near by. His first job was on another Goldcrest project, Hugh Hudson's ill-fated *Revolution* ('a salutary lesson for any would-be producer'). Macdonald tried to get a job with a London production company as a runner, but ended up doing work experience at the National Film and Television School. At the end of 1985 he headed for Los Angeles, where he studied producing at the American Film Institute, worked as a reader for writer and director Harold Ramis (*Groundhog Day*) and as director's assistant on Palace Productions' *Shag*. When he returned to England he worked as an assistant director on films including *The Big Man* and *The Long Day Closes* as well as on Scottish television series *Taggart* and *The Advocate*. At this time he also directed several documentaries and short films with his brother Kevin, who went on to win an Oscar for *One Day in September* (2000). It was during the making of one of these shorts that Macdonald's editor, Grace Hodge, introduced him to her brother John, who wanted to become a screenwriter. Although he had qualified as a doctor, John Hodge told Macdonald about an idea he had for a feature.

Shallow Grave follows three affluent twenty-somethings living together in a smart flat in Edinburgh New Town. They advertise for a new lodger but he dies soon afterwards in his bedroom of a drug overdose. The three flatmates discover a suitcase full of money in the dead man's room. They decide to keep it and dispose of the body secretly. As with *Trainspotting*, McGregor plays a character who double-crosses his friends and steals the loot. Just like *The Treasure of the Sierra Madre*, the audience watches greed corrode the friendship which glued the three characters together.

Macdonald and Hodge spent fifteen months developing the script, using £5,000 provided by the Scottish Film Production Fund, before approaching Channel 4. Hodge would write in the early hours of the morning when not treating patients, while Macdonald read early drafts working as a location manager on *Taggart*. Macdonald said that they both agreed that the script had to be perfect before financial considerations came in to play. Macdonald was determined to get the script to David Aukin, then head of Channel 4 Films, which at the time was giving roughly £700,000 apiece to twelve films a year. Macdonald managed to get the script to Aukin's driver, who presumably turned round and handed it to his boss.

Channel 4 said it would provide £800,000 – the amount it still pays for a television licence – if the newly formed Glasgow Film Fund would raise another £150,000. Macdonald swayed the fund, calculating that he would spend £500,000 in the city on hotels, food and the like for cast and crew. The question now was how to make the film for £1 million. Macdonald educated himself as to how US independent films were made, down to the minutiae of budgets and shooting schedules. His target demographic was the kind of audience that went to see *Reservoir Dogs*. Macdonald sees his key job as deciding how much each project should cost and what its value will be in the market. For him this is the most important creative decision that a producer makes. Every project has a value; it is just a question of judging it right. For example, the value of *The Full Monty*, which grossed about $260 million, exceeded its £1.9 million cost. Knowing that he only had £1 million to spend, Macdonald took his cue from Steven Soderbergh's *sex lies and videotape* (1989), which revolved around three people and three locations. He ensured that most of the script took place in one flat. This meant that most of the money could be spent making the flat look stylish. As with most artistic endeavour, restrictions turned out to be liberating.

Channel 4 then sent out the script to young directors, one of whom was Danny Boyle. The 37-year-old director began his career in theatre, first with the Joint Stock Theatre Company and then the Royal Court Theatre Upstairs, where he was artistic director between 1982 and 1985 and deputy director between 1985 and 1987. During this period he produced Howard Brenton's *Victory* and Edward Bond's *Saved*, for which he won a *Time Out* award. Boyle also directed five productions for the Royal Shakespeare Company. He started working for television in the late 1980s as a producer for BBC Northern Ireland, where he made, among other television films, Alan Clark's *Elephant*. As director, Boyle's television work included *Arise and Go Now*, *Not Even God Is Wise Enough*, *For the Greater Good*, *The Hen House*, *The Delorean Tapes*, *The Night Watch* and *Inspector Morse*. He then made the series *Mr Wroe's Virgins* for BBC2.

Boyle was hired in March 1993 and six weeks of full-time preparation began in August. Macdonald, Hodge and Boyle decided to work as a team, making equal creative contributions. They all worked for the same £25,000 fee and the same potential profit share. Boyle says that working collaboratively he had to sacrifice some of the ego and control he was expected to have as director. He did not subscribe to the auteurist view of film-making as a massive ego crushing everything in it path in pursuit of some extraordinary vision. Rather, working with Macdonald and Hodge and sacrificing some of his own vision had made him a better director. That said, all three of them fought continually during *Shallow Grave* and they all fell out. Macdonald later described making any film as a bit of a war and anybody who said it wasn't so was lying.

The three collaborators then cast the film together and lived with their lead actors – Ewan McGregor, Australian actress Kerry Fox, and Christopher Eccleston – for a week so that everybody could get used to each other. Macdonald had noticed working on other low-budget films that nobody ever seemed to agree on the kind of film they were making. Often potentially good movies go wrong because everybody is making a slightly different film. The writer is making a film 10 per cent different from the one the producer thinks he has commissioned; meanwhile, the director is making a film which has veered 10 per cent from the script. Before you know it, the project has skewed and film, being a frail object, cannot stand a 20 per cent difference from intent to delivery. In order to prevent this, Boyle compiled a scrapbook filled with images from magazines and photography books showing what he wanted to achieve. The six of them also spent time watching videos of films in roughly the same genre such as *Les Diaboliques* (*Diabolique*, 1955) and *The Grifters* (1990).

The month-long shoot began at the end of September 1993, with post-production taking three months. At one point *Shallow Grave* literally ran out of film, and a crisis meeting was held to raise money to buy extra stock. The film was ready by the spring of 1994 and went on to gross £13 million worldwide. The *Financial Times* praised the film's black comedy, while the *Guardian* called *Shallow Grave* 'a highly accomplished effort which mostly succeeds in being funny, scary and intriguing'. The *Observer* praised the film for its modest ambitions. Says Macdonald: 'I made *Shallow Grave* with the idea of making an entertaining low-budget film in the way that American independents are made. When somebody comes to see me I'm looking for that clarity. It's not difficult to get a film made. Getting a film seen and connected with an audience, that's hard.'

Hollywood tried to split the team up after the success of *Shallow Grave* and wooed each of them separately. But Macdonald felt it was important that the three of them stay in Britain to make another contemporary film, not rush off to the West Coast and make *Alien 4* (something which was offered). He compared the situation to being in a pop group that has made a great album. The obvious thing to do would be to go back into the recording studio and make another hit record rather than a string of solo albums. He also decided to get the rest of the *Shallow Grave* team back together for *Trainspotting*, reasoning that film-makers such as Woody Allen or Martin Scorsese always used the same core crew.

In terms of cost and scale, everything was bigger on Macdonald's third film *A Life Less Ordinary*. It took fifty days to shoot compared with thirty days for *Trainspotting*. The finished film too was longer than the other two by about four minutes. 'Everything was bigger and takes longer,' said Macdonald. 'It's very difficult after you've been king of the world, after you've been put on a pedestal. We were desperate to do something different and light-hearted.' Unfortunately, *A Life Less Ordinary* lives up to its title, being both lifeless and ordinary. Macdonald's attempt at screwball comedy is often painful to watch, although the producer has a touching faith that it will one day be rediscovered. Macdonald described the critical drubbing the film received as 'not very nice at the time, but it's good to be brought back to earth'.

Around this time, the team also made *Alien Love Triangle* for Miramax, a yet-to-be-released 26-minute film starring Kenneth

Branagh, Heather Graham and Courteney Cox. *Alien Love Triangle*, again written by Hodge, is about a man who discovers that his wife is actually a male alien who decides it is time to go home. Then there is a knock at the door and in walks Heather Graham in a green alien suit wanting her husband back. Macdonald describes the short as 'a mad episode from *Friends* set in a cottage in Hertfordshire'. Miramax commissioned the film as one of three shorts to make up a portmanteau horror movie like the 1945 British classic *Dead of Night*. But Miramax shelved *Alien Love Triangle* after deciding to develop one of the shorts into the feature *Mimic*.

Macdonald's next film was hyped as a *Lord of the Flies* for the Nintendo generation. Based on Alex Garland's cult novel, *The Beach* follows Richard, a young backpacker who is given a map to a secret beach paradise. Hooking up with a French couple, Richard discovers an idyllic hippy commune, unaware that he himself carries the germ which will infect utopia. The story covers the usual Macdonald themes of murder and mayhem, drug taking and the claustrophobic interdependency of a small group of friends. As with *Shallow Grave* and *Trainspotting*, Macdonald reveals a Scottish Calvinist's distrust of earthly delights, whether they be ill-gotten money, drug highs or a paradisiacal beach. He likes to dangle such attractions temptingly in front of the audience before showing the terrible price that comes with them.

With *Shallow Grave* and *Trainspotting* Macdonald controlled the projects, working with UK broadcaster Channel 4 and Anglo-Dutch studio Polygram Filmed Entertainment. But Macdonald relinquished some control to Twentieth Century-Fox on *The Beach*, marking the first time he had worked with a Hollywood studio. Although he had bought the rights to the book and put the package together, Macdonald let Fox fully finance the film. If things went wrong on the $50 million project, Macdonald wanted the safety net of the studio that had berthed *Titanic*. However, studio involvement also comes with a price tag, which can be pointless script suggestions and Hollywood's golden rule that films must have an uplifting ending. As screenwriter William Goldman put it: Hollywood films reassure; independent films unsettle. With *The Beach* studio executives had a problem with the hero lying to save his own skin, and they insisted on a redemptive finale. Macdonald found himself having to protect John Hodge's adaptation from Fox's 'script notes'.

Ewan McGregor assumed he would play Richard but was upset to discover that Macdonald had instead offered the part to Leonardo DiCaprio, at the time a teenage heart-throb because of *Titanic*. The line that Macdonald took was that changing Richard from an Englishman to an American would allude to the USA's involvement in the Far East. But McGregor grumbled to the press that the real reason he was dropped was because hiring DiCaprio meant Macdonald was now making a Hollywood film with a $50 million budget – nearly half of which was spent on DiCaprio. Success in America had never been the goal before, so the actor was nonplussed that it was now the team's main mission. Boyle spotted the female lead, Virginie Ledoyen, watching a movie at a German film festival. Macdonald remembered the film as being boring except for this exquisite French girl. Tilda Swinton was cast as the imperious leader of the beach utopia, unfortunately coming across like a former head girl of Cheltenham Ladies' College who's done a tour of duty at Greenham Common.

In a case of life imitating art, Macdonald next went in search of paradise but instead found trouble. He spent August 1998 looking for a suitable beach in Thailand, and found one in Maya Bay on Phi Phi Leh, a small island in the Andaman Sea. Maya Bay was part of a protected national park. However, Macdonald decided to widen the beach by getting rid of unsightly shrubbery and planting one hundred coconut palms (later reduced to sixty). He also lowered two sand dunes by almost five feet in two places. Local environmentalists protested with banners directed mainly at Leonardo DiCaprio, which proclaimed: 'Leo, stop killing national parks', and 'Don't rape our beach'. Macdonald protested that his team had to clear three tons of rubbish off the beach before filming could begin; he also pointed out that he had promised to make good any damage with the Royal Forestry Department. On top of its fee for using the beach the production gave the department an £85,000 deposit to be refunded when the beach was returned to its original condition (the bond was later repaid to Fox).

Shooting began on 15 January 1999 but immediately there were rumours of bribery and local Mafia involvement. It was claimed that Macdonald had to have DiCaprio protected by armed guards and that the production's filming permit was illegal. DiCaprio was told to lose twenty pounds of flab which he had gained through his notoriously hard-partying lifestyle. There were no physical disruptions on set but the production was attacked every day in the local press, while environmentalists sued the Royal Forestry Department. DiCaprio was then forced to issue a press release, pledging to 'remain vigilant' over the state of the beach (conjuring up an image of the star standing guard with a trident after everybody else had gone to bed). Macdonald summed up the mess as a nightmare of local politics. As if there were not problems enough, a lighting rig fell into the studio tank in which DiCaprio and Ledoyen were filming a love scene. Watching the crane tip into the water, director Danny Boyle was convinced everybody would be electrocuted, but happily the lights short-circuited.

On 16 April, while filming in northern Phuket, a sudden storm overturned a boat carrying DiCaprio, Swinton and members of the crew, throwing them into what were supposed to be shark-infested waters. *Entertainment Weekly* smirked that Leonardo DiCaprio had experienced a real-life version of his part in *Titanic*. Motorboats could not get near actors and crew members treading water for fear of slicing through them with propeller blades. Those in the water were also in danger of being clouted by heavy metal boxes full of camera and make-up equipment being thrown about by ten-foot waves. Cast and crew tried to swim to shore, which was miles away, but a diver screamed at them to swim out to sea because he knew they would get exhausted swimming against the tide. Everybody made it back to safety, but even blokeish crew members could be seen sobbing.

The Beach was released on two thousand prints in America and another three thousand worldwide to generally lacklustre reviews. The *Evening Standard* considered that the film-makers, previously known for their genuinely fresh films, had become middle-aged before their time. There was a feeling that although the film was as gorgeous to look at as a television rum commercial, it did not really go anywhere. DiCaprio was pretty much the same at the end of the film as he had been at the beginning (perhaps Fox had been right in fretting about the story's 'character arc'). And there was a seen-it-all-before feeling – oh look, here comes Robert Carlyle doing his Scottish nutter routine, and so on. The whole thing came across as a lightweight *Apocalypse Now*.

Macdonald is now in his thirties and worries about not keeping in touch with the core cinema-going demographic. As he points out, he is now married with small children and his concerns are not his audience's concerns. Because most films are aimed at 18- to 24-year-olds, Macdonald believes there is only a small window when producers are in touch with the taste of multiplex audiences. 'It's become more and more of a young people's business,' he says. 'I've got a young family and things change.'

His next film, *28 Days Later*, was made very much with the
multiplex audience in mind. Alex Garland, author of *The Beach*, told
Macdonald that he wanted to write an original science-fiction
screenplay. Macdonald and Garland discussed various ideas,
including science-fiction films such as *The War of the Worlds* (1953)
and *The Omega Man* (1971). The cliché of the zombie genre is a
starlet in a white nightie running through a forest as a zombie
lurches after her. Inexplicably, the zombie always catches said
screaming actress even though he has been shuffling along like an
old man in a nursing home. Garland's twist was a film in which the
zombies could sprint, hurling themselves at their victims. Boyle
started watching as many zombie movies as he could. Meanwhile,
Macdonald reined in Garland's excesses. At one point the script had
zombies clinging to exploding jets as they take off while others
partied on hotel balconies.

In May 2001 Macdonald met Peter Rice, head of Fox
Searchlight, the specialist film arm of Twentieth Century-Fox – the
company which financed *The Full Monty* – to pitch the idea to him.
Rice had worked with Macdonald before and immediately agreed
to co-finance the film equally. *28 Days Later* follows a handful of
survivors as they make their way from London to Manchester after
the rest of the population has gone berserk. Most people have
become psychotic after being infected by an experimental rage
virus. But when the survivors take refuge in an army base they find
themselves in an even worse situation than before. The budget was
set at $5 million, one tenth of the cost of an average Hollywood film.
Macdonald was going back to his low-budget roots.

The film begins with survivor Jim (Cillian Murphy) wandering
the empty streets of London one month after the virus outbreak.
There was not enough money to shoot these scenes on 35mm film,
so instead Boyle suggested shooting on digital video. Macdonald

wanted an anarchic feel to *28 Days Later* so that it would look more like a documentary than a well-crafted feature. In much the same way as documentary film-maker Alberto Cavalcanti grounded the classic Ealing shocker *Dead of Night* (1945) in reality, Macdonald wanted *28 Days Later* to feel as if it might have actually happened.

Again, Macdonald showed his flair for marketing, which is what makes him such a good fit with Kenworthy, whose own strength lies in script development. As a producer you must play to your strengths, even if it does take time and wrong turnings to find out what those strengths are. Knowing *28 Days Later* would appeal mainly to young males, Macdonald scheduled television advertisements during big football matches. Night-vision cameras showed audiences' shocked reactions to the film. Equally effective was a comic strip that ran down escalator panels in nine London tube stations showing what happened when the virus broke out – something which, according to market research, people thought they were paying to see but which is in fact only alluded to in the film because of the small budget.

Macdonald may have fretted about losing his touch, but *28 Days Later* went straight in at number one in Britain. It earned £6 million during its UK run, and, at the time of writing, has yet to open in the United States. Why *28 Days Later* works is because it sets itself a small compass and stays within it, eschewing most clichés of the genre. There are many strong images – rats fleeing humans, people starving to death in the street, a tower-block roof covered with hundreds of plastic buckets and washing-up bowls to catch rain-water in. Grainy, washed-out digital photography also helps the film, which is marred by a tacked-on upbeat ending (presumably to keep Fox Searchlight happy).

During the mid-1990s Macdonald had a free-market attitude to public funding for film. More government subsidy for the industry would lead to a lot of movies being made that nobody wanted to see. In 1997 Macdonald derided films being made with National Lottery money. One can sympathise with Macdonald's point of view at the time. If an idea is good enough, then it doesn't need soft money. If the market rejects a project, then surely it shouldn't be made? However, this argument ignores the fact that Hollywood controls 80 per cent of the European market. The studios would happily fill our screens with the lowest common denominator unless producers can supply British distributors with films that cost them nothing to finance. Nevertheless, it was something of a surprise when Macdonald and Kenworthy applied for £29 million of lottery money to run one of three film franchises that the government wanted set up. Without any consultation the Conservative government decided that the film industry qualified as a 'good cause' for money from the yet-to-be-launched lottery. After intense lobbying, producers got their snouts in the trough first, snuffling up nearly £100 million for three mini-studios (the original recommendation was to use all the money for a single £300 million publicly quoted company, but producers, panicked by the thought of not getting their trotters on the cash, diluted that idea). In May 1997 the government awarded one of the franchises to Kenworthy and Macdonald's company, DNA Films. Apart from the name linking the two producers, Kenworthy liked the connection with the building blocks of life. The plan was to make sixteen films over the next six years – one in the first year and three each year thereafter. No film would cost more than £4 million, with the lottery providing up to half of each budget. Macdonald's strategy was to run a company with low overheads that could survive on production fees alone. If one of the films proved a hit then profits would be ploughed back into the company.

However, there was much wailing and gnashing of teeth elsewhere in Wardour Street when the two producers won the franchise. After all, they had turned down offers to join other consortia, saying they were not interested in public money. On winning the franchise Kenworthy said that DNA would become the home for a new generation of British film-makers. He and Macdonald were natural collaborators because they both believed in writer-driven cinema. Even though their films did not appear similar, they had a shared approach to film-making, which prioritised getting the script right. Macdonald would be more concerned with running the company as he enjoyed deal-making. Kenworthy would see films through from beginning to end as his speciality was development. However, they then spent nine months haggling with the Arts Council of England over their contract. One source claimed they took so long to sign because they were taken aback by the amount of red tape involved. There were rumours that they were going to walk away from the franchise because they were not keen on the amount of public scrutiny they were receiving.

DNA announced its development slate in November 1998. Kenworthy said the franchise would not be pressured into putting films into production just for the sake of it. What nobody liked to admit, he said, was that finalising a script could take years. Out of eleven projects talked about, only three would become films. But some questioned where they were going to find time to run the franchise when each of them was starting work on big Hollywood projects. Macdonald was about to fly off to Thailand to begin *The Beach*, and Kenworthy was preparing the follow-up to *Four Weddings and a Funeral*.

According to Kenworthy, Richard Curtis had the idea for *Notting Hill* when they were shooting *Four Weddings*: 'One of the things Richard acknowledges is that however much you work at a screenplay you can only ever go a certain distance from its central idea. And its central idea is either exciting or unexciting, either it appeals to an audience or it doesn't. In *Four Weddings* the idea was the structure. You know there are going to be four weddings, but you don't know when the funeral is going to come. The central idea of *Notting Hill* was, what if the most famous woman in the world met an ordinary guy and fell in love?'

As with most film scripts, Curtis said that *Notting Hill* began with 'What if?' What if he turned up at his friends' house, where he used to have dinner, with the most famous person in the world, say Madonna? How would his friends react? Would some of them try to appear nonchalant? What would happen during the meal? And what would they say to him afterwards? This, then, was the starting point, the idea of a normal person going out with somebody intimidatingly famous.

It took Curtis five years to develop the idea and write the script, working on the film version of his *Mr Bean* television series at the same time. There were ten drafts of the screenplay in total. In the first draft the girl who eventually became Hugh Grant's sister was a potential love interest. Early on, the central dilemma was which girl should Grant choose – the famous film star or the girl who works in the record shop across the road? Meanwhile, Kenworthy was worried that somebody else would make a film about a celebrity falling in love with Mr Average because it seemed such an obvious idea. He first read the script when shooting *Lawn Dogs*, the film he made after *Four Weddings*, on location in Kentucky.

Once it was clear *Four Weddings* was gong to be a success, everybody told Kenworthy to enjoy the ride, because it was never going to happen again. Kenworthy agreed, which was partly the reason he wanted to make *Lawn Dogs* – he was not overtly worried about commercial success any longer. Most producers, he reasoned, spent their entire lives trying to make a hit film so now he could relax. He would go mad if he tried to cap the success of *Four*

Weddings with its follow-up. Instead, he decided to take baby steps: get a good script, improve it, collaborate with a good director, find a great cast – and just ignore the pressure of people badgering him about it.

One structural problem that Curtis wrestled with was the romantic comedy prerequisite that although the audience can see that two people are made for each other, they must be kept apart. In the twenty-first century, with mobile phones and email, it is hard for people not to be in contact. This is why Anna Scott, the film star character, keeps whizzing back to Los Angeles, and why Carrie (Andie MacDowell) in *Four Weddings* suddenly disappears. Indeed, in many ways *Notting Hill* is a confident retelling of *Four Weddings*. Once again there is a gauche hero, a group of friends – one of whom is disabled (this time in a wheelchair) – and a visiting American with a past who comes and goes. But second time around Kenworthy and Curtis went for a much more straightforward storyline and an old-fashioned princess and the commoner love story. *Notting Hill* was a sort of late 1990s version of *Roman Holiday*, the 1953 film in which Audrey Hepburn plays a princess playing hookey in Rome. (By the end of the twentieth century, celebrities had usurped royalty. The word 'celebrity' now covers everybody from Julia Roberts to the runner-up in a cable television reality show. If the Greeks had five words for love, surely it is time to invent some new categories of fame?)

Kenworthy picked Roger Michell to direct because of his eye for honesty. Curtis liked Michell because his BBC television series *Buddha of Suburbia*, about an Asian family in 1970s Britain, was about culture clash. Curtis felt *Notting Hill* was about the same thing. (Writing in *Sight and Sound*, Charlotte O'Sullivan noted that Henry James, that great chronicler of Anglo-American relations, would have been bewildered by the British being presented as 'innocents' in *Notting Hill*.) Kenworthy said that hiring Roger Michell, who has since gone on to have a career in Hollywood, was an attempt to recreate what Mike Newell brought to *Four Weddings*. The recipe was to take a highly fanciful screenplay and add to it a director who could bring out the truthfulness of each scene. The problem with comedy is that unless one is skilled at it, the temptation is to try and make it funnier. The moment you get actors doing what is known in the trade as 'playing it wide' – comenting on their roles through their acting – says Kenworthy, you're lost. For comedy to work properly, you must believe in the characters and let the humour shine through. By the end of the film the audience should feel as if it has just watched a documentary, even if the whole confection has been spun out of sugar. Like Newell, Michell felt the biggest challenge of the project would be keeping it grounded in reality. Michell liked Curtis's script because it was funny yet moving, while at the same time celebratory but sad. It also managed to convey something about what it was to be alive, said the director.

Meanwhile, Kenworthy paid the price for making Hugh Grant a star in *Four Weddings*. His fee for *Notting Hill* had gone up from just under $100,000 to $7 million. The producer then had to screw up his courage and pay $13.5 million for Julia Roberts, who had come down from her usual $20 million price tag. Roberts liked the script but felt her part was underwritten. She wanted to be funnier, Kenworthy remembered. The actress then went off to Borneo to make a documentary about orang-utans. Kenworthy knew a cameraman who was working on the programme and sent a present through him with a note attached: 'Pack your bags for *Notting Hill*.' Afterwards, Kenworthy confessed to having nerves about hiring one of the biggest film stars in the world.

Filming on the $43 million production began on 20 April 1998, with five weeks spent on location in London before moving to

Shepperton Studios. During shooting the film was referred to as *The Notting Hill Project* in order to let the rest of the industry know this was a working title. Kenworthy disliked *Notting Hill* because the film was about a relationship, not an area. One alternative was *The Famous Girl*, but his favourite was the tabloid-headline-sounding *Famous Girl Meets Boy in Bookshop*.

Rick McCallum, producer of the second *Star Wars* trilogy, once told Kenworthy that making a film was just the visible part of the iceberg. Marketing was all the activity underneath the waterline. For example, Kenworthy's film *Lawn Dogs* was marketed as a coming-of-age story with undertones of child abuse. In hindsight it had been sold completely the wrong way. *Notting Hill* set a precedent because it was the first British film to be launched in the same way as an expensive Hollywood event movie or sure-fire hit. Promotional tie-ins were done with Häagen-Dazs ice cream and Max Factor cosmetics. Said Kenworthy: 'You can't say which step is the most important. They are all important. You have to push everything to the best because it might be the one crucial thing that makes your film a success or not.'

The first rough cut of *Notting Hill* ran to more than three and a half hours. It was tested seven times during editing, three times in the San Fernando Valley alone. At one test screening 93 per cent of the audience said they would recommend the film to a friend. Previously the highest score for any romantic comedy had been 88 per cent. Kenworthy said testing was useful because sometimes the audience was laughing so hard they missed the next, even funnier, line. Watching the film with an audience allowed him to gauge the laughs and give jokes space by inserting reaction shots around them. He was also ruthless in cutting superfluous scenes, following Faulkner's dictum that first you must kill all your darlings. Sequences jettisoned included a long wedding scene and the couple

on their honeymoon. Kenworthy also cut what, to my mind, was
one of the funniest scenes in the film – William Thacker (Grant)
trying to explain to his uninterested parents that he is going out with
a movie star – because the audience wanted to see him meet
Roberts again. (William informs his mother about his tentative
romance with a well-known person. 'She's very famous and er . . .
er . . . odd,' he stutters. 'Not Fergie?' replies his mother.)

Notting Hill was given the widest release of any UK-produced film
to date, playing on 2,500 screens in the USA and 550 in Britain.
Kenworthy described the decision to release *Notting Hill* in America
on the same weekend as the new *Star Wars* film as either a bold act
of marketing genius or an incredibly foolhardy move. *Empire*
magazine said that Kenworthy and Curtis had hit upon the magic
formula again and that, as wish-fulfilment fantasy, *Notting Hill* was
pretty hard to beat. *Sight and Sound* praised Kenworthy for not only
repeating but also improving on a solidly successful commercial
franchise, calling it 'a landmark'. The *Sun* raved that the *Four
Weddings and a Funeral* team had done the unthinkable for British
cinema and made a follow-up film which was even better than the
original. Of course, there were dissenting voices. The *Daily Mail* felt
the film was a shade too cynical, calculated and anxious to repeat a
winning formula. *The Times* asserted that a glass of warm milk and a
plate of biscuits lying together on a pillow would have had more
sexual chemistry than Roberts and Grant. The *Observer* compared
the film to a gathering of tired alchemists struggling to recreate the
gold of *Four Weddings*, while the *Financial Times* complained that the
film remained 'glutinously lovable, strenuously feel-good. At the end
I wanted to rush out and join a crowd of Millwall supporters in a
chorus of *Smack My Bitch Up* to remind myself of the real London'.[4]

Despite the film's success, DNA Films was foundering. After
promising to make sixteen films over six years, so far Kenworthy

and Macdonald had got only four on to the screen. Apart from *28 Days Later*, DNA had made *Beautiful Creatures*, a pretty dismal thriller; *The Parole Officer*, a not-very-funny comedy starring television comedian Steve Coogan; and turgid drama *Strictly Sinatra*. (A fifth film, *The Final Curtain*, written by John Hodge and starring Peter O'Toole, went straight to television in the USA.) First-time directors were put in charge of *Beautiful Creatures*, *Strictly Sinatra* and *The Final Curtain*, which with hindsight Macdonald admits 'wasn't too smart'. Macdonald says that it was difficult to build a business using inexperienced directors, both in terms of reassuring potential investors and dealing with people who didn't really know what they were doing.

In September 2003 DNA and Fox Searchlight, the left-field subsidiary of Twentieth Century-Fox, announced they were going into business in a joint venture. Each partner would bring £16 million to the operation, which would release DNA's films world-wide. DNA would use what was left of its National Lottery money. 'I see it as Fox putting £16 million into the UK film business,' said Macdonald at the time – an investment decision not unconnected with *28 Days Later* earning more than $45 million during its American run. The spin was that the DNA/Fox joint venture would, at a stroke, create the second most important British film company after Working Title. It also allowed Macdonald and Kenworthy to pull the global distribution levers of Fox. Macdonald said that he saw no point in making films unless people had a chance to see them. The two companies he had established his name with, Film Four and Polygram Filmed Entertainment, had subsequently gone out of business. But one must question the justification for handing over £16 million of public money to Hollywood. The purpose of the franchises was, after all, to build film companies led by British distributors.

Kenworthy recently told the press that he is stepping back from DNA to concentrate on being a creative producer. Kenworthy said that Macdonald enjoys being a mogul much more than he does. He just wants to produce movies. However, just as Macdonald produced *28 Days Later* through DNA partly to avoid the flak he faced making *The Beach*, so Kenworthy tried to include DNA in *Love Actually* as much as he could. But Universal now had its own deal with Curtis and was hardly going to share profits on a sure-fire hit (just as Warner Brothers does not look for co-investors in its Harry Potter franchise). DNA has had to make do with a credit and Kenworthy's producing fee – Kenworthy even had to agree to share producer credit with Universal executives Tim Bevan and Eric Fellner.

Back in the school hall during the filming of *Love Actually*, everybody is fussing about on stage again. Kenworthy takes a moment to talk to me. As with Macdonald, who can come across as aloof, there is some wariness about Kenworthy. Interviewing him is a frustrating experience, as if there is a sheet of glass between us. Perhaps journalists have burnt both men once too often in the past. Kenworthy's working method is to be on set every minute of every day, rather than stay in the office as some producers do. 'Not that you're a back-seat driver, because obviously directors don't appreciate that. When you're on set it's not a democracy, it's a hierarchy and the director must be in charge of the crew's destiny. If you get the writer/director/producer relationship right I think the director can really appreciate having a whisper in the ear.'

Curtis is now standing on stage. He tells the audience it is time for the big shot of the day. Behind the stage curtains is the British prime minister, he explains, a bit like Tony Blair except that the fictional PM has not had a partner for five years. When the curtains open you will see the prime minister kissing a woman, says Curtis, and I want you to go completely wild.

Kenworthy wanted to be a director until he found out what producers did. Being a producer, he says, is about raising money, spending it wisely and exerting your influence in a million ways. The producer is the person who is there at the very beginning and at the very end. Everybody else comes and goes, including the director. But the producer is still there, plugging away, delivering all the elements to financiers so that they can recoup their money. For Kenworthy one of the exciting things about being a producer is that you do not need any skills to do the job. The producer is a middleman. All you have to do is persuade somebody to give you money, and if you do not have skills you can hire them. For example, if you don't know anything about business affairs you hire a lawyer. Or if you have no feel for screenwriting you can hire a script editor. This places the producer in the centre with skills running off him like the spokes in a wheel. He has several definitions of a producer. One is the driver of a runaway truck: at its height a film can be a juggernaut that you somehow have to steer to a successful conclusion. Another would be the conductor of an orchestra. But his favourite definition is that everybody working on the film should be making the same object. 'You could make a convincing argument that successful films are those where the spirit of the film goes all the way out to the edges – for example, that the costumes are perfectly matched to the script. The producer is the guardian of the spirit of the film.'

On stage a bored drummer and bass player have started an impromptu jamming session. An assistant director hands out disposable flash cameras for the make-believe parents to take photographs of their darlings. Kenworthy elaborates on the role of producer.

Since we work in an industry where most things aren't cheap, it's very wise to do a lot of talking. It was easy to get up a head of steam on *Four Weddings* because Mike Newell, Richard Curtis and I all had similar backgrounds, reading English at Oxbridge. We spent probably eight months doing nothing but talk about it, and I am convinced this had an awful lot to do with the final film. Within the central triumvirate of director, producer and writer there was no ambiguity. It always amazes me how much ambiguity a script can hide. You think that everybody reads the script in the same way but they don't. A script is in many ways an unsatisfactory blueprint for a film because it hides so much, much more than it reveals. In some ways the producer's job is to be the best interviewer in the world, getting the writer and director to talk and be absolutely in tune.

But perhaps the best example of Kenworthy's ability as a producer is the way he deepened *Four Weddings and a Funeral*. Curtis had the funeral take place in a beautiful Lake District panorama but Kenworthy changed this to a bleak, working-class area, in dramatic contrast to the weddings. This sombre sequence gives the film the moment of sobriety it needs to stop it from floating away like so much confetti. Curtis spent a whole month rewriting the single scene between Hugh Grant and James Fleet standing outside the funeral. Thinking about the relationship between Kenworthy and Curtis, one is reminded of Graham Greene's attitude towards Dickens, another popular storyteller. Greene wrote that the first two chapters of *David Copperfield* were supreme in the novel, unrivalled even by Proust or Tolstoy: 'How perfectly the idyll of Yarmouth is put in, with the menace of Mr Murdstone in the background. One dreads the moment when Dickens will fail as he always fails – with exaggeration, whimsicality, sentimentality.'[5]

Curtis jumps off stage and the music starts up again, except this time it is going to be played all the way through. The little girl is sensational, and when the gold curtains swing back to reveal Hugh Grant and Martine McCutcheon in a clinch, the place goes wild. If Curtis can capture one tenth of the atmosphere in the hall then surely he must have a popular movie. (In fact, *Love Actually* will prove to be in parts, as Kenworthy would put it, as thin as cigarette paper. What is so frustrating is that there are moments when Curtis appears to be standing on the continental shelf of his talent, ready to step off into something deeper.) 'Fantastic, really good,' says Curtis, pressing his fingers together in prayer. You can tell that he is pleased. 'Very jolly,' says the man from Universal Pictures, not looking up from his calculator.

4   Jeremy Thomas

The auteur

Junkies and the homeless living on the streets of downtown Los Angeles might have been surprised to see a woman hurrying past them in an expensive ball gown. The 72-year-old woman picked up the hem of her evening dress as she overtook the homeless pushing clothes in supermarket trolleys. Olivia de Havilland, one of the stars of *Gone with the Wind*, was caught up in the worst traffic jam in Los Angeles history. Cars were at a standstill. She was due to present an award at the sixtieth Academy Awards ceremony, and she was late. She still had ten blocks to go before she arrived at Los Angeles' Shrine Auditorium, where the Oscar ceremony was being held for the first time in forty years. Chicanos standing outside liquor stores must also have been surprised to see Meryl Streep and a nine-months-pregnant Glenn Close hurry past. Onlookers munching hot dogs and cradling babies gawped as Oscar nominees, presenters and their guests ran past taco stands and doughnut shops.

Also caught up in the traffic on 11 April 1988 was the man described by Italian director Bernardo Bertolucci as a hustler in the fur of a teddy bear. Thirty-nine-year-old producer Jeremy Thomas's film *The Last Emperor* had been nominated for nine Academy Awards. His film about the last emperor of China, who ascended the throne as a god in 1908 and died a gardener in 1967, had already won Golden Globes for best film, best direction, best script and best music.

Once inside the 6,000-seat auditorium, knowing that the event would be watched by millions of television viewers around the world only heightened the tension for Thomas. The atmosphere was electric. As *The Last Emperor* started winning awards for best original score, best costume design and best sound, part of him was thinking, Please God don't let me win because I can't go on stage in front of millions of people. He patted the speech in his dinner jacket pocket which he had written just in case. Then Bertolucci was up on stage collecting the award for best director. He got a big laugh when, referring to the self-gratification of awards ceremonies, he said: 'I was just thinking that if New York is the Big Apple, to me, Hollywood tonight is the big nipple.' *The Last Emperor*'s nine-Oscar sweep resembled that of a previous big winner, *Gandhi*. Like *Gandhi*, *The Last Emperor* was a big-budget, meticulously produced epic which had overcome the odds against filming in a difficult location. However, it lacked *Gandhi*'s high-mindedness, and some suspected its Oscar success was partly to do with the Academy thumbing its nose at Columbia Pictures, the studio behind *The Last Emperor*. Columbia had just sacked David Puttnam as chairman and chief executive in a coup d'état. The sometimes pious studio executive had been an early supporter of *The Last Emperor*, Puttnam had agreed to release the film in North America, Britain and elsewhere after watching just forty minutes of footage. In his speech Bertolucci had already thanked Puttnam for his efforts. (Despite this show of support Bertolucci was seen having lunch with Dawn Steel, Puttnam's successor, at the Russian Tea Room in New York one week later.)

Now the moment had come to announce the winner of the best picture. Comedian Eddie Murphy opened the envelope and announced: 'The winner is *The Last Emperor*, produced by Jeremy Thomas.' The auditorium erupted into applause and cheers as Thomas got up to collect his award. *The Last Emperor* was now the fourth most honoured film in the sixty-year history of the Academy Awards, after *Ben-Hur* (1959), with eleven awards; *West Side Story* (1961), with ten; and *Gigi* (1958), also with nine. 'This is a truly imperial evening for me,' Thomas began, peering past the television lights and seeing Robert Redford. He then thanked Bertolucci for inviting him on 'an incredible voyage of discovery'. The Oscar, he said, 'is a real affirmation for me that independent cinema can be epic and quite popular'. Backstage, Thomas was miffed by insistent questions about David Puttnam's role in the success of *The Last Emperor*. 'He didn't produce the film,' he snapped. (Much later he dipped his fingers into his dinner jacket pocket and pulled out his unread speech.)

Eighteen months earlier Thomas was pacing around outside the Hall of Supreme Harmony in Beijing. He had negotiated for months with the Chinese government for permission to film in the Forbidden City. This was the first time a Western film crew had been allowed to film inside the 250-acre enclave of the Chinese imperial family, which sits in the heart of Beijing surrounded by a moat with six main palaces and 9,999 rooms (only heaven has 10,000). Bertolucci had a line for the press about the Forbidden City being the set Hollywood would never have dared to build. Although Thomas was maintaining his usual equanimity, there was something about him that day which betrayed a certain impatience and anxiety. He was overseeing the biggest single shot of his career. Bertolucci and his cameraman Vittorio Storaro had spent all morning working out a difficult Steadicam sequence. The scene was the most epic in the entire film: the coronation of the infant Pu Yi as emperor. The script called for the three-year-old child to first wet his robes, and then scamper through the ranks of courtiers on the upper terrace outside the Hall of Supreme Harmony, lured by the tantalising sound of a chirping cricket.

The extras in the shot are ready, the lights are ready, the Steadicam operator is ready, even the cricket supervisor is ready. Everything hinges on the cooperation of the five-year-old Chinese–American toddler playing the infant emperor – and on the ability of the Steadicam operator to follow him smoothly as he darts through the ranks and picks out the actor hiding the cricket. Meanwhile, the completion bond company – the insurance people who ensure that a film is delivered on time and on budget – is breathing down Thomas's neck to make sure filming does not spill over into a second day. Thomas has been spending $50,000 on an average day, and a lot more on a huge crowd scene like this. Two thousand soldiers conscripted from the People's Liberation Army have been standing outside the Hall of Supreme Harmony since six o'clock that morning. They have been changing into antique costumes since the middle of the night, ordered to shave their heads and wear false pigtails. For days they have been drilled in how to bow in unison. Now they are baking alive in the heavy robes and costumes of Manchu courtiers under the September sun. Not only that, but they haven't been needed since they arrived. Some of them are practising kung fu kicks just to stay awake. Many of them are dying for a cigarette, but smoking is prohibited in that section of the Forbidden City. Rays shimmer slightly through the dust that blows off the Gobi Desert.

All of Storaro's cameras have been connected for video, and key personnel cluster around monitors to check the shot after each take. If five-year-old Richard Vuu chooses not to cooperate, he can push the film's budget into the red. An attractive young woman dangles various children's toys and clucks terms of endearment while endeavouring to keep out of camera range. Happily, little Richard is behaving comparatively well this morning. Bertolucci has promised the boy a ride aboard the high crane used for panoramic shots. (On previous days the director has looked as if he would like to drop the five-year-old from the selfsame crane.) But the boy is fouling up some takes by missing his path and ending up some yards away from the cricket. There are other hitches too. In one take the camera catches an unwanted glimpse of some lighting stands; in another, the Steadicam, which can only take short lengths of film, runs out of steam before the end of the shot. The tension is palpable. Thomas continues to pace. For *The Last Emperor* to succeed it must attract a vast audience, especially in the United States. Otherwise it will just be another art film – a $23 million folly with 19,000 extras. It is not as if Thomas is working with a director who is known for blockbusters. Bertolucci's last international success was sixteen years ago with *Last Tango in Paris*. Since then his films have met with lukewarm reviews and public indifference. The five-hour long *1900* (1976) closed within days of opening in America, and audiences also stayed away from *La Luna* (1979), about an opera singer committing incest with her drug addict son. This is the first time Bertolucci has attempted anything on this scale, and even the maestro had doubts first thing this morning. Will *The Last Emperor* revitalise Bertolucci's career with its lavish expenditure of money and magnificent crowd scenes? Or will the project turn out to be another stodgy Euro-pudding that will bore audiences from New York to Osaka?

And now the light is fading. Bertolucci still has not filmed the crucial final reverse shot from the back of the crowd. If he cannot pull off this shot before the light goes, the film will go over budget. The prospect of gathering thousands of extras together again is a nightmare. Against the odds, Storaro and Bertolucci get the last take they need. Thomas feels a weight being lifted from his shoulders:

'You forget how nerve-racking these things are because if you could remember them you probably wouldn't make another film.'

Bertolucci first became aware of Pu Yi's story several years previously when a friend discreetly placed two yellow volumes of Pu Yi's autobiography *From Emperor to Citizen* on his desk. (The book was actually ghosted by Chinese journalist Li Wenda and a committee of Communist Party hacks.) A few years later the Chinese approached Bertolucci about making a film of Pu Yi's life during the Venice Film Festival in 1983. Chairman Mao had always been protective of Pu Yi and would tell people that one day the story of the emperor who ruled three quarters of the world's population but died a municipal gardener would make a wonderful story for the West. The Chinese approved of the Marxist line Bertolucci took in *Il Conformista* (*The Conformist*, 1970), which explored the perversity of fascism. His membership of the Italian Communist Party also helped. The director started to think that Pu Yi was choosing him rather than the other way round. After all, his last two projects – adaptations of Dashiell Hammett's *Red Harvest* (to star Jack Nicholson) and Alberto Moravia's *1934* – had come to nothing. Even so, *The Last Emperor* was not Bertolucci's first choice of a movie to shoot in China. He really wanted to make a film of *Man's Fate*, but found that Andre Malraux's novel, which was set during the 1927 Shanghai uprising, touched too many open political sores. The Chinese were polite but firm. You really should think about making a film about Pu Yi, they urged.

Thomas had only met Bertolucci a few times when the Italian director phoned and said he wanted to meet him. Unwittingly, Thomas chose a Chinese restaurant in London's Chinatown. Bertolucci gave Thomas the two yellow volumes and asked him if he wanted to 'ride this tiger'. Thomas remembered that when Bertolucci brought him the project he knew it would be important, because of its rich historical subject-matter, and because Pu Yi's life was so extraordinary.

Pu Yi, the tenth and last emperor of the Ch'ing Dynasty (1644–1912) – was born in 1906. At the age of two he ascended the throne, where he remained until his abdication in 1912 following the proclamation of the republic by Sun Yat-sen. However, Pu Yi was allowed to remain in the Forbidden City in Peking (Beijing), and continued to rule over his court and some 1,200 eunuchs. In 1924, at the age of eighteen, he was expelled from the Forbidden City by local dictator Feng Yuxiang and took refuge in the north-east city of Tianjin. There he became a man of leisure and contemplated visiting the West, which had always fascinated him since the days when he had a Scottish tutor, Reginald Fleming Johnston, who was probably working for the British secret service. By 1934 the Japanese army had conquered most of northern China, and Pu Yi became the puppet emperor of the Manchurian state. In 1945 he was captured by the Soviet army and kept prisoner in Siberia with a small entourage until 1950 (one year after the Chinese Communist revolution). Stalin then agreed to return him to China as a war criminal. After spending another nine years in a Chinese prison while undergoing a process of 're-education', Pu Yi was freed by Mao, who arranged a job for him in the Beijing Botanical Gardens. On Labour Day 1962 the party rewarded Pu Yi with a new wife – his fifth – who worked as a nurse in a local hospital. Pu Yi died of cancer in October 1967 at the age of sixty-one just as the Cultural Revolution was gaining momentum.

In August 1984 television magazine *Broadcast* reported that Thomas was planning to make a six-part television series about Pu Yi. However, two rival television series were being planned by American writer and producer Alex Haley, author of *Roots*: one for the Chinese market with the script co-written by Yi's son, Prince

Aisin Pu Jie; and another for America. By October Bertolucci was reported in the Italian press to have abandoned the project after the Chinese plumped for the Alex Haley versions. However, Thomas was still negotiating with the Chinese authorities. The Chinese viewed him as the smartest overseas producer they had so far had to deal with. An early sticking point was special dispensation to film in the Forbidden City. He also drove a hard bargain. The head of the China Film Co-Production Corporation kicked himself later after agreeing to be paid in Chinese currency rather than dollars just a few months before the yuan was devalued by 20 per cent. By February 1985 Thomas had made the decision to condense the first draft from six hours to two and a half. In November 1985 *Screen International* reported that after two years of negotiations, the Chinese had approved the script by Bertolucci and his brother-in-law Mark Peploe. The $22 million film was due to start filming in March 1986 with Sean Connery playing the young emperor's Scottish tutor. The China Film Corporation for Co-producers published its unconditional agreement with Bertolucci in the English-language *China Daily*. However, the telegram giving final approval for the script – 'Glad reading how man who became a dragon turned back into a man. Congratulations' – had to be returned with a plea to insert the word 'approval' before the film's backers would part with their cash.

When it came to raising money for *The Last Emperor*, Thomas adopted an aphorism by Deng Xiaoping – 'It doesn't matter if the cat is black or white as long as it catches mice' – whenever yet another investor dropped out. Eventually he broke new ground by organising a consortium of five European merchant banks headed by Hill Samuel to underwrite the budget between them. The other banks were Standard Chartered Bank, Pierson Heldring & Pierson UK, Credit Anstalt Bankverein and Gota Bank UK. All five saw the long-term advantage of slipping a letter of introduction under the bamboo curtain. Thomas said the investment banks only came in because bankers saw it as a 'soft entry spot' to get to ministers – more like sponsorship than investment. (After *The Last Emperor* only one of the banks, Pierson Heldring & Pierson UK, had anything more to do with the film business, even though all five made handsome returns.) Half of the budget came in the form of an advance from US film financier Hemdale against a North American sale. Hemdale was representing Thomas when it came to selling the film to the US studios. Thomas's old friend Terry Glinwood was in charge of selling off all other markets (excluding France, Italy and Japan, which had already been pre-sold). United International Pictures (UIP), the overseas distribution joint venture between Universal, Paramount and Metro-Goldwyn-Mayer, mopped up all leftover countries.

By mid-May 1986 the start date for the film, now budgeted at $23 million, had slipped to 4 August. Peter O'Toole was now playing the Scottish tutor, although William Hurt had been considered. A 21-week shoot was planned. Thomas decided they would take everything with them, including twenty-five vintage cars in containers. Parmesan cheese, 2,000 kilograms of pasta, 500 litres of olive oil, and 22,000 litres of Italian mineral water were packed around the cars. The Chinese put Beijing Studio Number One at Thomas's disposal, even building a four-storey office to accommodate his assistants, interpreters, accountants and designers. *The Last Emperor* was the biggest film ever to be made without the safety net of a Hollywood studio underneath it. If anything went wrong Thomas would be on his own. He took a deep breath and pushed on with his high-wire act. Interviewed on set, Thomas admitted *The Last Emperor* was a large project for an independent to have taken on but that he was making it the way Hollywood would, yet without the inflationary costs of the parent studio's overhead. Watching Thomas at work, foreign correspondent Edward Behr, who himself had written a biography of Pu Yi, thought Thomas's composure made him the worthy, if unconscious, heir to the cool upper-class Boxer Rebellion heroes who manned the British legation.

At the time, the Forbidden City was attracting thirteen million visitors a year but the Chinese closed it down for Thomas. Not only that but the government stopped the Queen from visiting the Hall of Supreme Harmony while on a state tour. The film-makers were not to be disturbed, the authorities said. Thomas, Bertolucci and the crew then moved north to Dalian and Shenyang, and finally to Changchun in Manchuria near the Russian border. A pecking order quickly established itself. The Italians were at the top of the pyramid, followed by grumbling British technicians, and finally the Chinese, who, with few exceptions, did the manual labour. Thomas compared the filming to an escalator that you cannot get off. Every day on location was difficult, and in those days before mobile phones communications were garbled. The final prison interiors were shot back in the Cinecitta Studios in Rome over a five-week period. 'I had done difficult films before but nothing like the scale of *The Last Emperor*,' says Thomas.

Not surprisingly, *The Last Emperor* was released to general rapture. *Variety* praised Thomas for organising such an ambitious production, which it compared to an exquisitely painted mural of twentieth-century China. The *Village Voice* compared Bertolucci to a conductor marking Marxist time with one hand while whipping up fabulous visions with the other. Together, both hands made fascinating music, said critic David Edelstein. *The Sunday Times* predicted that Thomas would win an Academy Award for best picture because every penny he had raised was clearly visible on the screen. However, Nigel Andrews in the *Financial Times* criticised the film for being as meandering and purposeless as Pu Yi's life. It compared the film to opium smoke, whose gorgeous images (the beautiful costumes, the photography, the huge number of extras) bewitch the senses and befuddle the mind. Andrews admitted that the experience was lovely; but where, he wondered, was it all going?

Just as the film was about to be released in America, Puttnam was ousted from Columbia. Parent company Coca-Cola had grown fed up with his constantly justifying himself to the press about his frequently odd film choices. Indeed, Puttnam seemed to have gone out of his way to pick fights with, among others, Coca-Cola board member Bill Cosby, Warren Beatty and producer Ray Stark – the power behind the Columbia throne. Puttnam had even criticised comedian Bill Murray, star of Columbia's *Ghostbusters* franchise, in public for his greed. Thomas's film was caught between two studio managements – Puttnam's, which had bought the film, and the new management, which was both keen to discredit Puttnam and at a loss with what to do with this Chinese epic. One executive described *The Last Emperor* as a 'huge budget arthouse movie. You have to support it or you are an enemy of the arts'. The new management reneged on a commitment to the Cineplex Odeon chain to show the picture on 150 of its theatres. Surely, wondered the *Los Angeles Herald Examiner*, studio boss Victor Kaufman wasn't doing this to embarrass Puttnam further? Thomas still thinks the film would have earned more if Columbia had bothered to put it on additional screens.

Bertolucci described *The Last Emperor* as a journey from darkness to light. It was, he said, the story of metamorphosis from caterpillar to butterfly. *From Emperor to Citizen* closes with these words: ' "Man" was the very first word I learnt to read in my first reader, but I never understood its meaning before. Only today, with the Communist Party and the policy of remoulding criminals, have I learnt the

significance of this magnificent word and become a real man.'
Thomas and Bertolucci kept to the party line espoused in Pu Yi's
'autobiography', probably aware that not doing so would jeopardise
the production. However, *The Last Emperor* glossed over the truth.
Once released, Pu Yi was not allowed to lead the quiet life which
Thomas and Bertolucci recreate in the film. He was a celebrity,
whose humble gardening work was often eulogised in the Chinese
press. His last wife, Li Shuxian, later disclosed that when she
married Pu Yi – through no choice of her own – he was just as
incapable of looking after himself as he had always been. He could
not even tie his own shoelaces.

Jeremy Thomas was born on 27 July 1949 in London. Film-
making ran in his family. His father, Ralph, directed *A Tale of Two
Cities* (1958) and the *Doctor in the House* series. His uncle Gerald was
the maker of the *Carry On* series of comedies. As a baby he got
underfoot of godfather Dirk Bogarde, actor James Robertson Justice
and comedian Hattie Jacques at his boyhood home near Pinewood
Studios outside London. He later told director David Cronenberg
that his whole family had been infected by the virus of cinema. As a
child he had wandered around Pinewood's studio hangars and
remembered the making of such spectaculars as *Cleopatra* and *A Night
to Remember*. When he was a boy he often featured in background
scenes during the school holidays. When Thomas was twelve he
made an 8mm version of *Ben-Hur* using wheelbarrows instead of
chariots. He was educated at liberal private school Millfield, which
he left with five O levels. When he was a teenager Thomas hung
around Notting Hill Gate watching Nic Roeg, whom he would later
work with, direct *Performance*. His first job was working in a film
laboratory before switching to the cutting room. In the mid-1960s
the editor's bench was a recognised route to the director's chair –
David Lean was one example – and, encouraged by his father,

Thomas never doubted he would one day be a director. It annoys Thomas that today the industry is full of successful producers who know nothing about how to make a film. This could not happen in architecture. There are producers who only understand the financial side but Thomas is proud of his hands-on knowledge. For him it is absolutely essential that a producer understands every aspect of making a film, from how to operate the clapper board to grading colour stock.

Thomas was assistant editor and sound editor on a number of features, including several by Ken Loach. He also worked with another political film-maker, Tony Garnett. Loach and Garnett woke Thomas up politically, showing him the hard lives most people lead – worlds away from his privileged background. Thomas then edited a documentary, *Brother Can You Spare a Dime?*, by Australian director Philippe Mora. *Brother Can You Spare a Dime?* was a compilation of 1930s Depression-era footage. The distributor decided to release the film simultaneously on television and in a cinema in London's West End. There were just twenty-five people in the audience on the first night. This is not a release pattern that has been copied much since.

Thomas produced his first feature film, *Mad Dog* (1976), at the age of twenty-six. It was the story of Daniel 'Mad Dog' Morgan, a young Irishman who failed to make his fortune during the Australian gold rush. Morgan was convicted of minor theft and given a barbaric prison sentence. He went on the run and his cat-and-mouse game with the Australian authorities became legendary. Thomas and Mora decided that Dennis Hopper, an actor notorious for his drug-taking and bad behaviour, would be perfect as Morgan. They flew to New Mexico in a single-engine plane to meet Hopper. The actor met them carrying a gun and driving a truck that was full of bullet holes. He got the part. Once finished, *Mad Dog* was sold outright to an American distributor for money that never materialised. The distributor cut twenty minutes from the film and marketed *Mad Dog* as an action movie. The experience taught Thomas a lesson – from now on he would be involved in how his films were marketed. Marketing should begin the day one starts thinking about the project. After all, nobody cared about his films as much as he did.

His next production, *The Shout*, was an off-centre version of Robert Graves' short story about a man who returns to England after spending eighteen years among the Australian Aborigines. He enthrals a West Country couple with tales of magic, murder and the power to kill with a shout. Thomas's first choice as director was Nic Roeg, who had just directed *The Man Who Fell to Earth* starring David Bowie. Roeg said he would only direct *The Shout* if Thomas first put up the money for another project, *Bad Timing*. Thomas agreed, on the condition that Roeg found half the money himself. *Bad Timing* had already been cancelled twice, but Thomas pitched it to staid film company Rank as a *Third Man* for the 1980s. In fact, *Bad Timing* was a mosaic about a psychiatrist's obsessive affair with a young girl. Not waiting for Roeg, Thomas approached Polish director Jerzy Skolimowski after seeing his film *Deep End* (1970) at the London Film Festival. Thomas appreciated how Skolimowski had created so much tension from so little on screen. *The Shout* was made for £500,000 with stars including Alan Bates and Susannah York and was finished in December 1977. It shared the special jury prize at the Cannes Film Festival the following spring with Alan Parker's *Midnight Express*.

Meanwhile, the British music scene was convulsed by the energy of punk rock. Throughout the early 1970s record companies had tightened their stranglehold on the market, releasing either triple-gatefold-sleeve albums with Tolkienian pretensions or the happy-clappy pap of disco. Reacting to this, Malcolm McLaren, owner of a fetish clothes shop in London's King's Road, put together a band, the Sex Pistols, in 1975. The idea was that it didn't matter if you couldn't play guitar or your drummer hadn't got a sense of rhythm – just go out there and do it. The do-it-yourself attitude of punk chimed with the entrepreneurial vision of incoming prime minister Margaret Thatcher. Bands that came out of punk rock included the politically tinged The Clash, the more poppy Buzzcocks and, in America, Blondie. When the Sex Pistols broke up in October 1978 after a gig in San Francisco, McLaren decided to make a film about the band titled *Who Killed Bambi?* The pitch was Sex Pistols meet Russ Meyer – the American director obsessed with well-endowed women – in the land of anarchy. Thomas admitted later that Meyer was mainly interested in scouring Europe for women with large breasts. It is doubtful that he knew anything much about punk rock. The producer helped structure the now retitled *The Great Rock 'n' Roll Swindle* with pop video director Julian Temple. Thomas and Temple shot new footage with escaped convict Ronald Biggs in South America. The highlight of the film was a version of the Frank Sinatra classic 'My Way' sung by ex-Sex Pistols bassist Sid Vicious. At the finale of the song Vicious whips out a fake gun and starts shooting people in the audience, including his girlfriend, Nancy Spungen. On 12 October 1978 Spungen was found stabbed in Vicious's hotel room and he was charged with murder. While released on bail, Vicious overdosed on heroin and died on 2 February 1979.

By now Thomas was raising money for Roeg's next project, *Eureka*, a kind of *Citizen Kane* story based on the murder of Sir Harry Oakes, a self-made millionaire who stumbled across one of the largest gold strikes of all time. Oakes, whose friends included the former Duke of Windsor and Jewish gangster Meyer Lansky, was bludgeoned to death in 1943; his murder was never solved. David

Begelman, head of Metro-Goldwyn-Mayer, suggested the project to Roeg. At one point the screenplay, co-written by Roeg and Paul Mayersberg, ran to 1,800 pages. Meanwhile, Thomas had met Japanese director Nagisa Oshima at the Cannes Film Festival. Oshima wanted to adapt *The Seed and the Sower*, Sir Laurens van der Post's book about the relationship between a Japanese prison camp commandant and an English prisoner of war. Thomas agreed to produce Oshima's film as well, and in 1982 both projects began shooting.

Eureka went into production in January in British Columbia, Canada, with Gene Hackman playing McCann. Roeg was given $11 million and a supporting cast that, as well as his wife, Theresa Russell, included Mickey Rourke and Rutger Hauer. Expectations for the film were strong, especially for Roeg, who believed *Eureka* would be his masterpiece. However, Roeg's oblique style confounded MGM, which thought it was getting a straightforward thriller. The working title for the film was *Murder Mystery*. Begelman, *Eureka*'s original supporter, had been fired for fraud, and his successor found the film impenetrable. Four different studio managements at MGM sat on *Eureka*, not knowing what to do with it. Finally, after two years, the film was given a limited release in the USA and then quickly dispatched to video.

Thomas had more success with *Merry Christmas, Mr Lawrence*, which was a hit on its release in 1982. Oshima cast two pop stars in lead roles – David Bowie as British war prisoner Jack Celliers, and Ryuichi Sakamoto as camp commander Yonoi. 'Beat' Takeshi, then only known as a comedian, played a guard, while English actor Tom Conti played the Lawrence of the title. The $5.5 million drama, set in a prisoner-of-war camp on Java in 1942, was shot in the Cook Islands in September and October of 1982. As with *The Shout*, *Merry Christmas, Mr Lawrence* has an off-centre feel with a

Japanese director looking at Western culture. In the most famous scene, an adult Bowie dressed as a schoolboy remembers his brother singing in an English country garden. But what is unsettling is that the garden is lush and tropical, not England at all. The film roughly follows two parallel stories. Yonoi recognises that Celliers is at the same point as him on the spiritual ladder; both men are at a higher point than Lawrence or his counterpart, the guard Hara. Hara eventually learns enlightenment from Lawrence.

Thomas had now worked with Roeg, Skolimowski and Oshima. It was at this point that Bertolucci approached him about *The Last Emperor*, knowing his preference for working with auteur directors. At the time, Thomas confessed that the reason why he liked working with auteur directors was because he had aspirations to direct himself – which he would later do. He said he was in awe of directors because he knew how difficult it was to make a really good film. He self-deprecatingly called himself a director groupie. Thomas describes film as the art of collaboration but says the director is the prow of the ship. A producer can be an entrepreneur, an enabler and a promoter but he cannot be the author. This must be a writer/director with something specific to say.

Meanwhile, Thomas formed a joint venture with his friend Chris Blackwell, founder of the Island Records company. Blackwell, whose mother had a long affair with Ian Fleming, made a lot of money in the 1970s and '80s with Bob Marley and U2. The record company boss used some of his profits to launch a film distribution company in America, releasing Nic Roeg's *Insignificance* in 1985. That same year Thomas and Blackwell formed Recorded Releasing to co-distribute and market films from both companies on a fifty-fifty basis. By 1988 Thomas's production company Recorded Picture Company (RPC) had three subsidiary arms: Recorded Releasing, which distributed about eight films a year; Recorded Cinemas, which owned cinemas in London and Edinburgh; and Recorded Development, a script development company which provided seed money for projects, working closely with directors.

In October 1988 Japanese film company Shochiku-Fuji announced it would provide more than 40 per cent of a $120 million fund for the next six films Thomas wanted to produce. Thomas had made Shochiku a lot of money in Japan. The distributor earned about $10 million in film rentals from *Merry Christmas, Mr Lawrence* and $22 million from *The Last Emperor*. (A film rental is the amount of money left from each ticket sold once the cinema has taken its share. In Europe independent distributors usually get 44 per cent of box office, but in the UK the distributor's share is an average 27 per cent of revenue.) Shochiku's $50 million was to come through a mixture of direct investment and minimum guarantees. (A minimum guarantee is an advance a distributor puts up to help fund a film yet to be made.) In exchange Shochiku would keep all Japanese, Hong Kong and Macao rights to films, as well as a share of profits. The balance of the fund, called Filmtrustees, would come from a consortium of other distributors including Hoyts in Australia, AAA in France and Iberoamericana in Spain.

Thomas's follow-up to *The Last Emperor*, and the second film in what would become known as the Eastern Trilogy, had its seeds in *Bad Timing*. Theresa Russell can be seen reading *The Sheltering Sky*, a novel first published in 1949, in the Roeg film. Roeg told Thomas he wanted to adapt the novel. Paul Bowles' story of three American travellers venturing into the heart of Africa had already achieved cult status by the end of the 1950s. *The Sheltering Sky* follows an American couple, Port and Kit Moresby, who in 1947 set out with a friend across Morocco, hoping that a journey into the Sahara will heal the rift in their marriage. Instead, as they drift deeper into the desert, they encounter only oblivion. Port dies from fever, while Kit goes mad in an African village. Bowles described *The Sheltering Sky* to his publisher as an adventure story in which the adventure takes place on two planes simultaneously: in the actual desert and in the inner desert of the spirit. 'The occasional oasis provides relief from the natural desert, but the sexual adventures fail to provide relief. The shade is insufficient, the glare is always higher as the journey continues. And the journey must continue – there is no oasis in which one can remain,' he wrote.[1] Bowles, a writer whose prose can be ruthless in its lack of sentiment, thought of the title during a ten-minute bus ride from 10th Street in New York to Madison Square Garden, during which he also plotted the story. The title came from a popular pre-First World War song, 'Down Among the Sheltering Palms'. Bowles used to listen to it on his grandfather's phonograph. What fascinated him was not the melody but the strange word 'sheltering'. What did the palm trees shelter people from, and how could they be sure of such protection? The theme of the novel, he wrote, is 'don't believe in the sky, don't believe in anything except the fact it protects us from the dark, because beyond it is just blackness'.[2] Thomas described the book as a profound love story with a haunting tone that was impossible to put down once you started reading it. But Robert Aldrich, producer of *Whatever Happened to Baby Jane?* and *The Dirty Dozen*, had already beaten Thomas to the prize. Aldrich had bought the rights back in 1964 and spent the next nineteen years trying to make the book into a film. Thomas approached the veteran producer about buying the rights but his offer was refused. When Aldrich died in 1983 the rights passed to his son, William.

Meanwhile, Bertolucci's brother-in-law Mark Peploe and *Last Emperor* production designer Ferdinando Scarfiotti both kept badgering the director to read the novel. Bertolucci finally got round to it on one of his trips to China preparing to make *The Last*

Emperor. A chance meeting between William Aldrich and Bertolucci finally got the ball rolling. Bertolucci first told friends he could make the film for $14 million, but Thomas set the budget at a more realistic $22 million. *The Sheltering Sky*, trumpeted the press release, would reunite seven of the nine *Last Emperor* Academy Award-winners. In addition to Thomas, Bertolucci and Peploe, the creative team would include director of photography Vittorio Storaro, costume designer James Acheson, editor Gabriella Cristiani and sound recordist Ivan Sharrock. Principal photography began on the $25 million production in Morocco in September 1989. Every day of filming would cost $80,000. (When told the size of the budget, a rival film-maker wondered what the money was being spent on. The book was, after all, mainly about just three faces.) Thomas predicted that *The Sheltering Sky* would be an intimate, sensual film told against the striking backdrop of post-war North Africa. Like the palaces in *The Last Emperor*, said Thomas, the exotic locations would be a feast for the eye.

Few productions offer more logistical challenges than period road pictures. The crew shot in three different countries, each with its own problems. Every prop on *The Sheltering Sky*, from street signs to petrol pumps to camel saddles, had to be supplied. Tons of *circa-1947* rubbish had to be recreated for one shot. For another scene, Thomas had to ship in building materials to construct a French foreign legion fort in the middle of sand dunes. Filming ended in Niger, one of the poorest countries in the world. No film had ever been shot there before, so Thomas, like an army general, had to create his own lines of communication.

John Malkovich starred as Port Moresby, with Debra Winger playing his wife, Kit. However, rumour had it that the film's American distributor, Warner Brothers, imposed Winger on Thomas. The actress had a reputation for being difficult and she did not mix with the crew. Some of them referred to her as Norma Desmond, the histrionic film star of Billy Wilder's *Sunset Boulevard*, behind her back. Winger's character was based on Bowles' neurotic and talented wife, Jane, also a writer, whose work Winger had studied at university. Like Jane Bowles, who ultimately took up with an illiterate Moroccan woman, Winger stalked the Arab quarters by night in a cloak. Bertolucci was delighted by Winger's identification with Jane Bowles, claiming the actress had a wound inside her like an open mouth.

When shooting stopped in Tangier, the 160-strong crew chartered a plane across the Atlas mountains to Er Rachida, only to arrive in the middle of a flood – the first rain for eight years. (Somebody should hire out film crews to drought-stricken areas, as their arrival inevitably coincides with rainstorms.) Rain delayed the twenty-truck procession to the next stop, Erfoud, for another two days.

Again Thomas was taking a risk letting Bertolucci and Storaro loose in the desert. Although Storaro was acknowledged as a genius, he was also appallingly expensive. (One is reminded of the story about David Lean shooting *Lawrence of Arabia*, also in Morocco. Lean had become obsessed about the play of light in the desert and kept on shooting and shooting until his producer, Sam Spiegel, told him he couldn't go on for ever. 'Why not?' snapped Lean.) Storaro describes his work on *The Sheltering Sky* as follows:

For Bernardo one of the most important things is writing the story with a camera – it is like his own pen. He has his own special language of style. I have signed all this with light. I tell the story through the conflict of light and shadow, one colour in relation to another . . . the life of Port is in conjunction with the life of the sun. The sun's journey is like Port's journey though his own life. When Port dies there is a balance between sunset and moonrise. Then the moon follows what Kit is doing. Finally,

the moon has finished its own course when we see Kit at the end of her
story . . . then it is the end of the night and the incredible colour of the
sky announcing a new day.[3]

(At this point Storaro startled the *Sunday Times* reporter writing a
location piece by slapping him on the knee and beaming, 'Good
story, eh?' Storaro looked somewhat wounded later when he
realised the reporter was avoiding continuing the interview.)

If Storaro could be a bit of a humbug, then Bertolucci could be
down to earth. In one scene Winger had to lie naked on her back,
drifting round and round in the water of an oasis as she looked up
at the stars. She could see Bertolucci and the crew calling and
gesticulating from the shore. Expecting some profound piece of
direction from the maestro, Winger lifted her head out of the water
only to hear Bertolucci shouting: 'More tits, more tits.'

Bertolucci and Storaro spent weeks filming in the Sahara, where
it was acknowledged that the people with the hardest job were those
employed to erase all footprints in the sand after each shot. On the
whole, filming in North Africa was to prove more difficult than in
China. To get the permissions needed to set *The Last Emperor* in
motion was difficult, Thomas said, but the logistical problems of
producing *The Sheltering Sky* were more difficult still.

Winger nearly ended up being lynched on the very last day of
filming in Agadez, Niger. In the scene, Winger, dressed as an Arab
man, had to try to buy milk with useless banknotes. But onlookers
from the village thought she was having a real argument with a
street vendor. The crew lost control of the set as the crowd hurled
themselves at Winger. As the set disintegrated into chaos only two
people kept their heads – the Steadicam operator who carried on
filming and Bertolucci, who waited to shout 'Cut!' until the last
possible moment.

On the film's release Iain Johnstone, writing in the *Sunday Times*, praised Thomas for the scale of his achievement. At a time when the American studio system was supreme and independent cinema was struggling, he had managed to fund a hit movie from his London office, paralleling his achievement with *The Last Emperor*. Alexander Walker of the *Evening Standard* agreed that the film was produced with great assuredness but said that its overall effect was vague. Derek Malcolm, writing in the *Guardian*, decided that somewhere in this fat, lushly photographed 138-minute odyssey was a leaner, better film trying to get out. The *Daily Telegraph* criticised *The Sheltering Sky* for its ponderous self-importance, saying it displayed the same symptoms found in *The Last Emperor*. 'Bertolucci's account of Emperor Pu Yi seemed to substitute an ornate exoticism for genuine poetry,' wrote Hugo Davenport, 'offering hollow grandiosity in place of the intellectual complexity of his earlier work: unhappily, so does this new film.'[4] The *Sunday Express* summed up the problem by saying that although *The Sheltering Sky* looked beautiful, you know what they say about beauty . . .

Thomas's career can be viewed like a Venn diagram, those intersecting mathematical circles which explain the relationships between things. Paul Bowles provides the link between Bertolucci's epic Eastern Trilogy – the sweep of imperial China in *The Last Emperor*; the heartless majesty of the North African desert in *The Sheltering Sky*; and the pageant of a 2,500-year-old Buddhist legend in *Little Buddha* (1994) – and a trilogy of films based on notorious novels of the 1950s, '60s and '70s – the scatological, kaleidoscopic *Naked Lunch* (1991); the chromium fucking of *Crash* (1997); and the funereal *Young Adam* (2002). Norman Mailer wrote that Bowles 'opened up the world of hip. He let in the murder, the drugs, the incest, the death of the Square, the call of the orgy, the end of civilization'.[5] On a more prosaic level, Bowles was friendly both with mainstream

American writers of the 1950s such as Truman Capote and Tennessee Williams, and members of the Beat movement, including William Burroughs and Allen Ginsberg.

Like Bowles, Burroughs was living in Tangier in the mid-1950s. He had settled in Tangier – the Interzone of *Naked Lunch*, a 'notorious free port on the North African coast. A haven for the mongrel scum of the earth. An engorged parasite on the underbelly of the West'[6] – because of its liberal attitudes and the availability of drugs and young men. Six years before, Burroughs had killed his wife when a drunken William Tell-style dare went wrong at a party in Mexico. Joan Burroughs had urged him to shoot a glass off the top of her head. Instead, he put a bullet through her brain. The Mexican judge accepted that it was an accident based on the testimony of other party-goers. After paying a lawyer $2,000 and serving thirteen days in jail, Burroughs posted $2,312 in bail and was set free. He later came to the 'appalling conclusion' that he would never have become a writer if it had not been for his wife's death. Joan's manslaughter was, he wrote, the moment in time when he saw exactly what was on the end of his fork – hence the title of the book he was working on, *Naked Lunch*. However, this rationale only came much later during Burroughs' rehabilitation in the 1980s. The truth was that Burroughs disliked women, believing they literally came from another planet. For most of his life Burroughs was a militant homosexual.

Naked Lunch (1964) was written as a series of sketches or 'routines' with Burroughs shutting up the censor inside his head. He had previously written a hard-boiled pulp novel titled *Junky* under the pseudonym William Lee (a friend of mine sold his rare first edition of this in order to pay for his own heroin habit, which has a certain circularity to it). Now everything that was going on in Burroughs' mind was vomited onto the page: coprophilia, erotic asphyxiation, the apocalypse. The book's random structure anticipated his later cut-up technique, where he took a Stanley knife to other people's words and rearranged them as a collage, trying to do for writing what cubism did for painting. ('That's not writing, that's plumbing,' said Samuel Beckett, aghast.) His friend Jack Kerouac, visiting him in 1957, asked Burroughs why the manuscript was full of images of boys being hanged. Burroughs replied that he had no idea. He was just an agent getting messages from other planets who had not clearly decoded his orders. When *Naked Lunch* was finally published in England in 1965 it attracted such opprobrium that the *Times Literary Supplement* ran a special letters page on it for two months. Dame Edith Sitwell wrote to say that she would not be reading the book because she did not want to spend the rest of her life with her nose nailed to other people's lavatories. 'A revolting miasma of unrelieved perversion . . . literary sewage' was how a Massachusetts supreme court judge described it. However, when Thomas read it he found it difficult, disturbing and strong, and he knew he wanted to film it.

In 1984 the producer attended the Toronto Film Festival, where he met director David Cronenberg. Thomas thought the combination of Cronenberg and Burroughs would be a recipe for a wonderful film. The director was known for his visceral horror movies, most of which had a common theme of people mutating with technology or insects to become a new strain of life. The conversation turned to *Naked Lunch*. Stanley Kubrick had talked about trying to film it. Cronenberg said that he had been somewhat surprised to hear himself saying in an interview that he too wanted to adapt it. Thomas asked Cronenberg if he knew Burroughs, and the producer suggested the three of them travel to Tangier and scout locations with an adaptation in mind. And so the following year, producer, director and 71-year-old novelist flew to Tangier accompanied by Hercules Belleville, head of development at RPC, and Burroughs' assistant, James Grauerholz.

Once again, Thomas was taking a huge risk in adapting *Naked Lunch* for the screen. There was even less support for experimental writing in the 1980s than there had been in the early 1960s. Then at least underground publications were in vogue and it was fashionable to condemn American society. Since then America had only increased its hegemony and Reaganism was triumphant. Cronenberg decided that a literal translation of the book would cost $400 million to make and be banned in every country of the world – not an attractive proposition from Thomas's point of view. What Cronenberg planned was to fuse his writing with Burroughs' in much the same way that the Jeff Goldblum character mutates with an insect in Cronenberg's horror film *The Fly* (1986). The director decided to base the film on incidents in Burroughs' life – Joan's death and his days as an insect exterminator, for example. *Naked Lunch*, explained Cronenberg, would be a phantasmagoria about how Burroughs became a novelist. But he warned the producer that he did not want to make a special effects movie, even though there was a lot of science fiction and horror imagery in the book. This disappointed Thomas, because for him the monsters in *Naked Lunch* were one of the project's main selling points – a special effects film for adults. Cronenberg agreed to compromise, and the first draft of the script featured monsters weeping addictive fluids, typewriters which mutate into insects, and a woman tearing her face apart. California-based special effects designer Chris Walas started making creatures six months before filming was due to begin. Some of the creatures, called Mugwumps, would need fifteen puppeteers to operate them. Burroughs praised Cronenberg's screenplay for substituting imaginary drugs for the mundane heroin and marijuana of the novel. Thomas said it was difficult to translate any book exactly on screen, especially a book like *Naked Lunch*. It was really more the spirit of the book he was producing.

Predictably, *Naked Lunch* proved difficult to finance. Shochiku, the original Japanese backer, dropped out at a late stage because it thought the project was too perverse. Somewhat unwisely, even Thomas had described *Naked Lunch* as unfilmable in his sales brochure. Another Japanese company, Nippon Film Development & Finance, stepped in to fill the gap. Once again, tenacity and will-power had prevailed.

Principal photography on the $17 million film started on 21 January 1991 in Toronto with Peter Weller playing Burroughs and Judy Davis playing both Joan and another character, based once again on Jane Bowles. Like Debra Winger in *The Sheltering Sky*, Davis looked, in the words of critic Pauline Kael, like a fashionable illustrator's idea of a spunky lesbian. All interiors and special effects work were due to be filmed in Toronto before the team flew to Tangier in April for exterior shots. However, rising tension in the Middle East ahead of the Gulf War meant that no insurer would cover the production on location. The three-week shoot in Morocco was cancelled and Thomas had to do some quick thinking. He calculated that *Naked Lunch* would save $1 million if it were shot entirely in Toronto. Not only that but it would qualify as an official UK/Canada co-production, triggering government and state funding from Telefilm Canada and the Ontario Film Development Corporation. Sometimes, working inside a tight compass can be liberating – imagination, after all, costs nothing. Cronenberg rewrote the script over a weekend as the interior of a man's mind rather than a city swarming with monsters. The director later claimed that keeping the film studio-bound only heightened the claustrophobia.

Overall, reviews were admiring, even if Nigel Andrews in the *Financial Times* did compare the film to a television adaptation of

Casablanca with special effects by the Muppets. In particular the film was praised for capturing some of the book's dry-as-a-bone humour. (At one point, Judy Davis, having injected some insecticide, drawls: 'It's a very, uh . . . literary high. It's a Kafka high. You feel like a bug.') Writing in the *Guardian*, Derek Malcolm grudgingly admired Thomas for never producing anything easy.

However, by the early 1990s Filmtrustees was beginning to go sour. *Naked Lunch*, *The Sheltering Sky* and Karel Reisz's *Everybody Wins* together cost more than $60 million to make but grossed less than $6 million at the box office. Even Thomas's greatest triumph, *The Last Emperor*, only earned $18.9 million in North American rentals. Banks complained to trade paper *Variety* that Thomas was irresponsible with other people's money. Bankers were horrified by what they saw as Thomas's lack of concern. He did not even keep lenders informed about their losses, they complained. One colleague said that Thomas's passion affected his perception of the necessary balance between the creative and the commercial. On the other hand, the business had changed. Hollywood was squeezing out independent distributors such as Shochiku and Iberoamericana. Studios were releasing films that a few years ago only independent distributors would handle. Filmtrustees went into liquidation on 16 October 1992 with debts of $6.8 million after funding just three films. Thomas told me:

> Filmtrustees was a punctuation mark in my career. It took a certain amount of time to recover from that. I've tried to be a businessman but I'm a film-maker. I don't want any shareholders. Listen, I've been lucky in that I've got out of jail a number of times. Since then I've been around the board, passing Go, and now I can sustain losses. It's nice having a private company. You don't have to answer to anybody and you don't have performance figures. The films I want to do could not exist within the environment of a shareholder company.

Obviously, there is a split between one's enthusiasm for film as a film and the business side of it. I think you need that enthusiasm initially, that lack of reality, to mount something because the odds against making a film are so enormous. But as time has moved on, I have become more realistic about the numbers side of making a film, the realities of making various films on various budgets, and the potential of recouping costs for investors.

Thomas decided on a new strategy, buying the freehold on his Mondrianesque office building in a London side street and becoming as independent as possible. He started buying back rights to his old films in order to create a library – in short, to create value in his company: 'Buying back my movies is an emotional as well as a strategic decision. There is a method in my madness.' Now the plan was to increase Recorded Picture Company's output to two or three films a year. Editing and screening facilities were installed in the Hanway Street office, and a branch was opened in Los Angeles. Thomas recruited an in-house legal affairs team consisting of Peter Watson, formerly of investment bank Guinness Mahon, and Stefan Mallman, who used to work for German company Constantin Film. Watson and Mallman worked alongside Chris Auty, RPC's engaging managing director. Thomas says: 'Modesty has paid off. Push forward but at a steady pace. It's not a blunderbuss, it's a sniper rifle.'

Meanwhile, Thomas and Bertolucci started talking about the third film in the Eastern Trilogy, a project which would convey the teachings of Tibetan Buddhism. Buddhism had fascinated Bertolucci since he visited Kathmandu in the 1970s. His interest had first been sparked by a biography of Tibetan Buddhist Milarepa that he first read when he was twenty-one. Thomas may have been swayed by the fashion for Buddhism in the early 1990s. If nothing else, the film would have a built-in audience of fashion designers and Hollywood actors.

Little Buddha tells the story of a young American boy, Jesse, who is believed to be the reincarnation of a respected lama. A deposition of Tibetan monks arrive at Jesse's house in Seattle, and invite him to go on a journey to Tibet. Intertwined with this modern story is the legend of Prince Siddhartha, whose gradual enlightenment forms the pillars of Buddhist thought.

The $35-million *Little Buddha* was mainly shot in Bhutan, where no film director had ever been before. Only two thousand tourist visas were granted each year. Heavy equipment was transported to Kathmandu by road. Arriflex cameras, set materials, generators, kitchens, grip and lighting equipment – and large amounts of food – all had to be ferried from Calcutta to Kathmandu and Bhutan by a 400-mile trek over the mountains. During one expedition a truck was hijacked, and then hijacked again by its original drivers. The 300-strong English, Italian, Nepalese and Hindu crew also shot on location in India and Nepal. Thomas believed that audiences thrived on unique locations: 'It's a fantastically operatic venture and a creative artistic endeavour for the entire crew,' he announced. Key to the project's success was the involvement of technical adviser Dzongsar Khyetse Rinpoche, spiritual tutor to the Tibetan royal family and, it turned out, a dedicated cinephile who knew all of Bertolucci's films. Thomas told writer Kirk Ellis that everything was interconnected, echoing a tenet of Buddhist thought.

If Burroughs is like painter Francis Bacon with his screaming heads and blind monsters, then English novelist J. G. Ballard is the René Magritte of suburbia, juxtaposing the surreal with the flyovers and retail parks of west London. On the face of it Burroughs and Ballard were unlikely allies. Burroughs looked like an undertaker from the Midwest, while Ballard was an expat type, at home on the veranda sipping a pink gin. (I remember going to the opening night of an exhibition of paintings by Burroughs in the late 1980s. Wanting to meet Burroughs, and not seeing him in the gallery, I ventured upstairs and came to a door with a brass plaque inscribed 'Centre for Interplanetary Studies'. Feeling rather like Alice about to go down the rabbit hole, I pushed the door open and found myself pretty much alone in a library with Burroughs, Ballard and Francis Bacon, who was sitting in an armchair like a gloomy owl.) In the 1960s Ballard wrote a series of novels that embraced the apocalypse. In Ballard's view, drowned cities or a crystallising world were a trigger for evolutionary change. Driving home one night, he was nearly killed in a car accident, which got him thinking: What was it about traffic accidents that made people slow down to get a better look? Ballard put on an art exhibition of car wrecks, intrigued to see what people's reaction would be. The opening was chaotic – people got wildly drunk, fights broke out and one woman was nearly raped in the back of one of the exhibits. He then conceived of the first pornographic novel based on technology. When he submitted the manuscript, *Crash*, to his publisher, the editor said in her report that, 'the author is clearly beyond psychiatric help' – which Ballard took as the highest compliment. Part of Ballard's charm is his unashamed enthusiasm for everything that right-thinking liberal humanism opposes: bad television, big cars, pornography, multi-storey car parks and airport slip roads. *Crash*, published in 1973, tells the story of James Ballard and his wife, Catherine, who spice up their marriage by having sex with other people. Ballard has a near fatal crash, and is contacted by Vaughn, leader of a shadowy group sexually excited by automobile smashes. Vaughn is planning to murder Elizabeth Taylor by ramming his car into hers. That way, Taylor will be immortalised in a car tragedy just as James Dean was. Like any pornographic novel, everybody has sex with everybody else, but what makes *Crash* such a hoot is Ballard's tongue-in-cheek pseudoscientific prose style.

During the filming of *Naked Lunch* Thomas asked Cronenberg if there was anything he wanted to do next. Cronenberg replied that he wanted to adapt *Crash* and Thomas revealed he had bought the rights on publication, only to have spent ten years trying to set up the film. Cronenberg's agent warned him that *Crash* would end his career. Cronenberg's response was to fire him. Thomas decided that the way to get the film made would be to halve the budget and persuade the cast to work, in his words, 'for peanuts'. To save money he decided to shoot in Toronto rather than the gyratory systems of west London. Happily, Ballard thought Toronto was just right because it was a paradigm of an anonymous North American city. French company UGC was originally meant to finance the film, but backed out when it read Cronenberg's script.

Crash would be Thomas's most controversial film to date. Its premiere at the Cannes Film Festival was compared to past art scandals such as the first night of Stravinsky's *Rite of Spring* or the unveiling of Picasso's *Les Desmoiselles d'Avignon*. Against the wishes of jury president Francis Ford Coppola, *Crash* was awarded a special prize for 'audacity and invention'. Sniffing controversy, *Evening Standard* film critic Alexander Walker described *Crash* as containing some of the most perverted acts and theories of sexual deviance he had ever seen propagated in mainstream cinema. Walker later criticised Thomas for what he called his 'almost supernatural quietness', which might signal, the critic suggested, the producer's disturbed conscience. The unimaginative tabloid press picked up the story. The right-wing *Daily Mail* splashed a front-page article headlined 'Ban This Car Crash Sex Film'. The newspaper reported that culture minister Virginia Bottomley had called for *Crash* to be banned on the grounds of taste – despite her not actually having seen it. According to *Mail* reviewer Christopher Tookey in an inside article (headlined 'Morality Dies in Twisted Wreckage'), *Crash* promulgated 'the morality of the satyr, the nymphomaniac, the rapist and the paedophile' and marked 'the point at which even a liberal society should draw the line'. The newspaper urged its readers to boycott products made by Sony, parent company of Columbia TriStar, the film's British distributor, as part of its 'Campaign to Stop Depraved Movie Being Shown in Britain'. A coalition of Muslim and Christian fundamentalists threatened to join the *Mail* boycott unless *Crash* was banned.

Britain has a strange censorship system whereby the government does not have the power to ban anything. Instead, the British Board of Film Classification (BBFC) certifies films on behalf of local councils, which can then veto what people see. On 21 November 1996 Westminster Council banned *Crash* from cinemas in London's West End unless three scenes were cut and the film was given an 18 certificate. The BBFC had yet to make up its mind. One councillor said she was worried about impressionable teenagers being inspired to recreate scenes from the film. Thomas told the council that *Crash* had been seen around the world without one copycat incident. Traffic accident statistics had remained static. Chris Auty, co-executive producer of *Crash* with Thomas, pointed out that you could see impressionable teenagers, usually hugging a can of lager, queuing up outside Soho peep shows, whose premises were licensed by . . . Westminster Council. Thomas cancelled all further press screenings, hoping to damp down controversy and give censors breathing space to come to a measured decision. Celebrities including Jeremy Irons, Michael Palin and *Four Weddings and a Funeral* producer Duncan Kenworthy defended the film on grounds of artistic freedom. On 18 March 1997 the BBFC awarded *Crash* an 18 certificate without any cuts. But three days later Westminster Council extended its ban after a two-hour meeting. An absurd situation developed, whereby you could see the film in a ring of cinemas surrounding the West End but not in central London itself.

Meanwhile, Ted Turner, owner of the film's American distributor Fine Line Features, also said he was appalled by *Crash*. Fine Line executives, fearful for their jobs and not wanting to antagonise the boss, postponed its release to March 1997.

In truth, *Crash* is a drab little art film, about as sexually exciting as a gearbox oil change. In public Ballard praised Thomas and Cronenberg for going further than the novel. He compared the film to a chart where two axes – sex and technology – go off the scale to converge at some point in the future. True to the feel of Ballard's science fiction, *Crash*'s future world is not one of computers and the Internet, but of steel and metal. Screws, burnt rubber and rusty tin sheets are Cronenberg's metaphors for a crumbling society. Cronenberg said that the idea behind the film was that everybody in the twentieth century has been traumatised and overwhelmed, as if they have survived a car crash. What happens when one goes through a traumatic experience is that one shuts down emotionally. On the outside you may look normal but inside you are stitched together like Frankenstein's monster. You can still interrelate, explained the director, but the passion has gone. However, Martin Amis pointed out that back in 1973 the automobile could be seen as something erotic, conjuring up freedom and power. By 1996, however, associations pointed the other way, towards banality: car pools, lead-free fuel and asthma. Director Chris Petit made a more serious criticism, comparing Thomas's adaptations of *Naked Lunch* and *Crash* to a 'Classics Illustrated' take on literature, lacking flair or willingness to experiment. Novelist Iain Sinclair dismissed Cronenberg as the asset-stripper of the modernist canon.

By now Thomas and Auty were finding themselves on planes most of the time, selling films direct to sympathetic foreign distributors. Any countries they did not sell to themselves they handed over to a sales agent, with a different seller for each film. For example, London-based Majestic Film & Television sold the Bob Rafelson thriller *Blood & Wine*, Paris-based UGC International sold Bertolucci's *Stealing Beauty* and Los Angeles-based MDP Worldwide distributed *Crash*. Thomas decided it was unwieldy to work with so many people, and, more importantly, pay so many fees, and he decided to create his own in-house sales operation, Hanway Films. With hindsight, Thomas said his biggest regret was that he did not set up Hanway years ago. (A factor behind this may be that the sales agent is the first to see any money from a film, often making a profit before the movie has even been released.)

In the summer of 1997 Thomas directed his first feature film, *All the Little Animals*, at the age of forty-nine. Based on a novel that had fascinated him since he was a boy, *All the Little Animals* tells the strange story of Bobby, a brain-damaged young man; his wicked stepfather, Bernard De Winter (also called 'the Fat'); and a mysterious stranger called Mr Summers, who lives in the woods and devotes his time to burying dead animals. The screenplay was updated from the book's 1960s setting to the present day by Thomas's wife, Eski. Thomas had sat on the rights for years, resisting approaches from other directors as he waited for the right moment to try directing. As far back as he could remember he had always wanted to direct. But once he had achieved success as a producer, his producing career had taken on a momentum of its own.

Filming took place on location in London, Cornwall and the Isle of Man. When Thomas went on set the first day he didn't feel at all nervous. He knew where to put the camera and knew what he wanted from the actors. The most important thing was to be confident enough to command the set. However, sensing blood in the water, critics tore into the finished film. The *Guardian* review called *All the Little Animals* one of the silliest, most baffling films it had ever seen. The *Daily Telegraph* called Thomas's film 'downright unhinged'. *The Times* said *All the Little Animals'* blunt environmental message hung over the film 'like lead poisoning'. What was really puzzling, said the paper, was the question of why Thomas, who had bravely steered some of the most uncompromising works by Bertolucci, Cronenberg and Roeg to the screen, should have blooded himself with this nonsense. Thomas shrugged off the criticism, saying people judged his first film by the standards of directors he had worked with. He would still like to direct another film, although next time he would work with a good producer. Ironically his directing debut went over budget and over schedule.

Thomas has between eight and ten projects in development at any one time, but most of them get made. Projects in development at the time of writing include another J. G. Ballard novel, *Super-Cannes,* to be directed by John Maybury, director of the little-seen but imaginative biopic of artist Francis Bacon, *Love Is the Devil.* Another project is a big-screen version of *Kon-Tiki,* based on Thor Heyerdahl's 1947 voyage from Peru to Polynesia on a balsa raft, combining both Thomas's concern about nature and his love of the epic. 'I feel that there's a decent idea there and I'm prepared to spend time getting them right,' Thomas says. His most recent production has been *Young Adam,* the third film in his cult novel trilogy. Thomas says the project appealed because it was in the tradition of Ballard, Burroughs and Bowles. Burroughs once described Alexander Trocchi, author of *Young Adam,* as 'the cosmonaut of inner space'. Trocchi prostituted his wife and abandoned his children to pursue his dream of being a writer, but whatever talent he had was poisoned through heroin addiction.

Young Adam, which stars Ewan McGregor, Tilda Swinton and Peter Mullan, is a murder story set in 1960s Glasgow. McGregor plays Joe, a drifter working on a coal barge run by a husband and wife. They discover the body of a young woman floating in the canal, but Joe knows more than he is letting on. He begins an affair with the wife, seemingly reawakening her interest in life. At the same time an innocent man is arrested for the girl's murder. Despite knowing the truth about how the girl died, McGregor's character does not act. Like Adam in the Garden of Eden he is incapable of distinguishing between right and wrong.

Thomas's production is one of the most satisfying elements in this dream poem of a film. On the one hand, *Young Adam* is a meticulous recreation of pre-Beatles Glasgow with its out-of-season funfairs and paper-thin walls and faded geometric wallpaper. 'A banana!' exclaims a boy when given one as a present, because bananas were still exotic in early 1960s Scotland. As we go deeper into the film it is clear we have entered the curious logic of a dream. However, the pace is as monotonous as the journey of the barge Joe works on. Towards the end of the film you almost want him to throw himself in the canal and be done with it. Nevertheless, *Variety* described *Young Adam* as 'a resonant, beautifully modulated relationship drama', while *Screen International* said that this powerful, disturbing film marked the arrival of a boldly non-conformist voice in British cinema.

When a film is in production Thomas is on set every day, not to interfere (he hires a line producer to keep an eye on the director), but to show commitment: 'My job is to create an ambience and an efficient space for the film to happen. Once the location is found and the script is locked and the crew is hired, there's not too much to do if you've done your job properly. And it can be annoying to have a producer there because by their nature producers are always looking at their watch, and that can be counterproductive to creative people.'

Thomas's office is a higgledy-piggledy museum of his film-making career and souvenirs picked up on his travels. Not for him the minimalist cool of Los Angeles studio executives. Newspaper clippings about his films headlined 'A Movie From the Bounds of

Depravity' and 'The Great Annual Celluloid Wankfest' have been framed. Lying around the room are model cars, his father's directing chair, a cricket ball, a prop typewriter and a geisha doll in a glass box. On the walls are cartoons and Walt Disney's signature and a Wanted poster of *Carry On* star Sid James as the Rumpo Kid, across which the actor has scrawled 'Jeremy, Get that O Level or I'll Get You'.

'There is a clichéd view of the producer as a fairly vulgar, bombastic, aggressive person which, in a sense, you have to be to get things done,' he says. 'But if you deal with your problems in a sort of cultured manner it makes things easier.' If, as a producer, he has an individual style, he sees it residing in two qualities: independence and internationalism. Most British attempts at 'international' productions manage to hit only the tip of the iceberg before sinking somewhere mid-Atlantic (think *Revolution* or, further back, *Honky Tonk Freeway*). Instead, Thomas is a producer without a country, financing his films with money from backers scattered throughout the world. *Little Buddha* was financed entirely by the French, while all the money for *Crash* came from a Canadian company, Alliance Atlantis. It is hard to define the nationality of a finished film, he says, whether it is from the country of where the money came from, from where the production company has its offices or from where the story is set. But for Thomas these distinctions are meaningless – it is all world cinema. Thomas is aware that his natural home as a producer would be France, which has a rich film-making culture. In Britain, he says, cinema is still very much a seaside fairground attraction.

On the other hand, he has no desire to base himself in the United States as his contemporary David Puttnam did. He prefers to be a significant force in a smaller place he understands rather than be relatively unknown in the States, because the meritocracy in America is money. It does not matter what you have done or the sort of person you are – money is arbiter of all. At a pinch, somebody can be a financial failure but still be admired in Britain, which is not the case in America (although this is changing. Sometimes it seems as if America is a glimpse of our own future).

A running theme throughout Thomas's work has been a director from one culture giving his view of another. For example, Italian director Bernardo Bertolucci and his Eastern Trilogy or Japanese director Takeshi Kitano's dismissive take on America in *Brother* (2000). The problem with this approach is that you can end up with a cock-eyed film that leaves audiences cold. Most of Thomas's films involve unexpected violence, unusual sex, uncensored thoughts and strange dreams. He works on a different ideology from other producers, specifically working to his own taste and not working for the market. Most British producers, he thinks, are too genre-bound, recycling romantic comedies and comedy gangster films. Audiences have to follow Thomas, rather than the other way round.

There is a definite link in my taste. When a bullet hits a body it makes a hole. It has an impact. My taste has kept me in business. I don't keep remaking the same film but they are all a little bit left of centre. They are films that want to be popular but they're not mainstream. This allows me to tap into a market that is not served by the Hollywood studios. I take cinema very seriously, and although it is easier to make an exploitation film – and easier to sell – I think it is more satisfying to make something which people can take seriously and talk about.

Thomas has described cinema as the perfect meeting place of business and pleasure. 'I never want to leave this game,' he says, leaning forward. 'In fact the film business should be called the film game, because that's what it is – a great game.'

5   Marin Karmitz

The revolutionary

One of Marin Karmitz's earliest memories is having a gun held to his head. He was four years old. Having a pistol pressed against his temple was probably the defining moment of his life. The nightmare always stays with him. Even now, anything that triggers the memory or evokes the situation makes him feel incredibly violent. Anything that seems like blackmail or a threat or a feeling of being forced enrages him. Karmitz's father owned a large chemical manufacturing plant in Romania during the Second World War. Local fascists decided that the chemical manufacturer had supplied the vitriol used to murder Horia Sima, their leader. One evening, Iron Guards arrived with a lorry full of vitriol kegs planning to revenge Sima's death by dissolving Karmitz's father in acid. Luckily he had been warned and managed to escape with his brother and their chauffeur. But in his hurry to get out he left behind four-year-old Marin, his cousin and their mothers in the house. The top floor of the building had been rented to an attaché of the British embassy, and the Karmitz women and children sought refuge in the flat in an attempt to benefit from diplomatic immunity. The Iron Guards wanted to know where Karmitz's father was, and one of them put a gun to little Marin's head to force his mother to tell the truth. But the fascists panicked and fled when they heard the Romanian army outside in the street. Staff from the British embassy then arrived to rescue their attaché. Now the Karmitz women and children were left alone without diplomatic protection. Eventually the chauffeur came back and rescued them – but only after having been tortured by the fascists. He had kept his mouth shut.

Walking through the peach-coloured, high-windowed courtyard in Paris's 12th District where Karmitz has his office, it is easy to see why rival producers call him the Napoleon of French cinema. MK2, his film company, is a huge business spanning production, distribution, exhibition and sales of DVDs and videos. Its headquarters near the Gare de Lyon employs 150 people. MK2 also operates nine cinemas in Paris with a total of forty-four screens, some of which even have smart, bustling restaurants attached with a wine list drawn up by director Claude Chabrol. This makes it the third-largest cinema circuit in the city. MK2 is what is known in the film business as a vertically integrated company, encompassing production, distribution and selling of its catalogue. The seven Hollywood majors also follow the same model. In 2001 his films attracted three and a half million admissions, making MK2 the fifteenth most popular distributor in France. Of course, Karmitz has become rich in the process. *Challenges* magazine calculated his wealth at £45 million. In person he is a grave, urbane man who thinks before he speaks. He is beautifully dressed with clipped, steel-grey hair and rimless glasses. Like most film companies his office wall is covered with posters of films he has produced. But alongside them are sculptures and photographs of the modern French school up to the 1960s. Collecting art is one of his passions, clothes another. Simon Perry, former head of the European Co-production Fund and an old hand on the European film scene, describes him as a 'fantastically shrewd and clever businessman'. But more importantly, Karmitz has maintained a juggling act which probably could only happen in France. It would be naive to think that he has built an empire without treading on other people's toes. But unlike most Hollywood producers, who are just in the business of feeding the popcorn penitentiaries, Karmitz's films are actually *about* something. Karmitz himself argues that he may have become a capitalist, but his films remain linked to the attack on capitalism.

As a creative producer Karmitz is something of an exception in France. Since France was the home of auteur theory in the 1960s, producers there have often been relegated to the role of hand-maiden to auteur director. Philippe Carcassonne is the regular producer of Patrice Leconte (*L'Homme du Train*), for example. Christophe Rossignon and his partner Bertrand Faivre are the producers of Asif Kapadia (*The Warrior*). Elsewhere in Europe, producers have also been servants of master directors – in Italy Elda Perry produces films by comedian Roberto Benigni, while in Germany Uli Felsberg is the regular producer of auteur Wim Wenders.

Karmitz was born to a Jewish family in Bucharest, Romania in 1938. His family fled the country in a boat in 1947 when he was eight. Leaving behind everything they knew in Romania to become refugees must have been terrifying. After all, people can stand most things except uncertainty. The Karmitzes were rejected at the first two ports they sailed to, Beirut and Naples, but they were accepted into France at Marseilles. Ever since then Karmitz has had a love of France. When he was young he wanted to become an ambassador because it would give him a diplomatic passport and allow him to cross borders. He learnt to speak French in Nice and eventually he got a place at law school but dropped out after three months. He then enrolled at the Institute des Hautes Etudes Cinematographiques (IDHEC) cinema school in Paris as a camera operator, graduating when he was nineteen. He worked as an assistant director to a number of film-makers including Jean-Luc Godard on *Les sept péchés capitaux* (*Seven Capital Sins*, 1962), Jean Dewever on *Honneurs de la guerre* (*The Honours of War*, 1960), Jacques Rozier on *Adieu Philippine* (*Goodbye Philippine*, 1963) and Agnès Varda on *Cléo de 5 à 7* (*Cleo from 5 to 7*, 1962). Then he got a job as a photographer for the left-wing Libération press agency, but resigned after somebody was killed by an angry mob during a strike at a car plant. Karmitz felt that his colleagues in the press had fuelled the tension that led to the murder.

Left-wing politics and cinema – the two passions which have shaped Karmitz's life – were now becoming intertwined. Another producer had refused the subject matter of Karmitz's first outing as a film-maker, a short film about an umbrella being passed from hand to hand. (Accepting other people's hand-me-downs has been something of a pattern in Karmitz's career, as we will see.) The short was sold to the Gaumont Film Company and released around the world. The proceeds enabled him to pay back money owed to his father and set up a production company, MK Productions, in 1964. Over the next two years Karmitz produced twenty-five short films, which coincidentally won twenty-five prizes and an Academy Award nomination. He made enough money to allow him to direct two shorts of his own – *Nuit Noire, Calcutta*, which novelist Marguerite Duras wrote for him, and *Comédie* by playwright Samuel Beckett, who was also a friend. Karmitz's largely autobiographical first feature, *Sept jours ailleurs*, was chosen to open the 1968 Venice Film Festival. But Karmitz boycotted the festival in a show of left-wing solidarity with Italian director Pier Paolo Pasolini, and the opening film was not screened. Fellow French director Claude Lelouch decided to distribute *Sept jours ailleurs* in France, but it was only shown on a handful of screens, just enough for the critics to hail it as a triumph. Karmitz says that this vote of confidence by Lelouch was a turning point for him. Part of the reason for his support of directors is because he knows how valuable this kind of help is. It is just the kind of help he needed when he was starting out as a film-maker.

In May 1968 ten million French workers went on strike for a month. Students joined forces with militant workers and marched in Paris. Police broke up demonstrations on the orders of de Gaulle's right-wing government (although playwright Jean Genet noted that the students' endless theorising diluted any threat of revolution; in the end they were more interested in talk than action). The national strike was another turning point for Karmitz. He joined a banned Maoist political cell called The Proletarian Left. In his own words, he decided to become a militant connected to the cinema, putting his technical skills at the service of the working class. He was no longer a film-maker, he declared, but a tool to be used by the proletariat. Karmitz spent most of 1969 talking to young workers in factories in the industrial suburbs around Paris. Some of the workers, interested in the idea of a film being made about their working conditions, offered to collaborate on a screenplay. About fifty pages of script were then submitted to different groups of militant workers for deliberation. Karmitz was invited to meetings with workers and trade union representatives. Until now he had stammered as soon as there were more than four people in the room. But addressing workers' meetings gave him the confidence to speak in public. The finished film, *Comrades*, was premiered during the 1970 Critics' Week section of the Cannes Film Festival, and was later shown at the New York Film Festival. But Karmitz was not satisfied with the film. As a bourgeois intellectual he had failed in making a truly revolutionary film. Becoming a proletarian intellectual was a very long process, he explained to left-wing US film magazine *Cinéaste* in 1970. (This was a dizzying I-can-be-more-radical-than-you interview. The interviewer, in awe of Karmitz's uncompromising Maoist line, said that the problem with the American radical left was that it was a movement without anybody actually working class in it. It is the most bourgeois radical movement in the history of radical movements, he wailed.)

Karmitz's next film, *Coup pour coup* (*Blow by Blow*, 1971) was a fictional account of a group of female workers taking over a textile factory. The film was based on a number of factory takeovers in recent years in which women had been particularly active. Karmitz says he made the film for three reasons. First, women were doubly exploited at work and in the home. Second, women had struggled hardest since 'les évènements' of May 1968. Third, working-class women were never allowed to voice their aggravation, only working-class men. One of the themes of Karmitz's career has been giving a voice to people whose views are never heard in the media. He made a conscious decision not to behave like a 'bourgeois journalist' who only goes to a strike for a couple of days, talks to people and then reports back. He decided to immerse himself fully in the struggle for one year. Interestingly, the first cut of the film was full of arty editing – or 'elliptical montage' as it was called in the avant-garde press – but the women rejected it. Karmitz concluded that experimentation with form was very much a middle-class thing. *Le Monde* called *Coup pour coup* 'a new direction for French cinema'. It made such an impact that factory owners campaigned to have it banned. Unlike most artists, who, according to Karmitz, depend on nothing except themselves to communicate their subjective feelings about reality to an audience, Karmitz wanted to give a voice to people unable to speak. He considered what he himself had to say to be of little importance.

However, Karmitz was unable to find a distributor outside Paris for the film. This experience, and others, convinced him of the need to wrest distribution out of the hands of the big cinema chains. Their stranglehold on distribution was forcing producers to make entertainment rather than films of substance. His guiding principle has always been to 'work against the system while working within it', but setting up his own distribution company lay in the future.

By 1972 Karmitz had been ostracised by the insular French film community and was nearly destitute. He claims that he was under surveillance by the French interior ministry, and was stopped from travelling to America to take part in a demonstration. (People including his wife – a psychoanalyst – have accused him of being paranoid. Others have called him an intellectual terrorist.) He could not get a job as an assistant director – the person in charge of the day-to-day running of the set – or even as a director of commercials. Instead, he decided to make use of his experience of self-distributing *Coup pour coup*. He hired a one-screen cinema in the Latin Quarter for a year and showed films that he wanted to see. The venture was a success. In 1974, armed with a 500,000 franc ($90,000) bank loan – and against the advice of friends – Karmitz bought a restaurant in the then working-class Bastille area and converted it into the first MK2 cinema. Karmitz decided to name his company MK2 because the original MK Productions existed to produce short films. The company name was also a sly reference to one of Karmitz's other passions, the Jaguar Mk 2 sports car. The only other cinemas in the area showed either cheap martial arts films or porno movies. At the time, people thought he was mad to show only foreign-language films with subtitles. There were just two other cinemas in Paris showing subtitled films: one in the busy Champs-Elysées district and the other in the student Latin Quarter. Karmitz says that from the beginning of his career he has always been told that what he wants is impossible, but he has never been able to accept this word when it comes to cinema.

The three-screen 14 Juillet Bastille opened in 1974. In addition to three screens all showing 'difficult' films it also had a library and an exhibition space used for staging events. The second MK2 cinema opened two years later. Both showed the work of directors such as Godard, Wim Wenders and the Taviani brothers who had no other outlets for their films. Another innovation was introducing discounted cinema tickets for local residents. In 1996 Karmitz again defied the odds when he opened a multiplex in the 20th District, a run-down area notorious for street crime and drug dealing. Over the years all the other cinemas in the area had closed down. Almost a decade on, the Quai de Seine multiplex welcomes more than fifty thousand cinema-goers a year. Karmitz recently bought another building across the street, which will double the Quai de Seine's six screens. All of Karmitz's multiplexes show at least 80 per cent of their films in their original language. Another fourteen-screen multiplex, this time in the working-class 13th District, was due to open at the end of 2002. Subsequent cinemas have had restaurants attached, including one which had its wine list drawn up by director Claude Chabrol.

But it was not all clear blue skies. France has the most resilient culture in the world when it comes to standing up to Hollywood. This is fed partly by the French government's insistence that television companies and cinema owners recycle some of their turnover into domestic film production, and partly by the fact that, at the time of writing, films are banned from being advertised on television. Instead, French distributors advertise side by side with the US majors on the metro and billboards, maintaining a level playing field. But the truth is that most people prefer to watch American films. Commentators who predicted that the Disneyland theme park outside Paris would become America's 'cultural Vietnam' were proved wrong. By 1981 Karmitz was on the verge of selling the MK2 cinema chain. Turnover was down 30 per cent year-on-year as audiences went to rival cinemas to watch Hollywood imports. Furthermore, some MK2 cinemas had been ransacked several times by factions unhappy at the films being shown. Karmitz started talks with the UGC cinema chain and rival exhibitor Publicis about selling MK2. But something did not smell right and he decided not to sell. Later he found out that Publicis had cooked up a side deal so that UGC would buy the cinemas anyway from Publicis if its rival bought the MK2 chain. In the end Karmitz sat tight and rode out the difficult times. Since then there has been somewhat of a revival in popular mainstream French cinema from the mid-1980s with films such as *37.2 le matin* (*Betty Blue*, 1986) through to *Nikita* (1990) and *Le Fabuleux destin d'Amélie Poulain* (2001). There has also been an artistic resurgence with films pushing censorship boundaries of what is allowed to be shown on screen such as *Romance* (1998), *Baise-moi* (2000) and *Irreversible* (2002).

Karl Marx wrote that the means of production must be put in the hands of the workers. In addition to distributing other people's films, Karmitz decided to move into production. But when he started out he was, in his own words, 'the rubbish bin of French cinema'. Directors only came to him after other producers had refused them. This was how he came to be involved with two of his most famous films: *Au revoir les enfants* (*Goodbye Children*, 1987), Louis Malle's autobiographical account of Nazi-occupied France, and *La Vie est un long fleuve tranquille* (*Life is a Long Quiet River*, 1988), directed by Étienne Chatiliez. To date Karmitz has produced more than sixty films, many of which have won prizes at the Cannes Film Festival. Directors he has regularly worked with include Claude Chabrol, British director Ken Loach, the Taviani brothers from Italy and Iranian director Abbas Kiarostami. In recent times he has been sent on average more than a thousand screenplays a year from all over the world. He produces at most six films a year, which he sometimes has trouble finding – and even more difficulty getting made. He enjoys a reputation as a producer who does not overly meddle with things. However, Chabrol was angry when Karmitz halved his budget for *Poulet au vinaigre* (*Cop au Vin*, 1985). But at least, Chabrol said, Karmitz was professional enough not to meddle on set; he prepares in advance and leaves his directors alone. Karmitz pointed out that the price of this freedom is to keep budgets as low as possible. The more freedom a director needs then the cheaper the budget must be. 'There's a saying in France that you cannot have the butter and the money for the butter,' Karmitz told me.

But perhaps Karmitz's most enduring achievement as a producer, both artistically and in terms of problems solved, was making three films back to back with Polish director Krzysztof Kieslowski. The *Three Colours* trilogy has been ranked by some critics alongside *Citizen Kane* and *2001: A Space Odyssey* – two of the most important films ever made. *Sight and Sound* magazine recently proposed *Three Colours: Blue* as the most significant film of the last twenty or so years. Karmitz had wanted to meet Kieslowski for a long time after seeing *A Short Film About Killing* (1988), an indictment of capital punishment which was one episode in *Dekalog* (*The Ten Commandments*), ten films for Polish television illustrating the Ten Commandments. One day, Kieslowski's agent Nicole Kahn rang to set up a meeting between the two men. Kieslowski was in Paris for a conference of European writers and directors. Looking back on that first meeting, Karmitz remembered a Hasidic saying that every meeting should be miraculous. Isn't any miracle something that is longed for hard enough? wondered Karmitz. Kieslowski told Karmitz that he admired *Au revoir les enfants*. They then spent the next two or three hours discussing morality and ethics, and what they had in common despite being a Jew and a Christian. The conversation went to the heart of everything Karmitz had been thinking about for the past ten years. Film-making was never mentioned. But as the meeting was winding up Kieslowski said that he had an idea for a trilogy based on the French ideal of liberty, equality and fraternity. These three words, he said, express the essentials of life in much the same way as the Ten Commandments do. The subject touched a nerve in Karmitz because as a Romanian immigrant he had been a Jew saved by France. By the end of the afternoon Karmitz had committed himself to raising 120 million francs, and the next four years to producing the trilogy.

Kieslowski submitted a twenty-page treatment of *Three Colours: Blue* to Karmitz after a screening of his most recent film, *The Double Life of Véronique*, at Cannes. There was still no contract between them. Karmitz thought the treatment was sublime, although he did not say yes right away. He wanted to see what would come next in the treatments for *White* and *Red*. Karmitz then went through each of the treatments with Kieslowski, making suggestions before they considered the production as a whole. It was clear to Karmitz that there was continuity between the three films. The question was, should they film all three at the same time? Karmitz could not see how to separate them. The Polish director then went back to his scriptwriting partner, Polish lawyer Krzysztof Piesiewicz, and worked up each treatment into a 110-page screenplay. All three men then sat down and set about refining and tightening the screenplays, or solving some of the problems. Karmitz saw the script stage as being the area where he could contribute the most. Kieslowski was not familiar with France and could not speak French. The script, written from the perspective of a Pole, was full of things which seemed novel to a Pole about France, but would strike a Frenchman as commonplace. In particular Karmitz helped Kieslowski weed out the secondary characters so that he could concentrate on the main story. Karmitz said that he had not worked on the script for six months without being able to see the dross. Kieslowski wanted to involve Karmitz right from the beginning, pruning the screenplay to get to the essential part, so that understanding became both universal and unambiguous.

The producer's first test was to help pick the crew for all three films, suggesting people who would gel with each other. In the end the crew was made up of technicians from France, Poland and Switzerland, and five languages were spoken during filming. Karmitz also felt it was important to structure all three films as official co-productions between France, Poland and Switzerland – partly to tap national subsidies for film-making. France's Centre National de la Cinematographie put money into *Blue* while the Swiss government invested in *Red*. Poland's contribution came through its subscription to the Council of Europe-administered film fund Eurimages, which encourages co-productions and invested almost 10 million francs in all three films.

Juliette Binoche agreed to star in the first film, *Blue*, turning down the female lead in *Jurassic Park* to play the role. According to Binoche, Kieslowski's films are the truest to everyday life you can get, although they are stylised. The style, however, comes from within, rather than being placed on top. Kieslowski makes one questionable addition to film grammar in *Blue*. He fades to black whenever there is an emotional turning point. Often the camera will rest on Binoche, the screen will go black and the music swells. *Variety* noted that Kieslowski put his faith in his leading lady's face 'as few directors have done since the silent era'.

Blue is the story of a young widow, Julie, who tries to leave behind everything which gave her life meaning in the past – love, possessions, feelings for other people. It is about how far individuals are able to detach themselves from family, memory and material objects, the very things which define most lives. The first image is of the defective car axle that kills her husband and small daughter (all three films begin with images of technology, showing how dependent we have become on machines). Julie wakes up in hospital having survived the car crash. Realising what has happened, she tries to kill herself. But she botches her suicide attempt, and instead watches the funeral of her husband and daughter on television. Her husband, a famous composer, was working on a concerto celebrating the European Union when he was killed. Still recuperating, Julie is visited by a journalist who wants to know whether it is true that Julie herself wrote most of her husband's music (Kieslowski is taking a dig at the whole cult of auteur here). Returning home to her country house, Julie sets about destroying everything in her past. She burns her husband's music and gives instructions for all her possessions to be sold. She even sleeps with her husband's friend in order to obliterate his memory. But unlike her hysterical staff, she cannot feel any emotion. The key to Binoche's cold portrayal of Julie was a passage she came across in a book by French writer Anny Duperey: 'I suffered enough inside without having to show it as well.' In one painful scene, which was not faked, Julie drags her knuckles along a stone wall in an attempt to feel *something*. She moves to a flat in Paris, but the past comes to find her. It turns out that her husband was having an affair with a lawyer, who is now pregnant.

Eventually Julie comes in from the cold. She decides to complete her husband's concerto for the European Union, and tells her husband's mistress that she can live in the country house. She even revives her relationship with her irritating lover, who, as Geoffrey Macnab in *Sight and Sound* pointed out, has been pursuing her around Paris like a droopy St Bernard. In a way, said Kieslowski, love is contradictory with freedom. One longs for freedom but if one loves, one stops being free. If somebody is in love and is loved, said the director, it affects them in every possible way. All the senses react differently, because one has the desire to look through the eyes of the person one loves. In the final glorious moments, Kieslowski reconstructs a montage of Julie's life. We see the man who loves her, her senile mother who barely knows her, the hooker neighbour who has reawakened Julie's sexuality. On an ultrasound we see her husband's unborn child and on the soundtrack we hear, for the first time, the concerto he was working on when he died. It is set to St Paul's First Epistle to the Corinthians (1, 13): 'If I speak in the tongues of men and of angels, but have not love, I am a noisy gong or a clanging cymbal. And though I have phrophetic powers, and understand all mysteries and all knowledge . . . but have not love I am nothing . . . Love is patient and kind; love is not jealous or boastful: is is not arrogant or rude . . . Love never ends; as for prophecy, it will pass away; and as for tongues, they will cease; as for knowledge, it will pass away . . . So faith, hope, love abide, these three; but the greatest of these is love.'

Blue began filming at a hospital forty miles outside Paris. Shooting was scheduled to last for two days. But Kieslowski, who was used to filming in Poland all day long without a break, was enraged by French technicians wanting an hour off for lunch. In Poland there was also no concept of overtime: you stayed until the job was done, for no extra pay. On the second day Kieslowski pushed his team round the clock, filming for twenty-four hours straight. Yvon Crenn, the production manager, telephoned Karmitz and said that he had used up his entire overtime allocation in one day. Crenn complained that at this rate, the crew would die of exhaustion before they reached the end of shooting. Karmitz saw his job as producer as knowing when to intervene. He called Kieslowski's agent, Nicole Kahn, and said he wanted a meeting later that afternoon after the director had some sleep. When Kieslowski and

Kahn arrived, Karmitz told the director that, having worked for twenty-four hours straight, he had not arranged for any cars to pick up the crew. They could, of course, drive their own cars. However, he was not prepared to accept the responsibility in case there was a serious accident. Would Kieslowski therefore accept the responsibility instead? From then on the crew worked normal hours. Not for nothing did Karmitz consider a career in diplomacy.

One thing that struck Karmitz about Kieslowski was his working method. His background as a documentary film-maker meant that he worked fast. Everything was done in two or three takes with a small crew. He was also prepared to improvise. At the same time, Kieslowski would make time to think about what he was doing. Karmitz thought this kind of duality was rare among film-makers.

Blue premiered at the Venice Film Festival in 1993 and went on to win twenty-five awards. Fellow director Angela Pope put her finger on why Kieslowski is such a good director. His films, she said, have a kind of secular religiosity. It is as if Kieslowski is talking directly to you. The characters may not be remotely like you, and their everyday dilemmas are not yours, but, in some way, you are at one with them. But film magazine *Empire* dismissed *Blue*, saying that 'to call it cryptic would be to flatter it with the proposition that it makes some sort of skewed sense'.

White started filming in Paris on 9 November 1992. Karmitz puts in a cameo at the beginning as a man leaving the law courts on the Ile de la Cité. The film stars Polish comedian Zbigniew Zamachowski as Karol Karol, which literally translates as Charlie Charlie in homage to Chaplin. Karol is a Polish hairdressser on his way to court to be divorced. We first see him walking up a flight of steps. He spots a flock of pigeons wheeling in the sky and puts on a brave little face. Could this be a sign? Of freedom perhaps? At which point one of the pigeons shits on him. Indeed, Karol is dumped on from a great height throughout most of the film. His French wife, Dominique (Julie Delpy), is an utter bitch who tells the court that their marriage was never consummated – a fact confirmed by Karol. He is apparently so in awe of his wife that he has become impotent. Things have become that out of balance. (Kieslowski gave an unconvincing explanation for Dominique's anger, saying that it stemmed from her inadequacy.) By the end of the divorce proceedings Karol has lost everything – his wife, all his money, and the beauty parlour they ran together bought by his savings. In an ultimate act of cruelty Dominique makes Karol listen on the other end of a phone while another man ravishes her. Penniless, without his passport and on the run from police – Dominique has framed her ex-husband for an arson attack on their salon – Karol is reduced to busking in the metro. However, Mikolaj, a fellow Pole, recognises the sad tune that Karol is playing on a paper comb and smuggles him back to Poland in a suitcase. But baggage handlers steal the suitcase when the plane arrives in Warsaw. Instead of loot they find Karol, beat him up and leave him for dead. 'Home at last,' sighs the hairdresser when he opens one bloody eye in a snowy wasteland.

Karol has now been stripped of all his illusions. The veil has been torn. He has seen the war of everything against everything. Love may be delicious, especially in its early stages – 'At last, I am not alone,' the lover thinks – but ultimately everybody is by themselves. Religion is just a fairy tale – thumb-sucking for children. The only thing that counts is money – the getting of it and wondering why there is never enough. There is a Polish proverb, appropriated by George Orwell in *Animal Farm*, which says that everybody is equal but some are more equal than others. Karol is determined to become more than equal to everybody else. He falls in with a gang of black marketeers and, after a Chaplinesque stint as a bodyguard, outsmarts them on a property deal. Within one year, he has become a wealthy entrepreneur importing fax machines. But Karol can only achieve equality by turning the tables completely. He decides to fake his own death and tempt Dominique back to Poland with the promise of some money in his will. She will then be framed for his murder and thrown into jail. But watching his own funeral through binoculars he witnesses an unexpected thing. Karol is astonished to see Dominique crying over his grave. Could it be that she still loves him? Coming back to her hotel room, Dominique is somewhat surprised to see Karol sitting up in bed looking pleased as punch. Eventually they make love and Karol's impotency has vanished. Equality has been restored. (The colour white – the colour of the unconsummated marriage – is used ironically throughout the film. The first white we see is when a pigeon shits on Karol. When Dominique finally has an orgasm with Karol, the screen whites out with her screams of pleasure.) But the fake murder plot is still in place. Dominique is arrested for Karol's murder the next morning after the entrepreneur has vanished.

Shooting finished in February 1993, but Kieslowski came back to Karmitz asking for more shooting time. The director had an idea for another scene with which to end the film. Karol will visit the Warsaw prison where Dominique is being held. He looks up at her cell window from the prison courtyard. Dominique sees him and, through the bars of her cell, mimes that she still loves him and wants to remarry him. The final image is of Karol with tears streaming down his face. Karmitz agreed that this final sentimental touch – rare for Kieslowski – would give Dominique warmth and humanity.

White is a sublime comedy with a brilliant performance by Zamachowski. He plays Karol Karol with the deadpan expression of a Buster Keaton or Droopy the cartoon dog. Hollywood missed a trick by not signing him up (CUT TO: an executive in Burbank, California, barking into a phone: 'Get me Zbigniev Tchaikovsky ... I mean Zbigniew Zazachomsky ... Spiggy Zamachowska? ... Oh, the hell with it'). *Empire* described *White* as 'the most playful and accessible of Kieslowki's films to date'. Roger Ebert, writing in the *Chicago Sun-Times*, said that it was as if European films had a more adult, inward, knowing way of dealing with the emotions, and that Hollywood had not grown up enough. *Premiere* said that Kieslowski was among the most paradoxical of film-makers, having spirituality without having God. But not all the reviews were good. The *Daily Mail* described *White* as boringly acted and lazily directed, while rival tabloid *Today* said that none of it made sense or was remotely funny. Writing in the *Evening Standard*, Alexander Walker wondered if the grand design to shoot three interlocking films was a financial stratagem to ease the problems of raising the cash rather than any mere intellectual conceit. Talking about *White*, Kieslowski said that equality is impossible because it is contradictory to human nature – hence the failure of Communism. That said, Kieslowski maintained that every effort must be made to bring equality about, bearing in mind it will never be achieved.

Karmitz compared the 53-year-old director's stamina in making three films back to back to asking a top footballer to play three World Cup tournaments without a break over a nine-month period: the amount of energy he put into the trilogy was colossal, he said. Each film had a shooting schedule of forty-five days. There were breaks between filming so that Kieslowski could rest. Editing *Blue* began at the same time as filming started, with editor Jacques Witta putting scenes in the order they occurred during the story. Witta continued editing *Blue* after *White* had started filming; he then showed Kieslowski a rough cut of *Blue* in Poland. When he had finished shooting *White*, Kieslowski concentrated on refining *Blue* –

and so the process continued. However, Urszula Lesiak, Witta's assistant editor on *The Double Life of Véronique*, edited *White*, leaving Witta to concentrate on *Red*. The same Paris editing suite was used for all three films. Kieslowski also used the same core team – Karmitz, cameraman Slawomir Idziak and Emmanuel Finkiel, Kieslowski's assistant – as a sounding board during numerous screenings of each film in the trilogy. Doubtless because of his education at Lodz Film School, he would then canvas their opinion. For example, there were fifteen different versions of *Blue*. Of all the directors Karmitz has worked with, Kieslowski was the least precious. He would carry a notebook around with him and scribble down what others said about the work in progress. All of Karmitz's views went into the notebook. Either Kieslowski said no immediately, or he would come back with an explanation as to why he wanted to do something the way he did. But the important thing, says Karmitz, was that he listened to other people.

It was decided in advance that each of the three films would be an hour and a half long. The problem was cutting each film down to the right length. Karmitz brought his outsider's point of view to the editing process, picking out places where each film could be shorn. He always kept Giacometti's work in mind, whose spittle-thin figures said a great deal. For Karmitz, it is the way in which a great artist reduces things which defines their work as superior.

Red, the brotherhood panel of the triptych, is Karmitz's favourite film of the trilogy. The theme of the film was inspired by a poem written by Polish poet Wislawa Szymborska: 'But every beginning is only a continuation as the book of fate is always open in the middle.' *Red* is the story of Valentine (Irene Jacob), who is a model girl both figuratively and literally. When she is not sashaying down the catwalk she is the sort of person who helps old ladies deposit bottles into bottle banks (a recurring scene in each film and something which the other lead characters conspicuously fail to do). In short, Valentine – Kieslowski can be heavy-handed when it comes to symbolism – is a model girl with a model heart.

Red begins with the camera snaking at high speed along cables before plunging into the innards of a telephone network, zipping through wires and dipping under Lake Geneva only to reach a busy signal. Kieslowski, parodying the title of his earlier film *A Short Film about Killing*, summed up *Red* as 'a short film about the telephone'. It is about crossed lines and crossed lives – interconnectedness in an apparently haphazard world. The busy signal comes from Valentine's flat in Geneva. Her boyfriend in England tries her again and gets through this time. While Valentine is chatting on the phone we see the young man who lives next door going out for some cigarettes. They are, as yet, unaware of each other. That night Valentine drives home after her dance class – again passing her next-door neighbour – when her car thumps something. She has hit a stray dog, which she takes to the hospital. The next day she takes the dog back to the address on its collar, a creepy-looking house in a Geneva suburb. Pushing the door open she walks into the gloomy, red-tinged parlour. The only sound is the eerie pop and whistle of radio static. An old man, played by Jean-Louis Trintignant, is sitting listening to a neighbour's telephone conversation. The husband next door is pleading with his male lover on the phone. Valentine is appalled by this intrusion into other people's privacy. Who is the old man and where did he learn how to tap phone lines? 'What were you? A cop?' she asks, picking the highest profession she can think of against which to measure his fall. 'Worse,' replies the old man. 'A judge.' Worse because, according to Kieslowski, the worst sin is to pass judgement on other people. The director told the *Sunday Times* that he did not want to judge his characters because that would be an immodest thing to do; we can never see the causes of an event, merely the results. 'Deciding what it true and what is not,' the judge tells Valentine of his decision to retire, 'seemed to me a lack of . . . modesty.' Like the jurist in Albert Camus' novel *La Chute* (*The Fall*, 1964) the judge has come to realise that judging people is futile and vain. Valentine decides to go round to the neighbour and tell him what has been going on. But when she gets to the house she sees the teenage daughter listening to her father on an extension. From the knowing look on her face it is clear she understands everything. The next day Valentine goes back to see the judge and so their friendship begins.

At this point most French films would develop into a love affair between the judge and Valentine. Indeed, there is a distressing theme in French cinema of love affairs between older men and young girls – with the men getting older and the girls younger with each film, perhaps reflecting the desires of the middle-aged men behind the camera. But Kieslowski avoids the cliché and is therefore truer to life. The judge knows he is too old for Valentine and instead engineers a meeting between her and the young man who lives next door. The young man is a lawyer and a younger version of himself. The judge buys Valentine a ferry ticket to go and see her boyfriend in England, knowing the lawyer will also be on the ship. But the ferry sinks during a storm in the Channel. Watching television the judge sees the lawyer helping Valentine into a rescue boat. Also being helped onto the boat are the leading characters from the other two films – Karol and Dominique, Julie and her hangdog lover. In a neat twist Kieslowski has tied up all three films and handed the bouquet to the audience.

Red started shooting in Switzerland on 1 March 1993. One logistical problem was that the woman who lived in the flat the film-makers wanted to use for Valentine's apartment in Geneva insisted on being put up at the Hotel de Beys, the most expensive hotel in the city. Not only that, but Karmitz would have to pay all her expenses – bar, restaurant, minibar and telephone. The producer had no option but to cave in. Karmitz says he won Kieslowski's respect on the first day of filming. The first scene to be shot was the last scene of Juliette Binoche, Julie Delpy and the others on the rescue boat. Karmitz noticed that the boat was not moving and he started rocking it up and down to simulate buoyancy. Kieslowski saw what he was doing, and told some of his crew to take over.

Irene Jacob described filming *Red* as an 'overwhelming experience'. Kieslowski, she said, could seem quite brusque. *Red*, according to Jacob, is a dialogue between disappointed experience and a time when everything seems possible in one's life. Kieslowski sympathised with both points of view. Editor Jacques Witta said Kieslowski would get misty-eyed watching *Red*, which was partly a reflection on old age. With *Red*, said Witta, Kieslowski achieved most of what he had set out to do. His feeling of a job well done was one of the reasons the director announced at the Cannes Film Festival that it would be his last film.

For Karmitz one shot in particular showed how cinema could sometimes say more than painting, literature or even music. There is a moment when the camera moves away from Valentine having fun in a bowling alley and tracks along the Formica tables at the back of the hall to an empty lane. The camera rests on a smashed beer glass and a crushed packet of cigarettes – all one needs to know that an argument has just taken place between the young lawyer and his girlfriend. Any writer would need a long time to explain all that, but Kieslowski sums up a complex situation in one simple image.

Time Out called *Red*, somewhat predictably, a virtually flawless masterpiece and 'one of the very greatest cinematic achievements of the last few decades'. *Variety* agreed that *Red* was 'beautifully spun and splendidly acted'; Kieslowski was retiring at his peak. The *Sunday Times* gave the film possibly the highest praise, calling it simply 'a work of art'. Not everybody was impressed. The film's characters, wrote Christopher Tookey in the *Daily Mail*, inhabit 'that parallel universe called arthouse cinema, a world where people are randomly motivated to talk endlessly about philosophical questions to no effect, and so much is left unspoken and enigmatic that average filmgoers may find themselves thinking of Arnold Schwarzenegger with tears of gratitude'.[1]

Red premiered at the Cannes Film Festival in 1994 but the Palme d'Or for best film went to *Pulp Fiction*. Even *Pulp Fiction* director Quentin Tarantino admitted that *Red* was the better film. *Red* was not even nominated for the Césars, the French equivalent of the Oscars. As *Red* had been constructed as an official French/Polish/Swiss co-production with Tor Film of Poland and Cab Productions of Switzerland (allowing the trilogy to tap soft money in each country), Karmitz asked the Swiss to nominate it as their foreign language entry for the Academy Awards. But the Los Angeles-based Academy of Motion Picture Arts and Sciences refused its nomination on the grounds that *Red* was not a wholly Swiss film. Once again, Karmitz found himself without a country. However, American journalists and others petitioned the Academy to change its mind. In the end *Red* was nominated for best film, best director and best screenplay in the main awards, running somewhat incongruously beside *Apollo 13* and *Braveheart*. Karmitz and Kieslowski found themselves squeezed between Sylvester Stallone and Jodie Foster at the ceremony. However, armed with miniatures of whisky they had sneaked in, the two men kept nipping off to the fire exits to have a quick swig before taking their seats again. It was the only way to get through the ceremony, Karmitz said. The producer once remarked that although Kieslowski did not speak

French and he himself did not speak Polish, after a few glasses of whisky they understood each other perfectly.

To an extent the *Three Colours* trilogy is about colour – blue as the colour of memory, white as the colour of weddings and orgasms, and red the colour of blood and emergency services. On another level all three films are about alienation. *Blue* is about alienation from the past and one's memories; *White* is about the alienation between men and women; *Red* is about how communication keeps people apart. It could also be argued that the trilogy's themes of liberty, equality and fraternity ran through Karmitz's relationship with Kieslowski as well. Kieslowski needed Karmitz's money to give him the freedom to make the trilogy, while Karmitz needed the director's art. Their friendship was based on equality between their roles and equality between Eastern and Western Europe. Yvon Crenn, the trilogy's executive producer, partly attributed the success of the three films to the close relationship between the two men. They supported one another intellectually, said Crenn, which was the reason for the artistic triumph of the films. This was the first time he had seen such cooperation between a producer and his director, 'but then Marin is a producer who loves his directors, which is essential'.[2]

Although Kieslowski had announced at Cannes that *Red* was his last film and that he wanted to retire and read books, he started planning another trilogy dealing with heaven, hell and purgatory (*Heaven*, based on Kieslowski and Piesiewicz's script, was eventually filmed in 2001 by German director Tom Tykwer). Kieslowski died following a heart operation in March 1996 – the director was a chain-smoker with a big appetite for coffee, alcohol and food – and his death sent Karmitz into a terrible depression.

One of MK2's quirks is that it never uses big billboard campaigns to advertise films. Karmitz believes Parisians are pretty vigilant when it comes to watching out for new releases. If they don't like a film, it will die within a week or two regardless of the campaign. He dismisses those who say he is a better distributor than a creative producer. For Karmitz there is no point in making a good film and not marketing it well; distribution is part of what a producer does. This is why Karmitz prefers to be called an 'editeur et marchand des films' (publisher and dealer in films), the title of a 1985 retrospective of his work at the Cinématheque in Paris (there have also been retrospectives of Karmitz's career at the Museum of Modern Art in New York in 1989 and the Tel Aviv Cinématheque in 1992). He prefers this to the title 'producer', which makes him sound like a technician rather than an impresario.

Not surprisingly, Karmitz has strong views about what producers actually do. The producer's first job is to choose the script and the writer and then work on the screenplay to make it the best possible. He is also the first reader and the first critic of the screenplay. He is the person who helps the director to select actors, the crew and the look of the film. The producer deals with financial problems and is aware of the twin constraints of time and money. He is also in charge of relations with the outside world, during shooting and when the film comes out. His specific job is to carry the film along – before, during and after production – providing a unity for the entirety. Furthermore, and this is where Karmitz stands out, a producer should follow and look after the ways a film exists, both in the country in which it was made and internationally. In addition to being a publisher of films, he considers himself a 'film merchant' in much the same way that an art dealer is the intermediary between art lovers, journalists and the public. Not only does he ensure the film gets made but that it also finds an audience.

A producer must at the same time be a mediator and a supporter, never the enemy, of the director. Once Karmitz had to refuse a director's demands because the director was making them to cover up his inadequacy. But he has also supported directors who wanted to go over budget, provided what they wanted to do brought something to the film (the last sequence in *White*, for example). Above all, the producer must adapt to the director and serve him as a representative; the producer must not try to control him. Karmitz has had a lot of battles in his life but he cannot abide a confrontational relationship with a director. He wants to collaborate with the director as far as possible. Nevertheless, the producer's job is not to avoid conflicts but to resolve them when they arise. The director is the mother while the producer is the midwife – before, during and after the process – and also the paediatrician. The producer's job is to push the director to go as far as possible. 'When I was a director I would have loved to have somebody doing this work for me, but if I was directing I would hate anybody to interfere with my job,' Karmitz says. Younger French producers are now rejecting the cult of auteur, realising that films are made by at least two people. Some of them have started doing things 'the Anglo-Saxon way', buying the rights to a book and then looking for a screenwriter. 'But it's very timid and there is still a lot of resistance,' says Agnes Poirier, film critic of *Liberation*. 'There is a lot of hostility towards something that is considered alien and American.' The auteur myth also lingers on in Mediterranean countries, especially in Greece and Portugal, and the further one travels in Eastern Europe.

Sometimes Karmitz will be keen to work with a director but has to reject the script. Once the script has been approved he will go through it asking whether a particular scene is necessary in terms of its importance and its cost. One way to save money when making a film is to shorten the shooting time. He believes that films should never be any longer than 105 minutes, based on the accepted wisdom about the length of plays. Karmitz thinks this long-standing theatrical rule is probably based on people's biorhythms. Having films that are no longer than this also means cinemas can squeeze in five performances instead of four. In his view, films are becoming longer and longer for no apparent reason. Even popcorn movies are becoming loose baggy monsters – *Gladiator*, for example, was two and a half hours long, while *Minority Report*, based on a short story, clocked in at 145 minutes. Karmitz thinks film-makers are crazy to cut scenes already shot: they should have been cut in the script.

When it comes to choosing the crew Karmitz makes a point of asking each would-be crew member what specifically they will bring to the production in addition to their technical competence. This can lead to some interesting answers. During the shoot itself Karmitz does not do much, although he does look at the rushes every day. He makes a point of hosting three big dinners for everybody involved in the project, at the beginning, middle and end of the shoot. That said, given his film school background, he is proud that if things do go wrong he could step in as cameraman, sound engineer or editor. On Claude Chabrol's *Merci pour le chocolat* Karmitz became the film's costume designer, picking out outfits for Isabelle Huppert and replacing some of the background paintings on set. He even knows how to develop films in the processing laboratory. Karmitz is then the first person to see the finished film. By this point the director is too close to his work to be able to view it objectively any more. Karmitz's job is to bring a fresh perspective. 'The best directors accept my help; the worst ones don't.'

All of Karmitz's projects have one thing in common. France's television channels have rejected them for not being commercial enough. French broadcasters are obliged to recycle some of their turnover into domestic film production. Canal Plus, the pay-television broadcaster, invested nearly £90 million in national film production in 2000 – a quarter of all the money which went into French cinema. The company was involved in 80 per cent of films made. But Pierre

Lescure, its former chief executive, has said the channel must concentrate its money on fewer, bigger films. Karmitz feels that other producers are hamstrung by the demands of prime-time television, which they need cash from in order to get their films made. According to him, this dependence has led to a glut of bland, similar films. Mould-breaking 'nouvelle vague' films by Godard and Bresson would have a hard time getting made today because broadcasters do not want innovative work. 'The industrialisation of cinema and the globalisation of distribution have led to a uniformity of content,' says the producer. Creativity is no longer welcome. However, he has enough money to finance films himself, hold onto rights and build a library which can then be sold and resold – the ultimate objective in the film business (look how Warner Brothers continues to get paid for old cartoons made back in the 1940s). Karmitz produces what pleases and interests him rather than having to think about the market. For example, he decided to make a film with Iranian director Abbas Kiarostami – who in some ways has supplanted Kieslowski in his life – without even seeing a script, just trusting his instinct that the finished film would be good. He describes himself as one of the few producers left who can do exactly what he wants to, a claim shared by Dino De Laurentiis, his film-producing opposite.

According to Karmitz, two themes run through his work. The first: what is modern cinema? The second: defending the values that make people civilised in a language that is accessible and not academic. Throughout his career he has always rejected man's humiliation of man. Instead, his films have tried to show the need for generosity. What drives him is anger – anger at people who abuse their power, anger at censorship, anger at how the media is dominated by a handful of conglomerates. This anger goes back to his childhood, his being an immigrant and feeling excluded from society. Creative cinema can only exist, he argues, when it is opposed to the order of things. In this Karmitz most resembles fellow producer Christine Vachon, whose mainly homosexual-themed films are also against prejudice and commonplace ideas. For Karmitz, the failure of Communism has given way to blind consumerism, which is being fought by nobody and apppears to be unstoppable. What best defines his work is the desire to oppose: to go against accepted ideas, the merely fashionable and the poor accepting their situation.

He is dismissive of the commercialism of some young French directors, whose art he says is driven by their pressing financial needs, together with a desire to be loved by critics and the public. What surprises Karmitz is their ignorance of the history of cinema, literature and painting. They do not realise that what they are doing has, in most cases, already been done, and done better – with shorter plots, better-directed actors and more effective lighting provided by technicians with a better grasp of technique. Karmitz has denounced European film-makers who imitate Hollywood as collaborators, seduced by the lowest common denominator.

This does not mean that Karmitz is anti-American. On the contrary, he would love to work with directors such as Woody Allen or Martin Scorsese on the other side of the 'cellophane curtain'. But he knows he could never work in Hollywood, which is simply not his world (and it is not as if the studios are exactly knocking on his door, either). He believes the real difference between French and American cinema is creativity. There is a long-running argument in film circles as to whether cinema is a craft or an industry. Increasingly it seems as if Hollywood – which controls the global distribution pipelines – is only interested in remaking the same films over and over again (*Star Trek 10*, *Star Wars 5*, the third *Austin Powers*). Karmitz sees film-making as a craft like the haute couture fashion business, which each season designs a series of prototypes. (It could be argued that the nearest Europe has come to the industrial model is British producer Working

Title, which specialises in romantic comedies.) Karmitz is not interested in national films so much as films that aspire to be universal. Hollywood controls the world cinema business because its hands are on the levers of global distribution machinery. However, this is not enough to make universal cinema. For Karmitz, the universal is something which is human, something which 'elevates and transforms'. It is not a question of European cinema being opposed to American cinema but of defending the cinema of creation against the cinema of consumerism.

The universality of his films means that they sell well in other markets outside France. One recent success was *La Pianiste* (*The Pianist*, 2001) by Michael Haneke, which stars Isabelle Huppert (something of an in-house leading lady at MK2) as a repressed piano teacher in a love affair with a younger man. However, it is sometimes difficult to equate Karmitz's desire to make universal cinema with the films he actually produces. In *La Pianiste*, for example, Huppert's character, repressed to the point of insanity, urinates while watching teenagers making love at a movie drive-in, inhales greedily on used tissues in a pornographic cinema and asks her student lover to beat her while her mother listens.

Karmitz has strong views about what he calls Hollywood's cinema of propaganda against 'cinema of life'. He believes rival distributors filling up out-of-town multiplexes with dubbed American films are pursuing 'a policy of dumbing down based on special effects, gratuitous violence and contempt for law and order'. Clearly, he is not against violence per se but he is alarmed by violence for its own sake and he calls this the cinema of barbarians. This split between the multiplexes on the outskirts of provincial cities and upmarket cinemas in Paris is creating a two-tier culture with one type of cinema for the poor and another for the rich. Although governments no longer control economic or foreign policy, he does not understand why environmentalists can insist on nature being preserved, while something just as important, namely creativity, is left unprotected.

Now in his sixties, he believes that Europe and America are at war – 'a very modern war', one which is being waged through the communications industry. Media is America's number one export. Investment bank Merrill Lynch calculated that the seven Hollywood majors earned $31 billion in 2001, not including sales of films to television. Not only is it very profitable, but it is also a means of exporting ideas and a way of thinking – promoting the *pax Americana* around the world. As in any war, there are those who resist and those who collaborate for financial gain, such as heads of French television stations who buy American films at inflated prices. Or European companies such as Vivendi Universal and Intermedia who co-finance the US industry with millions of dollars, but stop short of making the same efforts for their own national film industries. But Karmitz does not believe that America has won. There is still a resistance. The future of cinema rests in what he calls the 'cinema of poor people', which exists all over the world – including America.

Later, as I had dinner in one of Karmitz's agreeably modern restaurants on the north bank of the Seine, I reflected that perhaps the key to his character was a photograph on his office wall. At first sight it looked like a snapshot of a beautiful, Julie Christie-like girl with tousled blonde hair, a snub nose and a cocky expression. In actual fact, Karmitz explained, it was a photograph taken in 1937 by Scuh Gotthard of a young miner, and the first to be printed using aluminium. It was therefore a photograph of historical importance, he said, portraying empathy for the working class while at the same time being an object of great aesthetic beauty. The photograph could almost be a metaphor for Karmitz's work, I thought, eating the last scrapings of my *brochette d'espadon* and *salade d'épinard*.

6   Christine Vachon

The rebel

In the early morning of 31 December 1993 two ex-convicts were driving north up Highway 73 into Nebraska. The country was as level as a lake, and there were few other cars. As the old Ford left Falls City – population 4,800 after fifty years of rural recession – its headlights fell on the round white storage tanks of a fuel plant, lit up like the Parthenon at night. It was there, one week before, that both men had beaten and raped a young woman called Teena Brandon. Twenty-one-year-old Brandon was no ordinary girl living in the Great Plains. Passing herself off as a cowboy called Brandon Teena, she had seduced one of the ex-convicts' girlfriends, Lana Tisdel. Not that many people in Falls City had been fooled by Brandon's Stetson-wearing, good ol' boy routine. Brandon was clearly a girl and not a boy. What stuck in 23-year-old John Lotter's throat was that his girlfriend was now going around town saying she was in love with this lesbian. Adding to his insecurity, both Lotter and his 21-year-old accomplice Thomas Nissen had been sodomised in prison. Now the two men were on their way to kill Brandon to stop her talking and sending them back to jail. The car turned west along Highway 73 from Falls City to Humboldt. The landscape was flat and limitless except for occasional twinkling farmhouse lights. Both men agreed they would have to kill anyone who happened to be in the shabby farmhouse where they had been told Brandon was hiding. Lotter and Nissen had been drinking for a week, and they were armed with a pistol and a hunting knife. Shortly after 2 a.m., they drove up the rutted track to the farmhouse and kicked in the front door. They found Brandon cowering at the foot of a waterbed in the bedroom. Lotter put the pistol up beneath Brandon's chin and squeezed the trigger at point-blank range, while Nissen shoved a knife into her liver. He then put the gun to the back of the head of Lisa Lambert, a 24-year-old unmarried mother. The third victim, a 19-year-old disabled black man named Philip DeVine, was murdered on the sofa in the living room. Lambert's nine-month-old baby boy was found crying in his cot the next morning.

On their way home, Lotter and Nissen drove the long way round, turning south from the farmhouse and right into Missouri before doubling back to Falls City. Their thinking was that any police officer who might stop the car would never link them to a crime committed north of the town. As they crossed back over the Big Nemaha River, Lotter rolled down a window and threw the gun and knife out into the frosty night air. It was something he had seen bad guys do in movies. But Lotter forgot that the river was frozen. The weapons were found lying on the ice in full view the next day. The knife, which belonged to Lotter's father, had been replaced in its sheath and the name Lotter was embossed on the leather.

Watching Nissen give evidence against Lotter at his murder trial was a film-maker from New York. Like Teena Brandon, Kimberly Peirce was the daughter of teenage parents, just fifteen years old in her case. Peirce too had been farmed out to a series of relatives and foster homes. And like Brandon, Peirce was sexually unconventional, describing herself as bisexual. The blue streak in her black hair hinted at her unconventional nature. But unlike Brandon,

who drifted into shoplifting and bouncing cheques, and at one point
was put in a mental hospital, Peirce excelled at everything she did.
She gained her first degree in English and Japanese literature at the
University of Chicago. She then moved to Columbia University in
New York, where she progressed from still photography to making
award-winning short films. She first read about Teena Brandon in
April 1994 when she was researching a story about a cross-dressing
female spy during the American Civil War. The extraordinary thing
about the case, Peirce thought, was that these people were not East
Coast sophisticates dabbling with their sexuality but a young couple
in redneck country. One day Peirce visited the farmhouse where
Brandon was killed. There was still blood on the wall and bullet
holes in the window. Peirce made a short film based on the Brandon
Teena story, but she did not have enough money to get the footage
out of the processing laboratory. Rose Troche, director of ultra-low-
budget *Go Fish*, suggested she get in touch with producer Christine
Vachon.

Vachon, once described by *Interview* magazine as an 'auteur
producer', was a pioneer of the so-called New Queer Cinema
movement. Her first feature was *Superstar: The Karen Carpenter Story*,
which had been banned by the dead singer's record company.
Subsequently she gained a reputation for being the gay saint of New
York independent film-making. Troche and *Go Fish* screenwriter
Guinevere Turner had turned to Vachon when making their
experimental black and white lesbian romance at weekends.
Vachon agreed to help because she felt that it would appeal to the
so-called lesbian community. With Vachon on board as producer,
Go Fish went on to earn $2.4 million at the North American box
office and another $400,000 in overseas sales. Vachon likes to joke
that she only works for the money and the glamour but she has yet
to see either one.

Like Marin Karmitz and Michael Douglas, what Vachon looks
for when taking on a new project is whether it has something to say
– passion rather than something polished. Often directors come to
her with a clear idea of what they want, but no idea of how to get
there – which is where she comes in. It was clear that Peirce did not
know one end of a grip stand from another, but she was articulate
about what she wanted. Vachon likes to work with directors with a
clear vision because working with somebody who is vague about
what they want can be, as she puts it, 'a pain in the ass'.

Vachon's artistic and political beliefs were instilled when she was
a child. Her father, John Vachon, photographed America's
underclass – those people left to rot as the divide between rich and
poor grows bigger. Her older sister was one of the founders of the
experimental Collective for Living Cinema. Vachon first got excited
about film at the age of twelve when her mother took her to see
Francois Truffaut's *Les Quatre cents coups* (*The 400 Blows*, 1959).
(Strangely, this was also the picture which hooked Harvey
Weinstein, co-chairman of Miramax Films, on movies, although he
thought he was seeing a porno flick.) Vachon climbed up the film-
making ladder, working as a location scout for music videos, script
supervisor, second assistant director, second-unit coordinator and
an assistant editor. She claims her rise from production assistant to
assistant director to unit manager was because she could not drive,
so she could never be sent away from the set.

Vachon met would-be director Todd Haynes shortly after he left
Brown University in Rhode Island, where he studied semiotics.
Together they set up Apparatus, a production company which
specialised in low-budget films. The thinking behind Apparatus was
that the budget was the aesthetic. If you wanted creative freedom,
then you could not have high production values – or put another
way, creative and financial decisions were inextricably linked. It is

ignorant to assume that 'creative' and 'financial' decisions are completely separate on a process as collaborative as film, says Vachon. All decisions about a project are important, even financial ones, because they contain the potential for what can be achieved by the director. Like Andrew Macdonald, Vachon believes that deciding the budget is one of the most creative things a producer can do.

Haynes wrote and directed *Superstar: The Karen Carpenter Story* (1987), a 43-minute biopic of the late 1970s pop singer who died from anorexia. All the characters were played by Barbie dolls filmed in miniature cardboard sets or against projected backdrops. Karen Carpenter's family were enraged by suggestions that they were somehow responsible for the singer's death and by intimations of incest between Karen and her songwriter brother Richard. Vachon made the film without securing any rights to Carpenter's songs, and lawyers at A&M Records blocked *Superstar* from being released. Vachon also produced Haynes's next film, *Safe* (1995), an Aids metaphor about a woman who becomes allergic to life. *Safe*, which gave Julianne Moore her first starring role, was set in the wealthy suburbs of California. Trying to make such an expensive-looking film for just under a million dollars made Vachon realise why so many low-budget movies were about heroin addicts.

Vachon thought Peirce's footage was amateurish and the script underdeveloped. Everything had been turned into fiction, whereas, as is often the case, the truth was more interesting. But Peirce herself was impressive and clear about why the story was important. Vachon decided that the director needed a bigger, grander palette. She encouraged Peirce to return to Nebraska and dig deeper into the story. Vachon too started attending the murder trials. And as Peirce started delving deeper into what had actually taken place, reality, as is often the case, became much more interesting than fiction.

Peirce spent five and a half years researching the story. She amassed ten thousand pages of notes and court transcripts and interviewed hundreds of lesbians, female cross-dressers and people who had changed sex to try to understand what was going on in Brandon's head. She struggled to distil hours of interviews and court transcripts into drama. Peirce and her writing partner Andy Bienen tried different ways of telling the story: putting the murder up front, then putting it in flashback. They also tried to fit the story into well-known templates – stranger rides into town (*Shane*) or *Romeo and Juliet* or *Pinocchio*. The question was how to get the audience inside Brandon's character as quickly as possible without being judgemental.

However, there were two other competing Teena Brandon projects. One was planned to star Drew Barrymore and the other Neve Campbell. Diane Keaton was hoping to produce the Drew Barrymore version after optioning Aphrodite Jones's non-fiction book about Brandon, *All She Wanted*. Producer Don Murphy (*Natural Born Killers*) was behind the Neve Campbell version. Murphy sent Vachon threatening letters through his lawyer, warning her not to go ahead with the project. Eventually Murphy threatened to sue the Toronto Film Festival where *Boys Don't Cry* was about to have its world premiere. Vachon had to ensure the festival would not get sued just one hour before the gala screening.

Although Lana Tisdel and her mother had signed contracts agreeing to be portrayed on film, Vachon discovered a couple of years later that there was something wrong with the signatures. Peirce would have to go back and convince both women to sign again; without their permission there would be no film. When it came to portraying Lotter and Nissen everything had to be in the public domain and had to have been witnessed by three different people. Then Tisdel sued Vachon and Peirce for defamation of character, perhaps encouraged by her lawyers. Peirce later admitted that actress Chloë Sevigny's portrayal of Tisdel was much more sympathetic than the actual person.

The overseas film division of United Artists agreed to finance the film. Peirce went to meet United Artists executives, but two days later the company pulled out. The problem was that nobody believed Brandon could be played sympathetically by a woman. One solution would be for Brandon to be played by a big star, which would reassure the audience. But Vachon was adamant about not having a star in the film, believing she would bring too much 'baggage' to the role. Meanwhile, Hart Sharp, a production company just down the corridor from Vachon's office, had money from another project which was no longer going ahead. Vachon used the Hart Sharp money to push *Boys Don't Cry* into production. Peirce was just one month away from shooting when Hilary Swank auditioned. As they watched her screen test it was as if somebody had turned the lights up in the room. What tipped the casting for Peirce was that Swank obviously enjoyed being Brandon as much as Teena had done. Vachon thinks *Boys Don't Cry* crossed over because of Swank's 'extraordinary, transcendent' performance. After all, it became clear from test screenings that this was not a movie most people were going to walk out of feeling good about things. Audience questionnaires compared watching *Boys Don't Cry* to being hit by a truck. Swank went on to win an Academy Award for best actress at the 1999 Oscars.

Shooting *Boys Don't Cry* proved upsetting for everybody – even the barber was in tears when he shaved Swank's head. Peter Sarsgaard, who played Lotter, vomited between takes filming the scene where Brandon is stripped naked. And Brendan Sexton III, who played Nissen, prompted the title *Boys Don't Cry* when he burst into tears filming the rape scene. He covered his face and apologised for crying, something which he said he had not done for years.

Peirce's first edit of the film was nearly three hours long. Vachon told Peirce gently that although the movie was, as she put it, 'an incredible experience', it might be *a little more incredible* if it was shorter. Twentieth Century-Fox saw the finished $2 million film and bought worldwide rights for $5 million. This scuppered the Diane Keaton project, which she had been developing for Rupert Murdoch's studio.

Boys Don't Cry follows Teena Brandon as she flees her home town and winds up in Falls City, where she falls in with a wild crowd. The first act is a series of rites of passage as Brandon makes every effort to be accepted. Her new white-trash extended family spends its entire free time boozing, smoking pot and partying. Act two follows the relationship developing between Teena and Lana, culminating in a seduction choked with sex. Brandon's secret is revealed in act three as Lotter and Nissen become her nemesis in an old Ford. *Boys Don't Cry* captures the pot-smoking vacuity of bombed-out teenagers and parents. (At one point Lana wonders plaintively if you can make any money singing karaoke.) Washes of electric guitar add to the atmosphere of inarticulacy and surrealism. But the film is marred by tedious self-conscious touches such as time-lapse photography of Falls City at night, something which has been done to death in television commercials. *Variety* compared *Boys Don't Cry* to *Rebel Without a Cause*, with two misfit girls enacting a version of the James Dean/Natalie Wood romance, 'searching, like their 50s counterparts, for love, self-worth and a place to call home'.[1] Vachon says that since *Boys Don't Cry* won an Academy Award it has been much easier to get actors to read her scripts. Robin Williams, for example, was persuaded to play against type as a sinister photo lab technician in *One Hour Photo* (2002).

Boys Don't Cry bears a family resemblance to *I Shot Andy Warhol*, a film Vachon produced in 1996. Like *Boys Don't Cry*, *I Shot Andy*

Warhol was a polished first feature ripped from tabloid headlines about women and sexual insurrection. It tells the story of Valerie Solanas, founder and sole member of the Society for Cutting Up Men (SCUM), who almost succeeded in murdering pop artist Andy Warhol in 1968. Solanas was a feminist lesbian and part-time prostitute who claimed that Warhol – almost malevolent in his passivity – had too much control over her life. 'I'm a flower child,' she told the young traffic cop she surrendered to hours after the shooting.

Valerie Solanas was born on 8 April 1936. Her father sexually molested her when she was small, before her parents divorced. Following the divorce Solanas, like Teena Brandon, was farmed out to various relatives. Contacted after the shooting, her father could not remember the last time he had seen his daughter. Solanas was sexually promiscuous by the age of thirteen, although many years later she told her publisher that she had only been in love once in her life, with a girl she met at boarding school. Despite her chaotic upbringing, Solanas enrolled at university, where she studied biology. At the same time, she started dabbling in prostitution to help pay for the fees. A bright student, Solanas grew disillusioned with academic life as she started developing her theories. With hindsight, Solanas was born in the wrong era, going to university in the Eisenhower white-picket-fence 1950s when she would have been completely at home in the burn-your-draft-card campus sit-ins of the 1960s. Young women were not supposed to have the kind of thoughts that Solanas did. She drifted to New York, where she earned money through prostitution while scribbling down what would become her manifesto. One money-making idea she had was accosting men on the street and getting them to pay for her to talk obscenely. Presumably they wanted a refund when she told them the dirtiest word in the English language was 'men'.

Written in 1967, *The SCUM Manifesto* was a fifty-page diatribe blaming men for everything that was wrong with the world. It advocated wiping men off the planet, initiating self-propagation of women by test tube, sabotaging the economy and exterminating every trace of the male society which women have colluded with. The male, wrote Solanas, will 'swim through a river of snot, wade nostril-deep through a mile of vomit, if he thinks there'll be a warm friendly pussy awaiting him'. Solanas also castigated women for being 'easily reduced to Mama, mindless ministrator to physical needs, soother of the weary, apey brow, booster of the tiny ego, appreciator of the contemptible, a hot water bottle with tits'. However, some men would be saved, including 'faggots', providing they help propagate the message that 'a woman's primary goal in life should be to squash the male sex'. Feminists of the day talked about *The SCUM Manifesto* as an ironic satire in the style of Swift's *A Modest Proposal*. Hearing this, Solanas wondered where on earth they got the idea she was being ironic.

Publisher Maurice Girodias had published the obscene *Naked Lunch* through his Olympia Press. Apart from Burroughs his authors included Samuel Beckett and Vladimir Nabokov. Girodias was impressed by Solanas's manifesto but did not want to publish it. Instead, he asked Solanas to write a novel based on her experiences. To celebrate her agreement Girodias asked her to dinner at *El Quixote*, the Spanish restaurant next door to the Chelsea Hotel where he was living. Solanas astonished Girodias by turning up in make-up and a 'memorable' red dress. The contract was signed in August 1967; Girodias paid her a $500 advance against royalties, with the promise of a further $1,500 in instalments. Only after signing did Solanas realise she had signed away not just her first novel, but the second and third. As her paranoia increased, she also believed she had signed away everything she was going to write for the rest of her life.

Meanwhile, she had advertised for actors to appear in a play she had written, *Up Your Ass*. One person who auditioned was transvestite Candy Darling, who hung out with the Warhol crowd at the Factory studio. (Once Warhol asked Darling how often she had a period. 'Every day,' Candy cooed. 'I'm such a woman.') Solanas lent Warhol a copy of her play, hoping he might produce it. Warhol read *Up Your Ass* but decided it was too obscene, even for him. Presumably he tossed the manuscript on a pile of other rejects and forgot about it; but when Solanas demanded it back, nobody had the nerve to tell her it was lost. Paul Morrissey, who directed films for Warhol, said that the pop artist saw something of himself in Solanas. Both were Catholic, born into working-class families. Both spent their childhood in poverty, were intellectually precocious and were bullied at school. Perhaps most importantly, both claimed to have rejected sex – although for different reasons. Solanas had experienced too much and Warhol too little. Solanas was growing increasingly frustrated with Warhol (she once said conversation with him was like talking to a chair). She was convinced he was going to produce *Up Your Ass* and take the credit. Her sense of rejection grew into paranoia and eventually developed into full-blown schizophrenia. Somewhere in the trajectory of that illness she shot Warhol.

But her intended victim was not Warhol but Girodias. On 3 June 1968 Solanas set off to the Chelsea Hotel with a .32 automatic and a .22 revolver in a brown paper bag. She asked for Girodias at the front desk but was told he was away on business in Montreal. She turned round and walked downtown to the new Factory office in Union Square. The decor showed that Warhol wanted to distance himself from the amphetamine-crazed freaks of the old studio. White walls and polished wooden desks had replaced silver foil and ratty couches. Solanas met Warhol just as he was entering the building, and they rode up in the lift together. One of the other people in the lift noticed that Solanas was wearing a fur coat even though it was a sweltering day. Warhol left Solanas by the front door and intercepted a telephone call from his friend Viva. Listening on the other end of the line, Viva heard what sounded like a whip being cracked and Warhol shouting, 'No, no, Valerie! Don't do it!' Solanas shot Warhol three times. Only one bullet hit but its wild path caused enormous damage, entering through the left lung and hitting the spleen, stomach, liver and oesophagus before penetrating the right lung and exiting through the side. She then shot visiting art dealer Mario Amaya, wounding him slightly. Karl Marx wrote that history repeats itself, first as tragedy and then as farce. In Warhol's case the process was reversed – three days later presidential candidate Robert Kennedy was assassinated in Los Angeles. Warhol complained that the Kennedy assassination kept him off the newspaper front pages. He never fully recovered after the shooting. When asked what would happen to his art collection after he died, Warhol replied that he was dead already. Weakened by the attempted murder, he suffered a heart attack on 21 February 1987 while recovering from a routine gall bladder operation. The judge decided that Solanas was mentally unfit to stand trial. She eventually pleaded guilty to first-degree assault and was sentenced to three years' imprisonment, one of which she had already served while awaiting trial.

There were many sightings of Solanas in the East Village in the late 1970s, sleeping on a bench in Thompson Square Park or sitting on a wall in St Mark's Place. By now Solanas looked like a tramp, dirty and unkempt. On 25 April 1988 the manager of a welfare hotel at 56 Mason Street, San Francisco, used his pass key to unlock her room. Solanas had not been seen for a week and the rent was overdue. According to the police report, she had been found kneeling on the floor of the one-room apartment, her upper torso facing down on the side of the bed. Her body was infested with maggots.

In 1987 Canadian television researcher Mary Harron was walking past a bookshop in south London when she saw *The SCUM Manifesto* in the window. Harron, who at the time was working for arts documentary programme *The South Bank Show*, was surprised by how good the writing in the manifesto was. As for Warhol, she felt that it was in his world rather than in the hippies or the radical politics of the 1960s that the seeds of contemporary culture could be found. Harron thought that hippies were old-fashioned, picturing some earth mother in a long dress holding a baby while some bearded hunk made things with his hands. Warhol, on the other hand, was about embracing the modern world with its 24-hour news channels, soundbites and celebrity equated to achievement. Indeed, Warhol had been too conservative in predicting that in the future everybody would be famous for fifteen minutes.

Harron originally planned to make a documentary for the BBC. The problem was there was almost no footage of Solanas and hardly anybody remembered her. She first pitched the project to arts documentary series *Arena*. But the idea of doing something even faintly sympathetic about somebody who tried to kill the world's most influential artist divided commissioning editors. It took Anthony Wall of *Arena* a long time to persuade colleagues to back the project. Harron kept working on her proposal when she moved to New York in 1991. Wall eventually gave her £150,000 to make the film, as well as a small research budget. Harron and her researcher Diane Tucker took four years to piece together the story of Solanas's life. Even when the script was in its final stages, more information would arrive and the story would have to be readjusted. Solanas's mother refused to talk to Harron or put her in touch with any relatives. Harron placed advertisements in newspapers across America while Tucker interviewed early feminists, some of whom remembered Solanas. Candy Darling's best friend, Jeremiah Newton, provided a great deal of material. But the people who surrounded Warhol were divided about whether to help. Some, like director Paul Morrissey, were hostile, while others, such as Factory photographer Billy Name, were sympathetic.

Harron had decided to make a fiction film before Vachon and co-producer Tom Kalin became involved. Dan Minahan, a *Late Show* colleague who would go on to direct for Vachon, was by now helping with the script. Harron and Minahan were both living in Los Angeles at the time, involved in a Fox TV news show called *Front Page*. Working on this tabloid news show supported them while they wrote the script.

American Playhouse, the feature arm of public-service broad-caster PBS, put up most of the budget, which nearly doubled from $1 million to $1.7 million. Samuel Goldwyn Company agreed to distribute in North America as part of its output deal with the broadcaster. Lili Taylor had signed to play Solanas while the script was still at treatment stage. Jared Harris was cast as Warhol and Stephen Dorff wriggled into a dress for Candy Darling. Harron knew it was important to get period details right. The Warhol Foundation gave its permission to reproduce paintings and Brillo boxes. Production designer Therese Deprez and her assistant Gideon Ponte made paintings from scratch. They located news-paper photos Warhol used and fabricated silk screens from them. The Warhol Foundation insisted that the paintings be defaced and shredded when shooting finished.

However, the finished film was somehow disappointing. Once again, non-fiction was more interesting than fiction. Perhaps 'mentally unbalanced woman shoots famous artist' was simply not a compelling enough story. Lili Taylor's soliloquies to camera were irritating, and the background was more interesting than the foreground. Writing in the *Village Voice*, Amy Taubin felt that Taylor as Solanas was never less than charming – her own choice to play the abrasive lesbian revolutionary would have been Vachon herself. In any case, *I Shot Andy Warhol* fell down the cracks as distributor Samuel Goldwyn went out of business and the film was dumped on Orion, who did not know what to do with it.

Sexual insurrection was also the theme of *Velvet Goldmine*, a fantasia about glam rock which Vachon produced in 1998. *Velvet Goldmine* examined the relationship between transgressive sexuality and history, tracing a line from Beau Brummell to Oscar Wilde and David Bowie. The film begins with the schoolboy Oscar Wilde being asked what he wants to be when he grows up: 'A pop star,' he replies. Just as Andy Warhol set the tone for the 1980s ('Making money is the best kind of art,' he once said), so director Todd Haynes believed that the gender-blurring of glam rock was a revolution still being felt today – like a stone thrown into the centre of a pond. Jim Lyons, Haynes's regular editor, said *Velvet Goldmine* was nostalgic for a period when people believed society was going to be more tolerant and homosexuality openly accepted. Vachon and Haynes began thinking about a glam-rock film during the writing of *Safe*. Vachon told trade paper *Screen International* in 1997:

> [Todd] was interested by the music, the time and the whole idea of examining that time . . . it suddenly seems like this intense explosion of complete fucking around and tampering with identity. And then America immediately turned it into heavy metal and in England it became Gary Glitter and it was gone.[2]

He had rediscovered the era and thought it would make great material.
Although he didn't have a narrative, he started to do a tremendous
amount of research. It's all about excess and as such was the complete
opposite of *Safe*.[3]

Haynes spent seven years developing *Velvet Goldmine*, while
Vachon spent two years trying to get it financed. She rang Scott
Meek at London-based television company Zenith Productions
while *Safe* was being edited. Would he be interested in paying
Haynes to write a script that he could not begin for a year? Meek,
who thought that Haynes was possibly the only film-maker he had
ever met who was touched by genius, jumped at the chance. Nicole
Kidman talked about playing the female lead before she got bogged
down in Stanley Kubrick's *Eyes Wide Shut*. Finally Jonathan Rhys
Meyers, Ewan McGregor and Toni Collette agreed to star. Michael
Stipe of rock band REM became executive producer in exchange
for assisting with the music. Stipe helped organise original and cover
versions of songs from the early 1970s by Roxy Music, Brian Eno,
Steve Harley, Marc Bolan and Iggy Pop. At least his phone calls
were returned, Vachon admitted. But New Line Cinema, the
subsidiary of Warner Brothers, wavered about financing the film.
Funding collapsed twice before broadcaster Channel 4 agreed to
put up most of the money.

Vachon then struggled through the most arduous shoot she had
ever done. Filming took place over eight weeks in London in the
spring of 1997. *Velvet Goldmine*'s $7 million budget was $1 million
short of the lowest number Vachon thought feasible. The script
contained 220 different scenes, and by the penultimate day they
were shooting five scenes a day at five separate locations. Vachon
described the last two days of shooting as 'excruciating', with the
very last scene to be filmed the most difficult. She wrote later that

she felt helpless asking Haynes to rush through so many important shots. It was, she said, a nasty impossible schedule, with the executive producer becoming hysterical, telephoning her to say that Haynes had no choice but to cut scenes. Haynes himself described the shoot as a nightmare. Every night he would go home wanting to shoot himself. (The cast, however, was having a whale of a time, in what the director described as true glam-rock style.) Vachon says that with hindsight she nearly broke the cardinal rule of producing – letting the movie get away from her. She has compared a film in production to a speeding train that gains momentum and is difficult to stop. Once it sets off down the mountain you had better get out of the way unless you want to lose a limb.

Producer and director then toiled through a lengthy post-production process, with the completion bond company, the overseer which guarantees a film will be completed on time and on budget and in accordance with the distribution contract, complaining about rising costs. Things became so bad that the bond company threatened to take control of the film: something it only does as a last resort. As Vachon put it in her autobiography: 'low-budget filmmaking is like childbirth. You have to repress the horror or you'll never do it again.'[4] A low-budget movie, she has said, is 'a crisis waiting to happen'. You have to stretch your abilities to the limit – and then keep pushing that limit. And when something goes wrong, you cannot just throw money at it. Ultimately, producing a low-budget film involves taking a leap of faith. One of the paradoxes of low-budget filmmaking is that you have to 'expect the worst and plan for the worst, and repress all thoughts of the worst'. Vachon compares independent film finance to a house of cards: if one element falls over, the whole thing can collapse. Therefore, as with any leadership position, the producer has to pretend to be confident at all times, which in itself can be draining.

Miramax Films picked up North American rights to *Velvet Goldmine* late into pre-production, but Vachon did not want Harvey Weinstein, its co-chairman, involved in any decision-making. Weinstein has a four-strong editing team which sometimes, under his guidance, re-edits other people's work. This alternative Miramax-approved version of a film is then presented to the director, and sometimes – as was rumoured with *The Shipping News* – is even released against his wishes. Weinstein's meddling has earned him the nickname Harvey Scissorhands.

Velvet Goldmine gets its title from a David Bowie song written in 1971 and released as a B-side four years later. Brian Slade is a Bowie-like singer murdered on stage at a London concert. But the assassination is revealed to be a stunt designed to boost his fading career. People start burning Brian Slade records in the streets and the singer disappears. Christian Bale plays a journalist assigned to write a feature about the forgotten rock star ten years later. Whatever happened to this platform-booted Icarus? asks his editor. The film then becomes a *Citizen Kane* pastiche as Bale cross-examines, among others, Slade's frowzy ex-wife (Toni Collette playing Susan Alexander Kane) and Curt Wild, an Iggy Pop figure played by a paunchy Ewan McGregor. The mystery is revealed to be that Slade and Wild once had an unhappy love affair. But who is the sharp-suited, bouffant-haired singer filling stadiums across America in 1984? Surely it couldn't be Brian Slade impersonating Bowie during the *Let's Dance* phase of his career? (Most of the audience, having dozed off by this stage, are beyond caring.)

Bowie astutely blocked Vachon from using his songs in the film. He claimed that *Velvet Goldmine* infringed on his own plans for a glam-rock musical which never materialised. More to the point, Bowie may have resented Haynes's disdain for his 'selling out' in the early 1980s, recanting his homosexuality. A production insider claimed that Bowie did not want to be reminded of what he had got up to in his youth. But without Bowie's music *Velvet Goldmine* becomes a pointless reconstruction, like watching *Amadeus* without Mozart. One would have thought it would be difficult to make a boring film about Bowie but *Velvet Goldmine* is stupefyingly bad. Haynes's whole premise is built on a fallacy. Bowie and Iggy Pop never had an affair (although Bowie's ex-wife claimed to have caught him in bed with Mick Jagger once). Bowie's notorious 'I'm gay and I always have been' interview with the *Melody Maker* in 1972 was probably calculated to shift record units rather than reveal his sexuality (he later described the remark as the greatest mistake of his career). At one point a teenage Christian Bale is shown masturbating over the infamous photograph of Bowie kissing Lou Reed. In fact, Bowie was shouting into the American singer's ear in a crowded nightclub. Vachon may have felt she was letting the movie get away from her, but she also made a far worse error not reining in the excesses of her director. *Velvet Goldmine* is, in its own words, as camp as a row of tents, like being stuck in a never-ending encore at a Marc Almond concert. (Sandy Powell went on to win an Academy Award nomination for her rainbow-coloured spandex catsuits and feather boas.) Vachon blamed the film's lack of success on its poor marketing. Channel Four, expecting *Trainspotting* in platform shoes, could not decide whether it was a gay movie or a rock movie. In any case, despite Haynes's protestations, the true story was more interesting than his fiction. The looks that the mascaraed brickies in Bowie's backing band exchange when he announces his retirement on stage in the documentary *Ziggy Stardust and the Spiders from Mars* are priceless.

'Gay sex as liberating transgressive act' is also one of the themes of *Hedwig and the Angry Inch* (2001). Like *Velvet Goldmine*, the film begins with a rock singer miming fellatio on stage with his lead guitarist. But this time we are not at the Hammersmith Apollo in 1973 but in a cheap restaurant in an American mall. And we are not watching a rock god but an East German transvestite who comes across as part Nico, part Farrah Fawcett and part Amanda Lear. Vachon wrote in her autobiography that the films she produces cannot be fitted into any category. She sees her job as making an alternative to the studio-processed schlock that has become more flagrant with the rise of entertainment conglomerates. 'I get told that, "You're not playing the game kid." And my response is: "Don't underestimate me because I didn't make 33 movies by playing your stupid game."' (One can imagine a Hollywood executive rubbing his temples as he listens to the pitch for *Hedwig*. 'Okay, Christine, let me see if I've got this straight. It's a rock and roll musical loosely based on Plato about a sex-changed German army wife on the road with a punk rock band?' Vachon eventually sees herself out and the executive sits alone for a long time, staring at his blotter pad. 'Jesus,' he says finally.)

Hedwig is the walk on the wild side that *Velvet Goldmine* never was. Hansel lives alone with his mother in East Germany in the 1960s (their flat is so small that he has to play in the oven). To the horror of his mother, who makes social realist sculptures of Stalin, Hansel becomes obsessed by pop music he hears on US army radio. One day a black American soldier picks up the teenage Hansel, and soon they are making plans to go back to the States as man and wife. But in order to get into the USA Hansel must first become a woman (his mother points out gnomically that in order to be free one must first leave something behind). But the sex-change operation, arranged by his approving mother, is botched – leaving Hedwig with the titular 'angry inch'. Deserted by her husband and dumped in a Kansas trailer park, Hedwig forms an all-girl band with some Korean army wives. One night she meets Tommy, the born-again Christian son

of the army base commander. Hedwig becomes Tommy's mentor
and the two of them start writing songs together (his copy of
Frampton Comes Alive is snatched away and replaced with *Aladdin
Sane*). The band becomes popular but Tommy, ashamed of his
feelings for Hedwig, runs away, taking the songs they wrote together
with him. Tommy Gnosis becomes a stadium rock star while
Hedwig's career nosedives. The somewhat garbled ending has
Hedwig throwing away her wigs and dresses when she realises she
does not need props to be loved. Like a Samuel Beckett character,
she will face the world alone. The metaphor of the film is taken from
Plato, the notion that mankind was once split into two parts by the
gods, and human beings are destined always to seek wholeness
through love. However, the film is saved from being irredeemably
arch by some good jokes (Hedwig describes herself as 'internationally ignored'). But its mawkish Elton John-like ballads betray
its roots as an off-Broadway show, while its punk rock songs sound
just the way stage musicals do when they are trying to be edgy.

First-time director John Cameron Mitchell, who plays Hedwig,
developed the story and characters in cabarets and drag clubs.
Mitchell, himself the son of a US army base commander, was well
known in the New York theatre scene. One of his innovations was
to get a punk rock band to be his backing group (how they laughed
when Mitchell counted down to songs five-six-seven-eight; they
were more used just to getting a nod from the drummer). The show
ran for years in a crumbling hotel in New York's meat-packing
district. Mitchell quit the show after performing seven times a week
over a ten-month period. However, the story was strong enough for
the show to continue without him (by now *Hedwig* had become a
cult along the lines of *The Rocky Horror Picture Show*) and successive
Hedwigs included actress Ally Sheedy (*The Breakfast Club*). One night
Michael De Luca, former president of production at New Line

Cinema, went to see the show and bought the film rights the next day. Mitchell was allowed to choose who the producer was going to be and he picked Killer Films, the production company which Vachon formed with Pamela Koffler in 1996. 'Killer has made some of the most interesting movies in recent years,' said Mitchell. 'Their group is very hands-on. They think the same way as I do. There's no bullshit, and there's no time for it, 'cause you don't have enough money. Bullshit only happens when you have the time and money to indulge it.'[5] Eight people from Killer went to see the musical, taking up a row of seats. Vachon says: 'I saw the potential of how it could open up. I mean, what is a great film? It's a story well told. I thought there was an incredible narrative line that would even be better served cinematically than theatrically.'[6]

If Killer Films has a formula then it is making projects Vachon feels passionate about because of the story and the director – and making them for the right price. Vachon says that she buys her freedom because she makes films for the right budget. Most Killer productions end up breaking even or making a profit. 'Budgets are often a mixture of "How much do I really need to make this movie?" and "What am I being told as I take this to market?" That's where the budget is born,' she told me. Sometimes the market does not tell her what she wants to hear, insisting that a project can only be financed with a major star. Sometimes the market will tell Vachon to slash the budget from $8 million to $5 million. Surprisingly, Vachon is sceptical about using government grants or soft foreign tax money to finance films. Her view is that if people just want to express themselves they should dance or paint. Because film-making is so expensive directors must remember the audience and make films people want to see.

There was never any doubt in Vachon's mind that Mitchell would make a great director, even if the actor had to go on a film-making workshop to be convinced. She sees working with first-time directors as an investment because she often works with them again. For example, she is now producing a second project with Mary Harron about 1950s bondage pin-up Betty Page. Nevertheless, working with first-time directors can often be difficult. Vachon has to call in favours because the director has none to call in. Of course, not every director wants to collaborate. Tim Blake Nelson, director of concentration-camp drama *The Grey Zone*, had his own 'sacred circle', the other members being his production designer and director of cinematography. Vachon stood a little way off during shooting.

Vachon put *Hedwig* into production on a constricting $6 million budget and a breakneck 28-day shooting schedule. Mitchell and his crew found themselves working twelve-hour days to get the film completed on time. (Despite the 'we're all in this together' line Vachon sometimes feeds the press, crew members often complain of rotten working conditions and excessive overtime while director and actors stay in better hotels. The crew of *One Hour Photo* worked such long hours day after day that they started wearing T-shirts saying '18 hour photo'.) But the hard work paid off when *Hedwig* won the audience award and best director award at the 2001 Sundance Film Festival in Park City, Utah.

In many ways Vachon keeps remaking the same film again and again. Her films are often about sexual transgressives – artists, prostitutes and others who, in Lawrence Durrell's phrase, have been deeply wounded in their sex. Robin Williams is a lonely photo technician, Sy, in *One Hour Photo* (2002), a kind of Travis Bickle in a dust-controlled environment, obsessed by what he thinks is the perfect suburban family. One wall of his flat is covered with hundreds of photographs of the Yorkins (Vachon's adopted daughter turns up later in one snapshot). He sees the happiest moments, like the birth of a child, birthdays and family holidays. But the wife has been taking photographs to reassure herself that the family really is perfect. Beneath the glossy 4x6 surface all is not well. The husband has been having an affair and neglecting his nine-year-old son. His wife is shallow and trying to keep everything intact on a surface level. As the technician's obsession grows so does his need to become part of the family. When Nina Yorkin ignores planted evidence of her husband's affair, Sy takes Will Yorkin and his mistress hostage. Later Sy confesses that he was sexually abused as a child.

Apart from the silly, overblown ending, *One Hour Photo* works well as a film. Like most first-time film-makers, writer and director Mark Romanek has made a film influenced by his favourite moments from other movies. *One Hour Photo* has a cold Stanley Kubrick feel – the SavMart where Sy works looks like the revolving space station in *2001: A Space Odyssey*. During his escape from police, running down a spiral car-park ramp, he looks like one of the astronauts plodding round the spaceship centrifuge in the same film. There are also nods to *All the President's Men*, *Psycho* and *THX 1138*. And for once Robin Williams turns down the volume on his performance.

Killer Films is situated in downtown New York on the corner of Lafayette Street and Great Jones Street. Vachon's office is hectic, with phones ringing and people running around, when I go and see her. The company takes its name from *Office Killer*, a film Vachon made with New York artist Cindy Sherman. John Wells, creator of television's *The West Wing* and executive producer of *ER*, pays the company's overheads – rent, salaries and the like – in exchange for a first look at whatever Vachon is working on (although Vachon describes it as a first chance to turn her down). On paper it looks as if Killer co-produces eight out of ten films it makes, but the truth is that Vachon wholly produces three quarters of her slate. The office has cheap partitions and finger-marked white walls, which I take to be a good sign. In my experience film companies with glass-ceiling atriums and leather walls tend to go out of business rather quickly. Vachon's fluttery assistant introduces us but it is clear Vachon has little idea about who I am. I have been warned that she can be spiky with interviewers. A couple of people have told me that she sometimes takes credit for work really done by others. But for the visiting English journalist Vachon is charm personified. However, she cannot resist peeking at her email every few minutes. A little attention deficit disorder is useful when you have this number of plates spinning, she tells me.

A tarot card reader once read Vachon's cards and asked if she was in the army. When she said no, the tarot card reader announced that according to the cards Vachon moved people around, just like the military. Vachon thought for a moment and could only agree. She has directed several short films – *A Man in Your Room* (1984), *Days Are Numbered* (1986) and *The Way of the Wicked* (1989) but says she does not want to direct a feature. She does not see producing as something that failed directors do because the two are such different disciplines. One would not ask a painter why he does not want to be a dancer. She sees producing as something separate and full of its own passion. Obviously a producer is no good without a good director, but she does not feel producing is the lesser job. She thinks film-makers outside the studio system need good producers, and there aren't too many around. Directing is the more glamorous position but that is fine with her. In any case, she likes looking at the project in its entirety rather than just concentrating on performances, which is the job of the director.

For Vachon the job of the producer is one of the great mysteries of the movie-making process. When asked what producers do, her reply is: what do they not do? The director has the luxury of despairing but the producer does not, otherwise the whole thing will spiral out of control. Occasionally, Vachon just feels like a cheerleader pushing everybody along, but on every film there is at least one thing that she has improved. As a woman she bumps against the double standard of how to command respect without being called a bitch. If you are a woman trying to run a film set you get labelled a bitch, whereas if you are a man you get labelled tough but fair. Some women producers make a point of firing somebody on the first day just to show who is in charge. Vachon knows her reputation is more in the direction of being a bitch than a fount of niceness, but she does not really care. It is not a popularity contest.

Early in her career Vachon embraced controversy. In 1991 she made *Poison* with Todd Haynes, three interlocking stories derived from works by gay French writer Jean Genet. The film's budget was $255,000, all of which had come through individual investors and arty foundation grants. However, right-wing activist Donald Wildeman complained to members of congress about *Poison*, which he said contained explicit scenes of homosexuals involved in anal sex. (Wildeman later admitted to not having seen the film). The National Endowment for the Arts (NEA), which had granted $25,000 towards the cost of editing the film, defended its decision. *Poison*, it said, illustrated the destructive effect of violence, and, taken as a whole, was 'neither prurient nor obscene'. But evangelist Pat Robertson and his Christian Coalition joined other conservatives in calling for NEA head John Frohnmayer to resign and for the organisation to be scrapped. By now broadcasters including ABC, CBS and CNN had picked up the story and Haynes went on national television to defend himself.

Four years later Vachon co-produced *Kids*, a documentary-style film which depicts a twelve-year-old girl losing her virginity to a boy who is HIV-positive. Considerable drug use is shown, and we see a group of teenagers attacking a black man. Miramax, which had paid $3.5 million for worldwide rights, found itself unable to release it. Parent company Disney was a member of the lobby group Motion Picture Association of America (Mpaa), and therefore unable to release a film with a NC-17 certificate. NC-17 means only those aged over seventeen can see a film. The certificate is usually reserved for pornography. Neither could Disney under Mpaa rules release a film without a certificate. Miramax was forced to set up a separate distribution company, Shining Excalibur Pictures, to release *Kids* – insulating Disney from controversy (a cynic would argue that Miramax encouraged controversy to guarantee more exposure). In Britain the film was released after the censor demanded cuts amounting to less than a minute of running time. Nevertheless, Warner Brothers cinemas refused to show the film, calling it 'despicable'.

One of the things that strikes you about Vachon is how she champions her directors. For example, she defended Todd Solondz for making *Happiness* (1998), his bleak retelling of Chekhov's *Three Sisters*. Solondz's breakthrough film, *Welcome to the Dollhouse* (1995), was one of the few films she wishes she had produced herself. *Happiness* asks us to feel sympathy for an obscene phone caller, a murderer and a paedophile. The obscene phone caller is a computer technician crucified with loneliness; the murderer is an obese woman defending herself against rape; the paedophile who drugs his son's classmates when they are asleep is, paradoxically, a good father. His conversations with his son are models of how a parent should speak to a child – simply but with honesty. And yet you choke on your popcorn when the tearful eleven-year-old asks his father if he ever wanted to sodomise him. 'No,' replies the father, 'with you I would have just jerked off.' Not surprisingly three distributors turned down *Happiness* when Solondz refused to soften the script. In the end October Films, a subsidiary of Universal Pictures, put up $2 million to finance the film. 'The projects I take on have something provocative about them that excites me. Any time a film starts up discussion and makes people think about the status quo, I think is good,' Vachon said at the time. *Happiness* won the international critics' prize at the Cannes Film Festival. But Universal and its owner, Canadian alcohol conglomerate Seagram, told October not to release the film. Vachon heard that the studio was not thrilled at the idea of one of its subsidiaries distributing such a controversial project. Universal cited a loophole in Solondz's contract that said the studio did not have to release anything it found morally objectionable. Good Machine International, the company selling *Happiness*, formed its own distribution company to release the film. Solondz pointed out that if *Happiness* had been expected to earn $50 million then Universal would have put it in cinemas, applauding him for his courage in going against the grain.

However, Vachon has by now been partially assimilated by the mainstream. The 'lonely photo lab technician stalks perfect family' pitch for *One Hour Photo* is much easier to grasp than the multiple-viewpoint glam-rock fantasia of *Velvet Goldmine*. In September 2002 Killer signed a one-year first-look deal with Warner Brothers. Like any other system, Hollywood survives partly because of its ability to assimilate those who prove a threat to it. Vachon has proved to Hollywood that her films make money. Comparing what they cost to make with what they gross at the box office, most of Vachon's films do better than those produced by the studios. *One Hour Photo* grossed more than $43.89 million worldwide (its director, Mark Romanek, previously directed pop videos for Lenny Kravitz and Nine Inch Nails). *Far from Heaven* (2002), Todd Haynes's recreation of a 1950s Douglas Sirk melodrama (on the face of it as pointless as copying a Rembrandt drawing using old brown ink) has so far earned $21.36 million. Making each film, she has said, is 'like reinventing the wheel. There is no obvious formula'. Ultimately, Vachon wants to be known as a great producer, not a gay producer.

Like many of the people described in this book, you sense that what lies at the core of Vachon – the final doll nesting inside the Russian doll shells – is low self-esteem. One pulls back the curtain and finds not a wizard but a frightened old man gabbling into a microphone. The flood of film magazine profiles about Vachon provides a kind of reassurance for her. Indeed, perhaps the thing that keeps making all the producers described in this book prove themselves again and again is poor self-image. Michael Douglas may always see himself as the son trying to gain the approval of the father who walked out on him. Marin Karmitz may always regard himself as an immigrant turned away from one port to another. Others described in this book may deep down think of themselves as the Jew, the lesbian or the homosexual. But one thing that all of them have in common is their absolute conviction in themselves as artists, in their ability to produce a film which achieves its full potential. As Vachon herself puts it: the 'producer as auteur, the producer as creative force, is sadly maligned.'

Afterword

Billy Wilder once told his cameraman to shoot a scene out of focus because he wanted to win an Academy Award for best foreign film, perhaps reflecting the disdain felt by a Hollywood professional towards the European auteur. Certainly, watching films like *One Flew Over the Cuckoo's Nest* and *Trainspotting* one gets the feeling of cool, disinterested minds – the inner circle of producer, writer and director – working together to do what is best for the project.

Recently, watching a typical auteur film, I was reminded that when I started writing I thought that using lots of long words and plenty of adverbs somehow made me more artistic. In much the same way this particular auteur director had used plenty of out-of-focus camera angles, while her actors were emoting like mad. Nobody could just open a door but they had to do so 'longingly' or 'fearfully'. Perhaps there is room for an academic book to be written dismantling the myth of the auteur, showing how iconoclastic directors such as Robert Bresson, Jean-Luc Godard and Andrei Tarkovsky relied on collaborators to help stamp their personalities on films. More recently, the study of semiotics, which succeeded auteurism as the fashionable theoretical scheme in university film studies, has eschewed the concept of individual authorship. It might be more correct to think of Hitchcock as a brand rather than just a single individual. One probably apocryphal story tells how Robert Riskin, writer of some of Frank Capra's best films, including *It Happened One Night* (1934) and *Mr. Deeds Goes to Town* (1936), was so fed up with all the talk in the late 1930s about 'the capra touch' that he marched into Capra's office, dropped 120 blank pages on the director's desk and demanded: 'Here! Give that "the Capra Touch"!'

But if some writer-directors can be called auteurs because a style or theme runs through their work, so the same can be said of certain producers, who may not be artists themselves but employ others to execute their vision. After all, it is the producer who stays with a project from conception to writing, casting, shooting, editing, marketing and so on through to its video release. The director just handles actors and is in control of the set. Years later, when everybody else has moved on to other projects, the producer may be the one still re-cutting the film for television.

Surely the test of any work of art is whether it succeeds in doing what it set out to do. Therefore the only question for any viewer is whether a film has succeeded on its own terms, as opposed to, say, judging its moral point of view. Most of the films made by producers profiled in this book give the sense of an exquisite piece of work, each element fitting together like a dovetailed piece of joinery. If a theme can be difficult to discern in the films of Michael Douglas or Marin Karmitz, it may be because these producers are canny enough to know that each film must stand or fall on its own merits.

My one regret in writing this book is that I was unable to persuade one Hollywood producer to take part, a man who fits my paradigm of a creative producer exactly. This producer's name, which is often as big as the titles of his movies on billboards, is synonymous with franchises and sequels. More often than not, like God, his films are made in his own image. But despite repeated emails and faxes, my interview request was politely turned down. Eventually I concluded that this was because the producer did not know me. F. Scott Fitzgerald's remark that 'We don't go for strangers in Hollywood' remains one of the truest things anybody has ever said about the movie business. But if this titan is one of the few who, in Fitzgerald's words, can keep the whole equation of pictures in his head, occasionally he can be just as fallible as the rest of us. Once, having lunch with a film-maker, the producer asked his companion what he was working on. The film-maker replied that he was planning a film set in the Renaissance. 'Oh yeah?' said the producer. 'Where's that?'

Notes

Frontispiece

1. Alfred Hitchcock, 'Directors are Dead', *Film Weekly*, November 20, 1937, p. 14.

Introduction

1. Philip French, *The Movie Moguls: an informal history of the Hollywood tycoons*, Weidenfeld & Nicolson, 1969, p. 2.
2. Bridget Byrne, 'Sam Spiegel: making cathedrals out of raw film', *Los Angeles Times*, 2 January 1972.
3. James F. Fixx, 'The Spiegel Touch', *Saturday Review*, 29 December, 1962.
4. Alan David Vertrees, *Selznick's Vision: Gone with the Wind and Hollywood Filmmaking*, University of Texas Press, 1997, p. x.
5. F. Scott Fitzgerald, *The Last Tycoon*, Charles Scribner's Sons, 1941, p. 10.

1 Michael Douglas: the star

1. Ken Kesey, *Kesey's Garage Sale*, Viking, 1973, p. 12.
2. Beverly Walker, *Sight and Sound*, autumn 1975, p. 216.
3. Reynold Humphries and Genevieve Suzzoni. *Framework*, vol. 11, 5, winter 1976–7, p. 23.

4. Michael Wood, *New York Review of Books*, vol. 22, 1, 5 February 1976.

5. John Parker, *Michael Douglas: acting on instinct*, Headline, 1994, pp. 113–14.

6. Annene Kaye and Jim Sclavunos, *Michael Douglas and the Douglas Clan*, W. H. Allen, 1989, p. 74.

7. Alan Lawson, *Michael Douglas: a biography*, Robert Hale, 1993, p. 53.

8. James Powers, *American Film*, July – August 1979, p. 34.

9. Annene Kaye and Jim Sclavunos, *Michael Douglas and the Douglas Clan*, W. H. Allen, 1989, p. 134.

2 Dino De Laurentiis: the mogul

1. Bernard Drew, *American Film*, December 1976 – January 1977, p. 9.

2. Peter Haigh, *Film Review*, vol. 27, 2, February 1977, p. 6.

3. Lorenzo Semple Jr., *The Complete Script of the Dino De Laurentiis Production of King Kong*, Ace Books, 1977, p. 3.

4. Herb A. Lightman, *American Cinematographer*, January 1977, p. 44.

5. Peter Haigh, *Film Review*, vol. 27, 2, February 1977, p. 6.

6. Bill Warren, *Cinefantastique*, vol 5, 3, winter 1976, p. 34.

7. Charles Champlin, 'A Ding-Dong King Kong Battle', *Los Angeles Times*, 5 November 1975, part IV, p. 1.

8. Paul Mandell, *Cinefantastique*, vol. 5, 1, spring 1976, p. 43.

9. Stuart Byron, *Film Comment*, January – February 1977, p. 20.

3 Duncan Kenworthy and Andrew Macdonald: the team

1. Todd McCarthy, *Variety*, 24 January 1994, p. 63.

2. John Hodge, *Trainspotting and Shallow Grave*, Faber and Faber, 1996, pp. 3–4.

3. Derek Elley, *Variety*, 12 February 1996, p. 79.

4. Martin Hoyle, *Financial Times*, 20 May 1999, p. 22.
5. Graham Greene, *In Search of a Character*, The Viking Press, 1962, pp. 45–6.

4 Jeremy Thomas: the auteur

1. Livio Negri, *The Sheltering Sky*, London: Scribners, 1990, back cover.
2. *Ibid*, p. 40.
3. Brian Appleyard, 'The Road to Morocco', *Sunday Times*, 2 September 1990, p. 55.
4. Hugo Davenport, *Daily Telegraph*, 19 November 1990, p. 21.
5. Norman Mailer, *Advertisements for Myself*, G. P. Putnam's Sons, 1959, p. 468.
6. David Cronenberg. *Naked Lunch: a screenplay based on the novel by William S. Burroughs*, second draft, 5 March 1990.

5 Marin Karmitz: the revolutionary

1. Christopher Tookey, *Daily Mail*, 11 November 1994, p. 55.
2. Yvonn Crenn, quoted in *Trois Couleurs: Rouge* production notes.

6 Christine Vachon: the rebel

1. Emanuel Levy, *Variety*, 6 September 1999, p. 62.
2. Louise Tutt, *Screen International*, 22 August 1997, p. 29.
3. Christine Vachon, quoted in *Velvet Goldmine* production notes.
4. Christine Vachon, *Shooting to Kill: How an independent producer blasts through the barriers to make movies that matter*, Avon Books, 1998, p. 1.
5. John Cameron Mitchell, quoted in *Hedwig and the Angry Inch* production notes.
6. Christine Vachon, quoted in *Hedwig and the Angry Inch* production notes.
7. Christine Vachon, quoted in *Happiness* production notes.

Bibliography

Books

Andrew, Geoff. *Stranger Than Paradise: maverick filmmakers in recent American cinema.* Prion Books, 1998.

Bahrenburg, Bruce. *The Creation of Dino De Laurentiis's King Kong.* Star Books, 1976.

Boorman, John and Donohoe, Walter. *Projections 5.* Faber and Faber, 1996.

Britton, Andrew. *Talking Films: the best of the Guardian film lectures.* Fourth Estate, 1991.

Cavassoni, Natasha Fraser. *Sam Spiegel: the Biography of a Hollywood Legend.* Little Brown, 2003.

Cronenberg, David. *Crash.* Faber and Faber, 1996.

Didion, Joan. *After Henry.* Vintage Books, 1992.

Dougan, Andy. *Michael Douglas: out of the shadows.* Robson Books, 2001.

Finney, Angus. *The Egos Have Landed: the rise and fall of Palace Pictures.* William Heinemann, 1996.

Fitzgerald, F. Scott. *The Last Tycoon.* Scribners, 1941.

French, Philip. *The Movie Moguls: an informal history of the Hollywood tycoons.* Weidenfield & Nicholson, 1969.

Haynes, Todd. *Velvet Goldmine.* Faber and Faber, 1998.

Hodge, John. *Trainspotting and Shallow Grave.* Faber and Faber, 1996.

Hughes, David. *The Complete Lynch.* Virgin Books, 2001.

Ilott, Terry and Eberts, Jake. *My Indecision Is Final: the rise and fall of Goldcrest Films.* Faber and Faber, 1990.

Jones, Graham and Johnson, Lucy. *Talking Pictures: interviews with contemporary British filmmakers*. British Film Institute, 1997.

Karmitz, Mann. *Bande a Part*. Grasset & Fasquelle, 1994.

Kaye, Annene and Sclavunos, Jim. *Michael Douglas and the Douglas Clan*. WH Allen, 1989.

Kesey, Ken. *Kesey's Garage Sale*. Viking, 1973.

Kezich, Tulio and Levantesi Alessandra. *Dino De Laurentiis: la vita e i film*. Feltrinelli, 2001.

Kipps, Charles. *Out of Focus: power, pride and prejudice*. Silver Arrow Books, 1989.

Lawson, Alan. *Michael Douglas: a biography*. Robert Hale, 1993.

Lippy, Todd. *Projections 11: New York filmmakers on filmmaking*. Faber and Faber, 2000.

Madsen, Axel. *John Huston*. Robson Books, 1979.

Mailer, Norman. *Advertisements for Myself*. G. P. Putnam's Sons, 1959.

Matthews, Charles E. *Oscar A to Z: a complete guide to more than 2,400 movies nominated for Academy Awards*. Main Street Books, 1995.

Morris, L. Robert and Raskin, Lawrence. *Lawrence of Arabia*. Doubleday, 1992.

Negri, Livio. *The Sheltering Sky: a film by Bernardo Bertolucci based on the novel by Paul Bowles*. Scribners, 1990.

Osborne, Robert. *65 years of the Oscar: the official history of the academy awards*. Abbeville Press, 1994.

Parker, John. *Michael Douglas: acting on instinct*. Headline, 1994.

Pierson, John. *Spike, Mike, Slackers and Dykes*. Miramax/Hyperion Books, 1995.

Puttnam, David. *The Moral Imagination*. University of Ulster, 1992.

Puttnam, David and Watson, Neil. *The Undeclared War*. Harper Collins, 1997.

Rodley, Chris. *Cronenberg on Cronenberg*. Faber and Faber, 1997.

Schatz, Thomas. *The Genius of the System*. Pantheon, 1988.

Semple Jr., Lorenzo. *King Kong*. Ace Books, 1977.

Silverberg, Ira. *Everything is Permitted: the making of Naked Lunch*. Grove Weidenfeld, 1992.

Sinclair, Andrew. *Spiegel: the man behind the pictures*. Weidenfeld & Nicolson, 1987.

Sinclair, Iain. *Crash*. BFI Modern Classics, 1999.

Stevens, Jay. *Storming Heaven: LSD and the American dream*. William Heinemann, 1988.

Thomson, David. *Showman: the life of David O. Selznick*. Alfred A Knopf, 1992

Vachon, Christine. *Shooting to Kill: How an independent producer blasts through the barriers to make movies that matter*. Avon Books, 1998.

Vertees, Alan David. *Selznick's Vision: Gone With the Wind and Hollywood Filmmaking*. University of Texas Press, 1997.

Wiley, Mason and Bona, Damien. *Inside Oscar: the unofficial history of the Academy Awards*. Ballantine Books, 1996.

Wolfe, Tom. *The Electric Kool-Aid Acid Test*. Weidenfeld and Nicolson, 1969.

Woods, Paul A. *Weirdsville USA: the obsessive universe of David Lynch*. Plexus, 1997.

Yule, Andrew *Enigma: David Puttnam, the story so far . . .* Mainstream Publishing, 1988.

Magazines and newspapers

AIP & Co.

American Cinematographer

American Film

Black Film Review

British Film and TV Facilities Journal

Broadcast

Cineaste

Cinefantastique

Cinema

Cinema Papers

Cinema TV Today

City Limits

Daily Mail

Daily Mirror

Daily Telegraph

Diva

Empire

Encore

Entertainment Weekly

Evening Standard

Exposure

Fangoria
Film Comment
Film Daily
Film Directions
Filmmaker
Films and Filming
Film Ireland
Filmmakers Newsletter
Films in Review
Film Review
Film and Video
Film West
Financial Times
Focus on Film
Framework
Gay News
Gay Times
Guardian
Heat
Hollywood Reporter
If
Independent
Independent Film and Video Monthly
Independent on Sunday
Interview
Jump Cut
Kinema
Listener
Literature / Film Quarterly
Making Films in New York
Mail on Sunday
Monthly Film Bulletin

Moving Pictures
National Film Theatre Programmes
Neon
New Yorker
Observer
Pact magazine
Photoplay
Premiere
Radio Times
Rushes
Scenario
Scotsman
Screen Finance
Screen International
Sight and Sound
Starburst
Stills
Sun
Sunday Express
Sunday Telegraph
Sunday Times
Take One
The Times
Time
Time Out
Today
Total Film
Vanity Fair
Variety
Video Business
Village Voice

Index

methuen

For more information on all Methuen titles,
visit our website at

www.methuen.co.uk

For sales enquiries about Methuen books
please contact

The Sales Department
Methuen Publishing Ltd
11–12 Buckingham Gate
London SW1E 6LB
Tel: 020 7798 1609
Fax: 020 7828 2098
sales@methuen.co.uk

Prices are subject to change without notice